# *The Spirit of Islamic Law*

## *The Spirit of the Laws*

Alan Watson, General Editor

The *Spirit of the Laws* series illuminates the nature of legal systems throughout the world. Titles in the series are concerned less with the rules of the law and more with the relationships of the laws in each system with religion and moral perspectives; the degree of complexity and abstraction; classifications; attitudes to possible sources of law; authority; and values enshrined in law. Topics covered in the series include Roman law, Chinese law, biblical law, Talmudic law, canon law, common law, Hindu law, customary law, Japanese law, and international law.

# THE SPIRIT OF
# ISLAMIC LAW

*Bernard G. Weiss*

The University of Georgia Press
Athens and London

Paperback edition, 2006

Athens, Georgia 30602

Designed by Walton Harris
Set in Trump by G&S Typesetters, Inc.

Printed digitally in the United States of America

The Library of Congress has cataloged the hardcover edition of this book as follows:

Library of Congress Cataloging-in-Publication Data
Weiss, Bernard G.
The spirit of Islamic law / Bernard G. Weiss.
p. cm.–(The spirit of the laws)
Includes bibliographical references and index.
ISBN 0-8203-1977-5 (alk. paper)
1. Islamic law. I. Title. II. Series.
LAW
340.5'9–dc21 98-10565

ISBN-13: 978-0-8203-2827-0
ISBN-10: 0-8203-2827-8

British Library Cataloging-in-Publication Data available

*To the memory of my mother and father,*

*Olga Josephine and George Christian Weiss, and*

*to their beloved Morocco, where it all began.*

# CONTENTS

# PREFACE

As is well known, classical Muslim jurisprudence encompasses two distinct disciplines known in Arabic as *fiqh* and *uṣūl al-fiqh.* Fiqh is the discipline concerned with the articulation of actual rules of law. I have elsewhere called it "practical jurisprudence." A medieval Muslim jurist in search of a statement of the law as it bore on a particular case or problem would turn to the literature of this discipline. Uṣūl al-fiqh, on the other hand, is concerned with questions having to do with the theory of law and with the methodological principles governing the formulation of rules of law. This I have called "theoretical jurisprudence."

All the Muslim schools of law (*madhahib*) cultivated both disciplines with equal care and energy, and all with equal fastidiousness kept the boundary between the two well defined. Jurisprudence was thus for jurists of all the schools a dyad of interdependent but nonetheless separate disciplines. That they devoted much energy to the study of rules is, of course, only to be expected. Without rules there is no law. What is remarkable is that they devoted at least as much energy to questions having to do with the justification of the body of rules that they so meticulously worked out. The sheer quantity of Muslim writings about rules of law—treatises, manuals, commentaries, glosses on commentaries, superglosses on glosses—is fully matched by the quantity of writings about theoretical and methodological underpinnings.

Western scholarship has tended to see the discipline of uṣūl al-fiqh as having carried on the task of justifying the law *retrospectively;* that is to say, it sees the discipline as having attempted to explore and lay out in an organized manner the methodological processes that had given rise to a body of rules that was already in existence. It is no doubt true to say that when the great classical works of this discipline were being written, the perspective of the discipline was indeed to a large extent retrospective. This is not to say, however, that Muslim jurists turned to the task of justifying rules as an afterthought. To the contrary, the business of formulating rules took place from the very beginning within a context of discussion of methodological and theoretical issues. As a discipline, uṣūl al-fiqh of course evolved in profound ways over time. But the roots of the discipline are certainly as ancient as the roots of fiqh itself. Furthermore, even after the discipline had matured and had become embodied in classical texts, Muslim jurists never lost sight of its practical value. Fiqh, as we shall see, was never a finished business.

This book relies primarily upon the literature of uṣūl al-fiqh, for it is in that literature that one finds the Muslim jurists most energetically and systematically addressing questions relating to the nature of law and of the law's authority, the sources of the law, the values enshrined in the law, and the religious underpinning of the law. The series of which this volume is a part seeks to explore the attitudes displayed by legal traditions on such questions. This book is—in keeping with the guidelines for the series—therefore not primarily a study of rules. To the extent that rules are discussed in these pages (particularly in Chapters 7 and 8), they serve to illustrate points vital to the understanding of the broader perspectives of the Muslim jurists.

Readers familiar with my previous publications will be aware that the focus of the present work upon the literature and concerns of uṣūl al-fiqh reflects the direction my research has taken throughout my career. In particular, it reflects the work that culminated in my book *The Search for God's Law: Islamic Jurisprudence in the Writings of Sayf al-Din al-Amidi*. But I am quite convinced that an apology for this focus is not necessary. Anyone conversant with the literature of uṣūl al-fiqh will have no difficulty, I think, with my basic contention that it is here, more than in the literature of fiqh, that all of the things that we are likely to subsume under the heading of "the spirit of Islamic law" are to be found. The following pages will suggest that that spirit embraces a number of salient features of Muslim juristic thought: espousal of divine sovereignty (the basis of everything else);

a fixation upon sacred texts that are the repositories of divine revelation; an uncompromisingly intentionalist approach to the interpretation of these texts; a frank acknowledgment of the uncertainty and fallibility of all individual human endeavor to capture the divine intent and a consequent acceptance of probabilism as the foundation of valid interpretation; a tolerance of legal diversity and a willingness to disseminate juristic authority among multiple schools; a moralistic bent grounded in a particular social vision; and, last, a preoccupation with the affairs of private individuals, and especially with family relations and contracts, coupled with a concern to define the limits of the power of government.

In preparing this book for publication, I was generously assisted by several people. Special thanks are due to Jeanette Wakin of Columbia University, who went over the entire manuscript with a watchful eye, made numerous suggestions for improvement of the text, called my attention to a number of factual errors or ill-considered judgments, and assisted me in rewriting certain passages. Any shortcomings that may remain are, however, entirely of my own making. I also thank Michael McOmber, who kindly developed a font containing the diacritics required for transliteration of Arabic terms, and Elaine Clark, who familiarized me with the computer procedures necessary to get the manuscript in final shape. Finally, I acknowledge a grant from the National Endowment for the Humanities in support of work on the manuscript that I did during the summer of 1995.

The transliteration system used in this book is basically that of the *International Journal of Middle East Studies.* Like the journal, I have not provided full transliteration for Arabic proper names (except in the Bibliography and in the bibliographic portions of the notes) or for Arabic words that have entered into English usage as evidenced by their inclusion in *Webster's Third New International Dictionary* (unabridged). Only the marks representing the *ʿayn* and the medial or final *hamza* appear in such words and in Arabic proper names. Thus words such as "Qurʾan," "Shariʿa," "hadith," "mufti," "kalam," and "qadi," which appear in *Webster's*, do not have vowel marks or underdots, whereas words such as *fatwā, ijtihād, ẓāhir,* and *ḥukm* do. However, where I discuss words in the former category *as Arabic words* (as when I deal with their etymology or their meanings in the Arabic lexicon), I revert to full diacritical marking, in addition to using italics. Such discussions are on the whole infrequent. Furthermore, in the glossary I provide full diacritical marking for all entries, whether found in *Webster's* or not.

I have not attempted in this book to avoid using the masculine pronoun with reference to God; nor have I used inclusive language, such as "he or she," when referring to the Muslim jurist considered in the abstract. Such usage, though indisputably desirable in contemporary self-expression, would, I think, be anachronistic in a book that seeks to be faithful to its premodern sources. I do not wish to put myself in the position of correcting the great classical jurists of Islam. Gender-related language issues are for contemporary Muslim writers, as for all living writers, to deal with. For the classical jurists (the most renowned of whom were all men), these issues did not exist.

# *The Spirit of Islamic Law*

# 1 The Formation of Islamic Law

Law, it seems, is integral to monotheistic religion. The world's sole creator is necessarily by right its sole ultimate ruler, legislator, and judge. All law worthy of the name must therefore originate with him. The human lawgiver is, despite his exalted position within the monotheistic scheme of things, only the mediator of the divine law to mankind. The words heard upon his lips become enshrined in sacred texts that are carefully preserved from generation to generation. Pious sages emerge to assume the task of interpreting these texts. Through their labors, the law becomes more fully articulated and its bearing on daily life made more clear. Government, too, becomes part of the ideal monotheistic order, for the law is understood to be the embodiment of a social vision that can be realized in this world only if power, an inescapable component of social existence, is placed in the law's service. Accordingly, monotheistic communities inevitably acquire or seek to acquire the character of monotheistic polities. In times when the divine law is ignored or forgotten, the monotheistic outlook finds expression in movements of social criticism and programs of renewal or in visions of millenarian fulfillment of the divine program.

This overall pattern is, of course, classically represented in the traditions and beliefs of Judaism, the oldest of the world's three principal monotheisms. Its most recent representation is found in Islam. In many ways Islam is a much more autonomous and complete representation of the classical pattern than is the intermediate monotheism, Christianity. Its own historical tradition portrays it as repeating the process of monotheistic formation from the ground level up. In particular, Islam presents itself to the world as the possessor of a law unique in itself and distinct from Israel's law.

Not so Christianity, which was founded by Jews who continued to see themselves as Jews despite their willingness to enter into an eschatological partnership with gentiles. The gentiles were in any case, to use Paul's language, seen as branches grafted onto the trunk of Israel (Romans 11:16–24). The point is that the first Christians saw themselves as heralds of an eschatological fulfillment of the hopes *of Israel* and could not regard divine law as other than the law of Moses. The "new commandment," or "new covenant," mentioned in the pages of the New Testament is a legacy of the renewal traditions of Judaism itself, which date back to biblical times. Never does it entail an intention to displace Israel's law. Jesus is, after all, presented in parts of the New Testament as the fulfiller of the Mosaic law, not its repealer. This fulfilling of the law is essentially a revisioning, not a total reconstruction. In Matthew's account, for example, Jesus increases the requirements of true righteousness by disallowing what Mosaic law had allowed, but he does not directly contravene Mosaic prohibitions or commands. Paul's reference to Christ as "the end of the law" must be understood in the context of the complexity of his thinking about the law in the context of eschatological salvation. The law of Moses remains throughout Paul's writings a standard by which conduct is to be judged.[1] Paul struggled with the realization that the gentiles also had their law and tried to accord validity to that law, but he could see it only as coexisting with the revealed law and as a more diffuse version of it that was "written on their hearts" (Romans 2:15). Thanks to the workings of conscience, the gentiles could achieve the essential righteousness of the Mosaic law; they "who have not the law do by nature what the law requires" (Romans 2:14).

Islam, on the other hand, was not founded by Jews, nor, for that matter, by members of any older monotheistic community. It does not reflect any of Christianity's consciousness of having emerged within a particular preexistent monotheistic matrix. The first Muslims are portrayed in Islamic tradition as decidedly distinct from Jews and Christians, and the setting in which Islam arose is portrayed as similar to that in which Israel's monotheism had arisen, a setting of pure paganism. The larger world in which Islam appeared was, of course, hardly devoid of monotheism; it was in fact a vast sea of monotheism. This larger world, however, does not constitute the original and decisive setting of Islam in Muslim sacred history; rather, Arabian paganism, called *jāhiliyya*, constitutes this setting. For the most part, the first Muslims are converts from paganism. The high point in the drama of Islam's triumph in the time of the prophet Muhammad is the destruction of the idols of the Kaʿba in Mecca. In this event the encounter of Israel's God with the deities of Canaan is revisited.

The reason for Islam's engendering of a new, autonomous body of sacred law has much to do with the fact that Islam developed in the context of a polity of its own making. Monotheistic law and monotheistic polity went hand in hand. Here again the resemblance to ancient Israel is noteworthy. Israelite history placed the giving of the law in the context of a wandering tribally organized desert polity that would subsequently establish hegemony over the land promised to the patriarchs. This history, along with the law itself, was of course shaped in the context of a sovereign kingdom built on the land of Israel. Despite its bifurcation into southern and northern centers of power after the death of Solomon, it remained in the thinking of prophet/idealists a single Davidic kingdom and in any case was able until the time of the exile to provide a context of political community within which the law could be further refined and at times revisioned. With the postexilic restoration, once again a context of political community in the land of Israel, this time with a new type of priestly leadership, was created, albeit under the watchful eye of Persian overlords.

Similarly, Muslim history places the revelation of Islam's law in the context of a polity based in Medina and portrays Muhammad as, like Moses, both prophet and ruler. (The revelations that came to Muhammad before the migration of the Muslims from Mecca to Medina are generally regarded as having little legal content.) Although a few modern Muslim revisionists have contended that it was not part of Muhammad's mission to create a state, the weight of Muslim opinion down through the ages has been on the side of the opposing view. The standard account of the life of Muhammad has him undertaking rather soon after his arrival in Medina in 622 C.E. (year 1 in the Muslim calendar) to set down in writing regulations governing the internal affairs of the community and the defense of the community against attack from the outside. Tradition would see this as the virtual charter of the Islamic state. Muhammad clearly held the reins of government in his hand; he was lawgiver (mediator of the divine law), judge, statesman, and head of an army.

Without denying the rootedness of the Islamic polity in the time of Muhammad, modern Western scholarship has come to see the period after Muhammad and the first conquests as more decisive for the building up of that polity and, with it, the law. Although the polity created under Muhammad's leadership was not exactly a desert polity, it did, like the polity under Moses, foreshadow greater things to come, and it too was tribally organized and, if not migratory, situated in an oasis settlement surrounded by a migratory desert population. The greater things to come were the conquests in the wake of which the Umayyad caliphate of Damascus would emerge (dubbed by later Muslim historians a "kingdom"). The Umayyad caliphate (661–750 C.E.) and its successor, the Abbasid caliphate, for a period of time (750 to about 950 C.E.) would do for Islam what the Davidic kingdom had done for the religion of Israel, that is, provide the political context necessary for the development of genuine law.

The details of the development of Israelite and Islamic polities and law differ enormously, but the main contours are at least similar. And just as Israel's law would be seen to be distinct from all other law, no matter what the influences from other legal traditions the modern historian may be able to detect, so Islam's law would be seen to be distinct, again, no matter what the borrowings. In both cases, a divinely ordained law unfolded in the midst of a developing political community whose needs it was designed to meet.

The development of law and polity in Christianity follows a rather different course. Christianity existed for three centuries within a polity that was very much *not* of its own making and that during much of this time was perceived to be alien to itself. When during the fourth century Christianity finally prevailed politically, it took over the empire within which it had spread, including its law. Thus Roman law would become the foundational law of the Christian world; there would be no distinctively Christian law. The *corpus juris civilis* of Justinian was the product of Christian compilation and the project of a Christian emperor, but it would not be seen as Christian law. During the Middle Ages, canon law would develop side by side with civil law, and to some extent the Bible would be used as a source but only alongside Roman law. There was no theologically grounded need to turn exclusively to scripture for law. The law of Moses—especially the Ten Commandments—would enjoy pride of place as an object of theological reflection, particularly in the context of discussions of sin and salvation, in which the interrelationship between law and grace always loomed large. But biblical law considered purely as law enjoyed no such pride of place. Classical Christian thought eventually turned to the idea of natural law as a way of justifying law, reflecting Paul's readiness to validate the law that was written in men's hearts.

The post-Constantinian Christian world was always conscious of having appropriated the empire within which it had spread together with its institutions of government and law. In the world of Islam, all such consciousness was resisted. Islam spread throughout the world with a very different kind of consciousness, a consciousness of bringing a new law and polity to areas it overran, of inaugurating a new religiopolitical era. The Muslims did not appropriate an empire but rather created one. For Christians, the Roman empire remained Roman. The caliphal empire was decidedly not Roman (nor, for that matter, Sassanian); it was Arab and Islamic. Islam's mission was precisely to bring to the world a new polity and law, replacing all outmoded polities and laws.

Though the seeds of the new Islamic order were planted in the time of the prophet Muhammad, its full maturation required the labors of subsequent generations of Muslims. The building up of the Islamic polity was largely the achievement of the first caliphal dynasty, that of the Umayyads, which established itself in Damascus in 661 in the wake of civil wars that had marred the later years of the short-lived Medina-based regime of the earliest caliphs. The Umayyads took seriously the social vision that had been heralded by the Prophet and saw themselves as its executors, dubbing themselves "caliphs of God."[2] Heirs of the Roman (Byzantine) administrative tradition, they took decisive measures to de-Romanize their empire and give it an Arab and Islamic character. Although they used Byzantine bureaucratic machinery and personnel, they regarded things Roman as alien in spirit to the new order they stood for. Rome was still the enemy, with a vestige of its former power yet well established in Constantinople. The new Islamic empire had been destined to defeat and replace Rome. The change was symbolized in the adoption of Arabic early in the eighth century as the language of administration.

In the realm of law, the great contribution of the Umayyads was their establishment of a new caliphal system of justice. Judges within the system were given the title of qadi, which distinguished them as bearers of caliphal authority within the judicial realm. The qadis were in the strictest sense delegates of the caliph or a provincial governor and could be appointed or dismissed at will by their superior. Since the governors were themselves subordinate in authority to the caliph, the entire system was pyramidal, with the caliph standing at the pinnacle as the ultimate source of all authority, judicial, administrative, and legislative. The Umayyad program called for a centralized, autocratic approach to the implementation of the Islamic social vision.

The qadis, through their case-by-case decisions, laid important foundations for the subsequent development of Islamic law. They did not have a body of law to work with that could easily be identified as Islamic, and therefore they based their decisions on their own judicial discretion and sense of equity. The law available to them was an amalgam of Roman law and the older indigenous law of the various areas of the empire, including elements both of Arab tribal law and ancient Near Eastern law.[3] This complex the qadis applied, modified, or ignored as they saw fit. Their decisions gained authority not from the legal material as such, none of which had for them any intrinsic authority, but rather from the status they enjoyed as delegates of the caliph. The justice that the qadis meted out carried authority as caliphal law. As the years passed—particularly in the final quarter century of Umayyad rule—the decisions of the qadis had the cumulative effect of producing a sizable body of precedents that historians of Islamic law, following Joseph Schacht,[4] have come to call Umayyad judicial practice.

But notwithstanding the socioreligious aspirations of the Umayyad caliphs, Islamic law as we now know it was not destined to emerge directly out of Umayyad judicial practice or, indeed, out of the circles of power. Not judges but scholars who lacked official connections with the caliphal regime were to play the key role in the development of a body of law suited to the Islamic polity. These scholars did not, of course, work in a vacuum. The practice of the qadis was their starting point. But it was only a starting point, something to critique as a first step toward a wide-ranging and politically unfettered formulation and systemization of an ideal law of God. The scholars were preoccupied less with the law as it actually was, to the extent that this could be determined from judicial practice, than with the law as it ought to be.

As the ranks of scholars swelled, the caliphal regime soon found itself competing with the scholarly community in the shaping of Islam and Islamic law. The qadis represented caliphal officialdom; the scholars stood distinctly outside the sphere of officialdom. The fact that qadis were sometimes recruited from the ranks of the scholars does not invalidate this important dividing line. If such persons were in any way influential in the process that would give rise to Islamic law, they were able to exercise this influence in their capacity as scholars, not as judges. For in the burgeoning Islamic society, authority was fast becoming linked to personal piety and religious knowledge, not to power. This development had its origin in the earliest days of Islam and gained momentum during the conquests, when Arab Muslims found themselves forming in each major region, along with non-Arab converts to Islam, fledgling religious communities caught up in the pressing task of thinking through the implications of their newfound faith.

In such a situation the caliphate, no matter how determined it was to shape the new Islamic order, could not hope to control the development of a grassroots spiritual leadership. The scholars formed just such a leadership and did so quite spontaneously and quite independently of the imperial regime and its aspirations. They were in fact more than jurists in the usual sense of that term, for they attended not just to the law but to much else besides. Their horizons were far-reaching, encompassing a whole way of life inclusive of many details of day-to-day living that lay beyond the sphere of what usually counts as law. At a much later date, Islamic usage would find a word to express the totality of norms—legal, moral, and ritual—that these pious scholars endeavored to articulate, the word "Shariʿa" *(sharīʿa).* Since the Shariʿa includes norms beyond those that constitute law in the strict sense, it is incorrect to equate Shariʿa and law *simpliciter* as is often done. On the other hand, law is clearly a part of the Shariʿa, in Muslim thinking, and must always be understood as such.

It was inevitable that law considered as a body of enforceable norms would be a major concern of the pious scholars of the later Umayyad period and after, for the Islam they were seeking to articulate was, as we have noted, an Islam that had grown up within the context of an expanding empire. The scholars were very conscious of living within a polity that had to be reckoned with in their envisioning of an ideal Islamic order of society. Though these scholars were not generally part of caliphal officialdom, they were clearly men of affairs who were incapable of envisioning an Islam without Islamic government and law. They shared with the Umayyad regime the conviction that the expansion of Islam through the vehicle of the caliphal empire was foreordained by God and that it had in fact been the mission of Islam to replace fallen empires with a new political order. It was therefore inevitable that they should have devoted a major part of their reflective capacities to the subjects of government and law and that Umayyad judicial practice should have been a major object of their attention.

In the later Muslim accounts these scholars of early Islam would be characterized as *ahl al-raʾy,* "people of opinion." Although the term became pejorative in some circles, it was not intrinsically so; those so named were people whose opinion on matters of law and morality counted, the people who spoke with authority. It must be borne in mind that when these scholars began the work of formulating the law, the textual canons of Islam were as yet not fully defined, particularly that vast body of texts known as hadith. Unlike the later scholars of Islam, these early scholars were therefore not primarily exegetes. When they expounded the law, they expressed their personal sense of what was in Islamic terms proper and just with respect to each particular case that came within their purview. The authority with which they spoke was largely personal. They were in fact the sages of early Islam.

Although Muslims came to see themselves as constituting in principle a worldwide community called the umma, real community remained local, and each local community had its own scholar-sages. Communities of Muslims existed in all the cities where the conquering Arabs settled—Basra, Kufa, Damascus, Fustat, Qayrawan, and so forth—as well as in the original Muslim settlement of Medina. Modern scholarship has singled out Kufa in Iraq and Medina in Arabia as the two most influential centers of legal development. Their influence is, however, most visible when seen retrospectively, that is, in the light of the fact that Sunni Islam's three most widespread schools of legal doctrine were to emerge from these centers, the Hanafi school from Kufa and the Maliki and Shafiʿi schools from Medina. Kufa was furthermore the primary birthplace of Shiʿi legal development.

In each center, the scholars disagreed with each other from time to time on points of detail, and where the differences could not be resolved, toleration seems to have prevailed. On the other hand, the scholars seem quite early to have discovered among themselves a significant measure of agreement and in time were able to articulate a body of shared doctrine. Thus did the earliest schools of legal doctrine—what Joseph Schacht called "the ancient schools"[5]—emerge in the major centers. As scholars from different centers came into increasing contact with each other and became aware of doctrinal differences between the schools, an atmosphere of interschool debate and polemic arose, prompting the schools to shore up their doctrines with ever more persuasive arguments.

Two important developments in legal argumentation occurred. First, legal argumentation became more sophisticated as concern with maintaining the consistency of the law increased and as the use of reasoning by analogy in the extension of the law to new cases became more refined. Reasoning by analogy is a method of argument that by its very nature leads to assimilation of like cases and thus to more generalized statements of the law. Discrete cases give rise to broad categories, and as these categories are organized under major headings, the law assumes a more systematic character. This development was well under way by the end of the Umayyad period. Though the method of reasoning by analogy would have its detractors, both among Sunnis and Shiʿis, it would eventually become firmly established within the mainstream Sunni schools (though never among the Shiʿis).

The second development had to do with the locus of legal authority. The earliest scholars appear to have made statements about the law on their own authority, without seeking to attribute these statements to an earlier or higher authority. They were all, of course, strict monotheists who in principle recognized God as the ultimate source of all authority. This conviction was shared by all Muslims and could not be called into question. But divine authority was of little value if it was not channeled through human instruments. The scholars seem to have regarded themselves, and to have been regarded by others, as able to articulate the mind of God on issues of law and daily conduct. The fact that they were guided largely by their own sense of propriety and justice did not render their very human deliberations at all incompatible, in their view, with the principle of divine authority. The notion that divine justice is essentially at one with an uncorrupted human sense of justice, which has a checkered career in the history of Islamic thought, had roots in this early period when the formulation of the law was not yet perceived as a primarily exegetical enterprise.

Among the scholars themselves in each community, circles of younger disciples formed around various older scholars, their masters. This development was an inevitable outcome of transmission of legal learning from one generation to the next. By the end of the Umayyad period, each legal school had a number of prominent masters who were thought to give especially authoritative expression to the school's doctrine. After the fall of the Umayyads and the rise in 750 of the second caliphal dynasty, that of the Abbasids, this trend continued. A new generation of masters arose, replacing the old, only to be superseded in time by yet another generation. As the generations passed, a retrospective singling out of certain masters of the past as uniquely authoritative occurred, and the most definitive elements of school doctrine came to be seen as harking back to them. In this manner there emerged out of the major regional schools what Schacht called "personal schools," meaning schools named after an eponymous founder.[6] Of the four major schools of later Sunni Islam, all of which are of the personal type, three emerged, as we have already noted, out of earlier regional schools: the Hanafi school out of the Kufan school and the Maliki and Shafi'i schools out of the school of Medina. The eponymous authorities of these schools were Abu Hanifa, Malik ibn Anas, and Shafi'i. (The fourth school, which—as we will see in the following pages—was to emerge under somewhat different circumstances, was named after Ahmad ibn Hanbal.) Shi'i legal doctrine, as it developed, would also be connected in a special way with a prominent authority who lived roughly the same time as Abu Hanifa, namely Ja'far al-Sadiq, and Shi'i law is accordingly sometimes characterized as Ja'fari law. Unlike the Sunni eponyms, however, Ja'far al-Sadiq would be counted among the infallible Imams of the Shi'i tradition.

Norman Calder, in a seminal study of the early literature of the three above-mentioned Sunni schools,[7] has elicited evidence of two different tendencies in these schools' thinking about authority. He sees the earliest literature as containing two basic types of material: on the one hand, expository material in which the doctrine of the school is set forth discursively in a format of responsa and, on the other hand, polemic material in which doctrine is supported by "authority statements" (exempla). In the expository material (also called dialogue material by Calder), statements of the law (responsa) are placed under the authority of great masters of the school, most often the eponymic founder, whose word is usually treated as final and without need of further argument or appeal to higher authority. This fixation upon the authority of the masters served the internal needs of the school in the setting down and consolidating of school doctrine, particularly doctrine related to hard cases. It did not serve the needs of the school in the context of interschool debate. The polemic material therefore attributes statements of the law to figures belonging to the earlier generations of Islam, whose authority would be recognized by all the schools. Included in this material are not only statements of companions of the Prophet but also statements of the Prophet himself.

As one follows the development of scholarly thinking about authority in subsequent juristic literature, one notes, according to Calder, a greater frequency of citations of statements of the Prophet and a change in the role of the great masters from that of authority figures in their own right to that of conduits of prophetic teaching. The masters no longer merely state the law; they also supply an exegetical grounding of the law in sayings of the Prophet or accounts of his deeds. This trend heralds the dawn of what is to become the classical understanding of authority and approach to justification of the law. It represents the triumph of the perspective of a distinct class of scholars known in Arabic as *ahl al-ḥadīth*.

The term *ahl al-ḥadīth*, which I shall translate as "hadith specialists," denotes a body of scholars whose history reaches back into the Umayyad period and whose labors were for an entire generation or so largely, if not entirely, independent of the labors of the scholars belonging to the earliest regional schools of law. They too were seeking to elaborate norms that would govern the day-to-day affairs of Muslims but refused to allow mere human judgment or insight to be decisive in the articulation of those norms. They saw their task as the gathering, ordering, and memorization of nothing less than the very words of the Prophet or accounts of his deeds. These were distinguished from the divine words contained in the Qur'an and came to be known collectively as the Sunna (custom or tradition) of the Prophet. The main difference between the hadith specialists and the early law schools had to do, not with acceptance or rejection of the idea of Sunna as such, but with the issue of how the Sunna was transmitted. During the Umayyad period, the law schools had come to view their school doctrine as authoritatively representing the Sunna. The hadith specialists saw the narrative material that they collected—the hadith—as the sole authoritative representation of the Sunna.

The point of view of the hadith specialists proved to be irresistible in the end, even for the law schools. As the regional schools were being transformed into personal schools during the early Abbasid period, the concept of Sunna as represented by hadith infiltrated school thinking more and more, preparing the way for its ultimate triumph. Thus in the school literature of the ninth century, we find prophetic hadith entering into arguments for legal doctrine with ever greater frequency, until finally appeal to hadith along with the Qur'an becomes the standard type of argument.

But hadith material could be, and was, fabricated. Modern Western scholarship has in fact thrown doubt on the authenticity of the great majority of hadith narratives and has predicated the very growth of the hadith corpus upon a process of legal and theological dialectic in which conflicting doctrines were increasingly put into circulation by casting them in the form of prophetic dicta. That fabrication occurred was openly and freely acknowledged by the Muslim legal schools themselves, and scholars therefore had to be able to demonstrate the authenticity of any hadith narratives they cited. The methods of authentication that were developed for this purpose, however, focused on transmitters, not, as Western scholarship would have it, on the actual content of the narratives. And Muslim scholarship was of course much less skeptical about the results of authentication efforts than Western scholarship has tended to be.

It had been understood among the hadith specialists themselves that a hadith had no authority unless accompanied by a chain of transmitters called an "isnad" *(isnād)*. A scholar of the law had to scrutinize with great care the isnad of each hadith he used in order to ascertain that the transmitters met the agreed-upon tests of trustworthiness, that they had direct transgenerational contact with each other, and that there were no gaps in the chain of transmission. If a scholar was remiss in his evaluation of an isnad, any argument for a rule of law that he might propound, based on hadith, would be vulnerable to criticism from other scholars.

In order to facilitate this text-critical aspect of the legal scholar's work, certain specialists in hadith busied themselves, during the ninth and tenth centuries, with the gathering of hadith narratives into written compilations. The result was the emergence of the classical hadith books, which contained only hadith narratives judged to be authentic by the compilers, along with the isnads upon which that judgment was based. Henceforth, legal scholars could turn to these books and make their own judgments regarding the reliability of particular narratives. Typically, the material in these books was arranged under topical headings that were of interest to legal scholars. They were clearly compiled as tools of legal study.

As the schools of law with which we have been concerned in the preceding paragraphs (Maliki, Hanafi, Shafi'i) were incorporating increasing amounts of prophetic hadith into their legal argumentation, the fourth of the surviving Sunni schools of law, the Hanbali school, emerged from within the ranks of the hadith specialists themselves, claiming Ibn Hanbal, a renowned compiler of hadith, as its founder. The development of the Hanbali school during the century or so after the lifetime of its founder followed, interestingly enough, a course that was just the reverse of what happened within the three other schools. Starting with an uncompromising fixation on hadith narratives as a prime source of law, the Hanbalis moved gradually in the direction of greater use of certain methods of legal reasoning that continued to survive within the other schools along with the massive incorporation of hadith. We will consider these methods in due time.

Shiʿi thinking about hadith and the role of hadith in the formulation of the law followed yet a different course of development. In one respect Shiʿi thinking was similar to Sunni; it, too, would come to see hadith as the proper embodiment of the Sunna. It would be more inclusive in its conception of the Sunna, however, for the Shiʿi Sunna embraces sayings and deeds not only of the prophet Muhammad but also of the Imams. We will explore the Shiʿi doctrine of the imamate more fully in a later chapter. Here it is sufficient to note the reason for juxtaposing the Imams and the Prophet as repositories of Sunna, which is that Shiʿi doctrine deems the Imams—descendants of the Prophet and his successors as political heads and specially enlightened spiritual guides of the community—to be, like the Prophet, endowed with infallibility. For Sunnis, infallibility of an inspired individual ends with the death of the Prophet, while for Shiʿis it ends with the death of the Twelfth Imam two and a half centuries later.

The adoption of prophetic hadith (supplemented, in the case of Shiʿis, by hadith relating words and deeds of the Imams) as a major source of law second only to the Qurʾan resulted in the transformation of the exposition of law into a largely exegetical enterprise. Whereas the qurʾanic text was of relatively modest size and the amount of strictly legal provisions in the Qurʾan was in any case meager, however important for certain areas of the law such as family and inheritance law, the body of hadith texts was enormous, and a much greater part of the law would be anchored in hadith than in the Qur'an. Once exegesis—the extraction of law from texts—had, thanks to the increased dependence on hadith, become central to Islamic jurisprudence, scholars of the law were presumed to be masters of all the appropriate hermeneutical skills, and the tools of Arabic philology, which were fast developing around the same time, quickly became vital implements of legal study.

Just as the recognition of hadith as a source of law assured that legal scholarship would become largely an exercise in exegesis, so also the writing down of hadith in the great compilations helped to foster the literary character of the law. Whereas in the early stages of its development—that is, until near the end of the eighth century—the law found expression primarily in the dicta of living scholars, now it was becoming, and would remain throughout its subsequent history, a law of books. This bookishness of the law was also fostered by the emergence, along with the written compilations of hadith, of written compendia of substantive law. Originally themselves compilations of transmitted juristic dicta (responsa, authority statements), these eventually took the form of authored works, including both lengthy expositions and shorter manuals. The manuals, which were typically abridgments of larger works, were in turn frequently the object of commentary. As the literature of commentary proliferated, it gave rise to a proliferation of glosses and superglosses—all this, of course, over a span of centuries. These school texts became an object of study in their own right, for which mastery of the established hermeneutical skills was as requisite as for the study of the Qur'an and hadith. Eventually, in the eleventh century, an entire educational institution, the *madrasa*, would emerge, whose primary function was to train scholars in all the disciplines entailed in legal study.

Looking back over the development of Islamic law as recounted in the preceding pages, we cannot fail to be impressed by a point of great importance for the understanding of the Islamic legal tradition. Despite the many transformations that occurred in the course of the law's development, one thing remained unchanged. The elaboration of the law had been, nearly from the beginning, the work of private scholars unaffiliated with officialdom, despite aspirations of the caliphal regime to the contrary; and it was to remain so throughout subsequent centuries. Like the Umayyad caliphate, the Abbasid caliphate that succeeded it in 750 C.E. had ambitions to shape the development of Islamic norms, especially in the realm of religious dogma, and it undertook to bring the scholars of the law under its influence, even to the point of instituting an inquisition. But the Abbasid program of caliphal domination over the shaping of Islam was no more successful than that of the Umayyads had been. Led by none other than the great uncompromising hadith scholar Ibn Hanbal, the scholars of the law were able successfully to vindicate their independence vis-à-vis the caliphal regime and to establish once and for all their monopoly over the exposition of the law. The caliphate had to give up all claims to legislative powers and to resign itself to being—or at least to giving the appearance of being—the instrument of implementation of the law of scholars, the law of books. Something on the order of an Islamic rule of law would become for all time the normal state of affairs. Judges alone would be part of the caliphal regime (or, later on, the regime of the sultanate); the real bearers of the law would have their niche elsewhere in Muslim society.

The bookishness of the law helped to undergird the autonomy of legal scholarship and to prevent interference from the central regime. Certain definitive texts—the Qur'an and hadith, to begin with, but also certain major compendia of law—enjoyed canonical status with authority that was firmly and deeply entrenched within Muslim society. These texts formed the basic curriculum for the colleges of law (madrasas), which themselves had financial resources independent of government revenues. The canonical texts, the madrasas, and the communities of scholars who congregated in them thus all became immovable rocks of Islamic society that the ruling regime would never be able to challenge or dislodge. The scholars of the law, far from being beholden to the regime, were in a position to make the regime answerable to them. The independence they enjoyed made it possible for them when necessary to adopt a critical stance, although the community of scholars have rarely defied or denounced the regime.

Despite their many differences, the four surviving Sunni schools of law—the Hanafi, Maliki, Shafiʿi, and Hanbali schools—have, since the time of their final maturation, shared a common vision of the law, its sources, and the methods of its elaboration, and we will turn to that vision in the remaining pages of this chapter. We may begin with the overarching concept of the Shariʿa. As stated early in this chapter, the Shariʿa includes law and much else besides law, and it is misleading to equate Shariʿa and law. There is in fact in classical Arabic no precise equivalent of the English word "law" in the ordinary, everyday sense. The law contained within the Shariʿa must therefore be identified with reference to concepts and provisions that we can without hesitation characterize as "legal." For one thing, the Shariʿa clearly contains rules as well as provisions for the judicial application of these rules and for their enforcement by means of state-supplied sanctions. We can have no difficulty in speaking of these rules as rules of law. To return to a point made earlier, the scholars of the law elaborated the Shariʿa with an eye always on judicial practice and on the conduct of government. Not wanting the ruling regime (whether it was called the caliphate or, as in later times, had some other name) to shape the Shariʿa, they themselves nonetheless shaped it with the regime very much in mind, always viewing the coercive power of the regime as the necessary instrument of its implementation.

In archaic Arabic the term *sharīʿa* means "path to the water hole." When we consider the importance of a well-trodden path to a source of water for man and beast in the arid desert environment, we can readily appreciate why this term in Muslim usage should have become a metaphor for a whole way of life ordained by God. Reciting words from the first chapter (*sūra*) of the Qurʾan in their daily prayers, devout Muslims call upon God to "guide us along the right [or straight] path." Though another word for "path" is employed in this qurʾanic verse, namely *ṣirāṭ*, the prayer signals a basic theme that runs throughout the Qurʾan and throughout the life of the Muslim, a theme that is integral to the concept of the Shariʿa. This theme is divine guidance. Without guidance from God, humans are without direction and are liable to stray from the right path, for just as surely as there is a right path, there are also wrong paths. And just as the right path leads ultimately to happiness and fulfillment both in this world and the world to come, the wrong paths lead to sorrow and pain in both worlds.

The right path, the Shariʿa, constitutes an entire way of life. It em-

no word for "law"

braces right ways of worshiping God, of interacting with fellow human beings, of conducting one's personal life, even of thinking and believing. The concept of the Shari'a is the most comprehensive concept in Islam. Indeed, it forms the very core of Islam. The term "Islam," after all, means "submission," and the Shari'a is the divine delineation of the life of submission. To submit to God is to follow the path that God has ordained, nothing more and nothing less. Even mysticism in Islam—the mysticism cultivated by Sufis—comes ultimately under the rubric of the Shari'a in that it represents its experiential dimension, its inner essence (*ḥaqīqa*), its secrets (*asrār*).

Despite its centrality, the term *sharī'a* is seldom defined in the classical literature of Islam, which otherwise defines key terms carefully. We may extrapolate a definition of the term, however, from a phrase that appears throughout that literature, namely *al-aḥkām al-shar'iyya*. The term *aḥkām* (sing. *ḥukm*), though most commonly translated as "judgments," is in this context best rendered in English, I think, as "categorizations." The objects of these categorizations are our human acts. Strictly speaking, the term *ḥukm* is elliptical; it stands for *al-ḥukm 'ala'l-fi'l bi-kawnihi kadhā*, "the categorization of an act as such-and-such." The term *shar'iyya* is a qualifier derived from the same Arabic root as *sharī'a*. The full phrase *al-aḥkām al-shar'iyya* may be translated as "the Shari'a categorizations" (using "Shari'a" as an adjective) or even as "the categorizations that make up the Shari'a." Since God is the author of the categorizations, we arrive at the following definition of the Shari'a: it is the totality of divine categorizations of human acts. The categories entailed in the divine *aḥkām* comprise several sets, only two of which need concern us here.

One of these sets embraces the following five categories: "obligatory" (*wājib, farḍ*), "recommended" (*mandūb, mustaḥabb*), "neutral" or "indifferent" (*mubāḥ*), "disapproved" (*makrūh*), and "forbidden" (*ḥarām, muḥarram, maḥẓūr*). Of these categories, two quite naturally lend themselves to being subsumed under the heading of law, namely the obligatory and the forbidden; for it is in the nature of law to prescribe—that is to say, impose obligation—and to forbid. Law is a body of rules, and a rule is in essence the categorization of an act as obligatory or forbidden. Classical Muslim thought employs two interrelated criteria to distinguish the divine categorizations of human acts as obligatory or forbidden—the divine rules—from other categorizations: blame (*dhamm*) and punishment (*ʿiqāb*). Blame in classical Muslim thinking is the ground of justified punishment. To be deserving of blame is tantamount to be deserving of punishment. In these pages we will focus on punishment, or punishability, as the factor that renders an act obligatory or forbidden. In the case of the obligatory act, it is omission that is punishable; in the case of the forbidden act, commission. The sanction of punishment gives the categorization of acts as obligatory or forbidden an absolute and uncompromising character (*jazm*), in other words, the character of rules. Genuine rules do not brook noncompliance.

In contrast, the categorizations of human acts as recommended or disapproved are regarded in the classical texts as entailing no such sanction. These categorizations allow, in other words, the option of noncompliance inasmuch as the noncompliant person will not be regarded as liable to punishment. The only negative consequence of noncompliance is the loss of an opportunity to increase one's piety; but there is no real fault in this, no mar on one's personal record, no penalty to be incurred. These categorizations of human acts are thus decidedly not rules; they decidedly do not lend themselves to being subsumed under the heading of law. We thus have in these categorizations a major component of the Shariʿa that cannot with good reason be called law, and yet this component is as integral to the Shariʿa as is the strictly legal component. It is important always to bear in mind that the Shariʿa is as much concerned with recommending and disapproving as it is with prescribing and forbidding.

The middle category of the Shariʿa—that of "neutral" or "indifferent" (*mubāḥ*) acts—is also not, strictly speaking, a category of law, since the law has no special interest in acts that lie, not simply outside the categories of the obligatory and the forbidden, but also outside the categories of the recommended and disapproved. If these latter categories are not categories of the law, then neither can a category defined in relation to them be a category of the law. "Neutral," it should be noted, is not simply a residual category comprising acts left over after all other acts have been categorized. An act may be categorized as neutral ab initio on the basis of revealed directives. As a category that lies midway between the decidedly nonlegal categories, however, the category of neutral can have no strictly legal relevance.

I have deliberately refrained from translating *mubāḥ* as "permitted," preferring to reserve this translation for *jā'iz* and *halāl,* which are categories quite distinct from *mubāḥ* in Muslim juristic thought. These categories embrace acts defined simply as "not forbidden," which is precisely what "permitted" means. As binary opposites, *halāl* and *ḥarām* are frequently translated as "lawful" and "unlawful." These are clearly categories in which the law has an interest. In principle, the category of the permitted or lawful, considered as a binary opposite of the category of the forbidden or unlawful, is inclusive of obligatory acts, or duties. It is rarely, if ever, the practice of the Muslim jurists, however, to speak of duties as permitted. For all practical purposes, therefore, the category of the permitted occupies the middle ground between the forbidden and the obligatory.

But the rules of the Shari'a—the divine categorizations of acts as obligatory, forbidden, or permitted (in the sense just indicated)—do not in practice always function as rules of law in the ordinary sense of that term. In the classical literature of Islam, one finds a great deal of attention being given to obligations, or duties, and prohibitions in regard to which no thought is given to enforcement or implementation through mechanisms of an earthly penal system. This is abundantly true of duties that lie in the realm of worship, but it is also significantly the case with respect to duties in the realm of social relationships. The fundamental preoccupation of Muslim thinking about the Shari'a is with duties that human beings have toward God and with sanctions that belong to the world to come, not to this world. The Shari'a rules exist for the primary purpose of fostering obedience to God, not obedience to temporal authorities, however much the latter may be enjoined. Therefore, we cannot automatically equate the rules of the Shari'a with law. We need further criteria to use in distinguishing rules of law from other Shari'a rules. Such criteria are, as has already been intimated, supplied in the Islamic procedural (adjective) law and entail notions such as judicial applicability and enforceability. We may therefore characterize as rules of law those rules of the Shariʿa that the temporal authority and its judicial representatives are likely to apply and enforce.

The second set of categories entailed in the concept of the Shariʿa embraces the categories "valid" (*ṣaḥīḥ*) and "invalid" (*bāṭil*). The notion of validity has to do with correctness of performance considered as a criterion of whether a duty has been discharged or a transaction duly executed such that it (the transaction) may be considered to be in effect. Each of the five daily prayers, for example, is an act of worship that embraces many elements, including bowing, kneeling, prostrating, and the recitation of certain phrases. If the prayer is not performed correctly, it is invalid and a basic religious duty has not been discharged. It is as though one has not truly prayed. Similarly, if a sale is concluded in a manner that does not conform to the basic requirements of a contract of sale, the sale may not be regarded as having produced the effect of a transfer of ownership. Or if a man and a woman enter into a marriage in a manner that does not conform to the basic requirements of a marriage contract, the couple may not be considered to be truly married, and sexual intercourse between them will be illicit.

Again, as with the first set of categories, both a legal and a moral dimension are involved. Whether a marriage contract, for example, is valid or invalid is clearly an issue of law, and one has full warrant in speaking of legitimacy of sexual intercourse and eligibility to inherit from the spouse as legal effects of a valid marriage. At the same time, this issue is fraught with moral implications; for if a marriage contract is improperly concluded and thus invalid, any subsequent sexual intercourse must be deemed an act of disobedience toward God, a sin. A valid marriage contract, on the other hand, renders sexual intercourse acceptable, even laudatory, in the sight of God. The validity or invalidity of human transactions frequently impinges on one's moral standing before God. Since the Qur'an enjoins humans to fulfill their contracts, validity can translate into the existence of duties under God—that is to say, moral duties—and invalidity into their nonexistence. Thus as with the categories "obligatory" and "forbidden," so with the categories "valid" and "invalid" one needs criteria extrinsic to the categories themselves to distinguish the legal dimension from the moral. Again, procedural law contained within the Shariʿa will be decisive, and the notions of judicial applicability and enforceability will enter in.

Since this is a book on Islamic law, the focus throughout the following chapters will be on the part of the Shariʿa that constitutes law. While it is not appropriate to call the law simply the Shariʿa (for reasons just mentioned), we may certainly *describe* the law we shall be exploring as Shariʿa law, using the term *Shariʿa* as a qualifier (and thus as a translation of *sharʿī* as distinct from *sharīʿa*). Shariʿa law, then, is what we shall be considering, and since we shall be dealing with the pious scholars of the Shariʿa primarily in their capacity as expositors of Shariʿa law I will throughout the following pages refer to them as jurists and will call the principles that they expounded jurisprudence.

It is a presupposition of Muslim juristic thought that the law of God has not been given to human beings in the form of a ready-made code. Law is not sent down from heaven as a finished product. Rather, it is something that human jurists must elaborate on the basis of textual sources. Preeminent among those sources are the Qur'an and the body of hadith narratives in which are recorded the Sunna of the Prophet, his sayings and deeds (to which the Shiʿis add the sayings and deeds of the Imams). Also to be included among the textual sources are texts that record statements on points of law on which the jurists have agreed, which may therefore be regarded as expressions of their consensus. The authority of consensus is, as we shall see, grounded both in the Qur'an and the Sunna, and its role is differently understood by Sunnis and Shiʿis. On the whole, the textual sources contain rather few precisely worded rules of law. If they were filled with such rules, they would not be true sources in the Islamic sense of "sources" (*uṣūl*) but rather codes, statements of the law. It is the business of the jurists, not of prophets, to provide such statements.

The Arabic term *uṣūl* literally means "roots." The rules that the jurists produce are called, on the other hand, "branches" (*furūʿ*) or "fruit" (*thamara*). The extraction of rules from the sources is often called "harvesting" (*istithmār*). The work of the jurists is thus described by means of agricultural metaphors. Only the roots (that is, the sources) are given; the branches, or fruit, is not but rather must be made to appear; and for this to happen human husbandry is required. The jurist is the husbandman who must facilitate the growth of the law—the fruit, the branches—out of the roots.

In carrying out this task, the jurist must first explore to the fullest possible extent the meaning of the texts in order to determine what rules are contained within that meaning. This task requires him to employ the skills of a philologist and to be well versed in Arabic lexicography, morphology, syntax, and stylistics. The meaning of a text must include for him not only obvious or literal meaning but also metaphorical meaning and implied meaning. When he is satisfied that he has harvested whatever rules of law lie within the text's meaning thus conceived, he may then, according to Sunni theory, attempt to see what further rules may be gleaned by way of analogy (*qiyās*) with rules already determined. The use of analogy is reckoned by the four Sunni schools as a fourth source of law, following the Qur'an, the Sunna, and juristic consensus. It is, however, not a source in the sense of being something *from which* rules may be extracted, a category that includes only the textual sources. Rather, it is a method *through which* rules of law may be constructed on the basis of previously determined rules. Shi'i jurists reject the use of analogy, replacing it with rational intuition (*'aql*) as the fourth source of law.

The derivation of law from the textual sources through interpretation or the use of analogy entails a variety of issues some of which will be explored later in this book. First, however, we will explore the theological foundations of Muslim thinking about the law.

# 2 Divine Sovereignty and Human Subordination

Classical Muslim jurisprudence is deeply rooted in the monotheistic outlook described in the opening paragraph of the previous chapter. The Muslim jurist cannot even begin to think about the law except in the context of a worldview predicated upon the existence of God. Given that God exists, it follows by an inexorable monotheistic logic that he is the one to whom mankind must first turn as a source of law, for he alone is the ultimate sovereign, the possessor of all original rights. God's sovereignty derives from his status as creator and requires no further justification beyond sheer creatorship. The ultimate power in the universe is the power to create, and that is possessed by God alone. Ultimate authority and ultimate power are thus coterminous. Before the Creator, man is powerless; his affairs and his destiny both in this world and the next are entirely in the creator's hands. Man's position vis-à-vis the creator is therefore necessarily that of a subordinate or subject. The Psalmist gives cogent expression to this fundamental principle of monotheism: "Know that the Lord is God! It is he that made us, and we are his" (Psalm 100:3, Revised Standard Version).

The Arabic terms most commonly used in Islamic literature to characterize the Creator-creature relationship are *rabb* and *'abd,* "Lord" and "slave." The word "Lord" connotes not only sovereignty but also proprietorship. The Creator is the original owner of all that he creates; he possesses full property rights over his creatures. For this reason, "slave" best conveys the true meaning of *'abd,* notwithstanding the currently widespread preference for renderings less jarring to modern ears. A slave is one owned by another, and that is exactly what man is before God. God's slaves in fact have no original rights whatsoever, no rights apart from those granted by God, who alone possesses original rights.

It is not as though God is a harsh Lord and man a wretched slave. To the contrary, God makes provisions for man's well-being; the whole world of nature exists for man's benefit. In the life to come lie the rewards of paradise for those who are faithful. The law itself exists for the good of man, and man is assured that the requirements of the law will never be a burden greater than man can bear. Various epithets applied to God in the Qur'an connote love and compassion. Nonetheless, the lordship or sovereignty that God possesses by virtue of his creatorhood remains the fundamental consideration in the rationalization of the divine provenance of the law.

But how do we know that God exists? This question came to be formally addressed by Muslims within the discipline of theology, not of jurisprudence as such. But it is a question in which any monotheistic jurisprudence clearly has a stake, since without a divine being there can be no divine law. Therefore, as theology—or *kalām* ("discourse"), as it was commonly called in Arabic—developed among Muslims, it came eventually to be seen as a handmaiden to jurisprudence. Indeed, many of the Muslim jurists regarded their jurisprudence as logically grounded in kalam; from kalam it drew its most fundamental postulates (*mabādi' kalāmiyya*), among which the existence of God was primary. These postulates were the starting point of jurisprudence; without them jurisprudence could not proceed.[1] Consequently, every jurist should also be a theologian. It is in fact a common practice in the literature of modern Islamic studies to call many of the great jurists of Islam jurist-theologians.

Not all the jurists of medieval Islam looked with favor upon kalam. Some were in fact adamantly opposed to it, and one renowned jurist, Ibn Qudama (d. 1223), wrote a treatise denouncing it as forbidden under the divine law.[2] These opponents of kalam, however, were by no means themselves devoid of theological reflection. What they objected to principally in kalam was the extension of theological inquiry into the realm of divine attributes. For them the attributes assigned to God in the Qur'an were a given to be accepted without discussion of any kind. One should not attempt to fathom their meaning. Only God could know his own nature; such knowledge was not given to man. The existence of God, however, was another matter. It *could* be known. On this all Muslim jurists, whatever their attitude toward kalam, agree. And to the extent that they took up the task of explaining how God's existence could be known, they were engaging in genuine theological reflection.

This theological reflection was inspired by the Qur'an itself, which alludes repeatedly to the "signs of God" (*ayāt allāh*) in the natural world and calls upon humans to ponder them. These signs consist, not of static objects, but of processes: the falling of rain, the growth of plants, the development of complex forms of animal life, the movements of the celestial bodies, and so on. Especially marvelous, in the qur'anic reckoning, is the development of human life in the womb, which begins with a mere drop of semen and then proceeds through various transformations: the semen becomes a clot, the clot becomes a small lump, and the small lump is eventually transformed into a wondrous composite of flesh, bone, and blood (Qur'an 22:5; 23:14). Classical Muslim thought universally contends that if we contemplate these processes with open and receptive minds, allowing them to work upon us as the signs they are, we will find welling up within us the knowledge that they are the handiwork of an unseen but entirely real Artisan.[3]

The phrase "with open and receptive minds" places an important condition upon our contemplation of the signs. The fact that some human beings are not convinced of God's existence can only mean that their contemplation of the signs has been obstructed by prejudice and faulty upbringing. Classical Muslim thought is unanimous in affirming that the ability to know of God's existence is a native endowment of the human mind, part of what is called in Arabic *fiṭra*, the natural God-implanted inclination to be a believer.[4] This fiṭra is, however, fragile and easily corrupted. If the signs are to have their full impact on human minds, the fiṭra must be restored. This restoration process can occur only through a recognition of and turning away from the corrupting influences that have been at work on one's mind.

When the fiṭra is restored and contemplation of the signs is unfettered by corrupting influences, there emerges, it must be emphasized, a confident and unshakable *knowledge* that God exists. In classical Islam there is no place for the modern, largely existentialist idea of the "leap of faith." Nothing as foundational to Islam as God's existence is to be taken "on faith" in the meaning ordinarily given to that phrase in contemporary English. The Arabic term commonly translated as "faith," namely *īmān*, is better translated as "belief," which, though wide-ranging in its meanings, is less likely to carry the misleading connotations of "faith." In Islam, belief is holding something to be true (*taṣdīq*), and one holds a thing to be true only because one *knows* it to be true.[5] Belief and knowledge are thus closely interrelated, if not identical. Both find expression in "witness" (*shahāda*), which is a fundamental duty in Islam. Witnesses bear testimony not to what they have accepted "on faith" as true but only to what they know to be true. The notion of knowledge by faith construed as knowledge acquired in the absence of convincing evidence is unknown in classical Muslim thought. It is inconsistent with the notion of signs.

Within kalam circles, demonstration of God's existence developed into much more complex argumentation that adhered to the canons of logic inherited from Aristotle. Reflection upon the natural processes—the signs mentioned above—came to mean the application to these processes of formal methods of discursive, that is to say, syllogistic, reasoning, or reasoning from premises to conclusions. The natural processes themselves were seen as a kind of raw material upon which the discursive mind worked. The sign or proof of God's existence was now something that existed within the human intellect, in contrast to the qur'anic signs, which existed in the natural world external to the intellect. Proofs of God's existence were seen as the internal product of the intellect's reflection upon external natural phenomena.

Interestingly enough, these syllogistic proofs of God's existence reached their highest point of development in disputes, not with atheists, but with theistic philosophers. Atheists were quite marginal in the world in which Islamic thought was formed. This world comprised principally polytheism and flawed forms of monotheism, some of which existed (in the view of the theologians) among the Muslims themselves. The practitioners of kalam drew a clear distinction between theological reflection of the sort they engaged in and the more strictly philosophical tradition represented by the likes of Avicenna and Averroës. The latter they called *falsafa,* which, like the English "philosophy," derives from the Greek *philosophia.* Although both falsafa and kalam were influenced by the ideas and methods of argumentation of the Greek philosophers, the former absorbed much more of the worldview of the Greeks than did the latter.

The tenets of falsafa that troubled the practitioners of kalam included the doctrine of the eternity of the world. The philosophers maintained that the world emanates necessarily from God and must therefore coexist eternally with him. This assertion contradicted the prevailing view among Muslims that the world had been created out of nothing at a fixed point in time and that its creation resulted from a free exercise of the divine will. In order to combat the philosophers' view, the practitioners of kalam developed arguments to show that the world could only have come into existence at some point in time. But arguments for the creation of the world in time, though directed against theists who maintained the eternity of the world, could easily be transformed into arguments for the existence of a creator that might be directed against atheists. Even if atheists were so uncommon as to count for little as adversaries to be dealt with, the impulse to achieve systematic completion required that the issue of God's existence be dealt with.

Since the arguments in question all proceeded from the world to God, they may be classified as cosmological arguments. The most commonly used of these arguments may be further classified as "arguments from contingency," since they begin with something known about the world through direct experience and thus necessarily, namely the fact that it is made up of things that come into existence after having been nonexistent. We first become aware, through direct sensory experience, that particular things come into existence after having been nonexistent, and then through inductive inference we become aware that this is true of all the things that we experience; nothing in our world lacks a beginning. Taking this irresistible knowledge as our starting point, we begin to reason our way to God.

Such reasoning, as developed by many theologians within kalam circles, takes the form of a succession of syllogisms. The first is a disjunctive syllogism (either $x$ or $y$ is true; $x$ is not true; therefore $y$ is true) and proceeds as follows. (1) Each of the things that exist in our world must exist either because it is in its nature to exist or because something other than it has brought it into existence. (2) Each thing cannot exist for the first reason, because if it did there could not be a time when it did not exist, and this contradicts our experience of things in the world as having come into existence after having not existed. (3) Therefore, each thing exists because something other than it has brought it into existence.

Having reached the conclusion that all things in the world we experience owe their existence to something else, we may proceed to the next level of argumentation. That to which a thing owes its existence must itself exist either because it is in its very nature to exist or because something other than it has brought it into existence. If it exists because something other than it brought it into existence, then the same disjunction must be applied to that other thing; it too must exist either because it is in its nature to do so or because something else has brought it into existence. If the latter holds true, the same disjunction once again arises. If we continually choose the second element in the disjunction, we end up with an infinite regression: A owes its existence to B, B owes its existence to C, C owes its existence to D, and so on ad infinitum. But an infinite regression is impossible. Sooner or later the first element in the disjunction must hold true, and when it does we find ourselves in the face of an eternal, necessary being that is (or who is) distinct from the world of temporal things that we directly experience.

The impossibility of an infinite regression—though originally propounded as a way of showing, contrary to the philosophers' affirmation of the eternity of the world, that the world had a beginning in time—thus becomes the centerpiece of an argument for God's existence. It too had to be argued for, and the argument took the form of a hypothetical syllogism. (1) If there were an infinite, that is to say, beginningless, series of temporal things (that is, a series of things each of which was brought into existence by its predecessor), the world would not exist in the present moment. (2) The world exists in the present moment. (3) Therefore, an infinite series of temporal things is impossible. The hypothetical statement itself (the first premise) was based on the principle of the nontraversability of an infinite, which was inherited from Aristotle. If the series of temporal things had no beginning, then a forward progression from one thing to the next would have no place to begin, and it would be impossible for such a progression to reach the present moment. Thus the world would not exist in the present moment.

It should not be supposed that the foregoing paragraphs reproduce arguments for the existence of God in a form that may be found throughout the literature of kalam. The above account of the arguments is intended, rather, to give the reader an impression of the *type* of argumentation that has been widely employed among Muslim theologians, especially from the twelfth century onward. Arguments conforming to this type could be formulated in a variety of ways.[6] The various formulations all reflect the conviction that the knowledge of God's existence is something that must be acquired through a process of discursive reasoning that proceeds from premises to conclusion. God's existence is thus a conclusion emerging from premises that are rooted in our direct experience of a contingent world. Until we have progressed from premises to conclusion we are in a state of temporary agnosticism, not truly knowing whether or not God exists. Theism emerges as the outcome of our reasoning.

Although opposition to kalam was at times fierce, and especially during its formative period, in the long run time proved to be on its side. Antikalam sentiment did not vanish entirely, but its representatives became fewer and fewer as time passed. Most of the jurists of later Islam embraced kalam as a valuable handmaiden to jurisprudence, and several incorporated into their more theoretical writings (*uṣūl al-fiqh*) chapters on the "theological postulates" (*mabādi' kalāmiyya*) of jurisprudence. Eventually kalam was commonly admitted into the curriculum of the madrasas, after having for centuries been relegated to the domain of private study. The study of kalam thus became an important adjunct to the study of law.

This eventual triumph of kalam betokened the high value that had come to be placed on the more refined forms of theological argumentation with which kalam had come to be associated. While the qur'anic summons to reflect on the signs of God in nature would always constitute a primary stimulus to theological reflection, the methods of argumentation acquired from the Greeks and employed in kalam were now seen as useful tools with which to carry out the qur'anic mandate. The canons of valid reasoning were, after all, neutral. They could be wrongly employed—as the Greeks themselves had done to some extent and also the Muslim philosophers—or rightly employed, as was being done in kalam.

The value of kalam was not, in the view of at least some jurist-theologians, limited to the domain of scholarly discourse. Lay people, those outside the circles of scholars, could also benefit from it. The conviction that this was so led Muhammad al-Fuḍali, a nineteenth-century scholar, to write a treatise whose Arabic title (*Kifāyat al-ʿawāmm fīmā yajib ʿalayhim min ʿilm al-kalām*) can be rendered as, "A [Summary] Sufficient for the Common People of What They Are Required to Know of the Science of Kalam."[7] That Fudali should have considered it imperative—a matter of duty—for nonscholars to know a certain amount of kalam is significant. Whereas Ibn Qudama had six centuries earlier pronounced kalam forbidden for all Muslims, now Fudali transformed it into a requirement for all Muslims. The reasoning undergirding Fudali's treatise is crystal clear. Obedience to the law of God must be grounded in a knowledge of God. The knowledge of God is not innate but results from a reasoning process. All human beings, scholars as well as nonscholars, must therefore be urged, as the Qur'an does indeed urge them, to engage in the reasoning that leads to the knowledge of God, otherwise the very notion of a divine law will be without validity. Although the knowledge of God as such is not innate, not part of the inborn fiṭra, the ability of humans to reason their way to God is, and nonscholars as well as scholars are in possession of this ability. The fiṭra is universal.

But the reasoning humans engage in does not just lead them to a knowledge of God. More important, it ushers them into a covenantal encounter with God. To know God is to know him as a presence before whom one stands in a covenantal relationship. There is no other way to know God. The notion of covenant is not usually associated

God + Man = relationship
+ covenant

with Muslim thinking about God's relationship with humans. It does not seem to have the salience that it enjoys in Jewish and Christian thinking. Yet the notion is very much present in Muslim thinking, even if in less obvious ways. It may in fact be said that in Islam, no less than in the Judaeo-Christian tradition, law is inseparable from covenant.[8]

Muslim thought was bound to reflect on the divine-human covenant if for no other reason than that the Qur'an itself speaks of it in a number of highly significant passages, the Arabic designation being either *mīthāq* or *ʿahd*. A particularly seminal passage is 7:172: "And [remember] when your Lord brought forth from the Children of Adam, from their loins, their seed, and made them testify against themselves [saying]: Am I not your Lord? They said: Yes, verily. We testify. [This was] lest you should say at the Day of Resurrection: Lo! of this we were unaware." Although neither mīthāq nor ʿahd appears in this verse, qur'anic exegetes are in general agreement that the verse is about the covenant. In fact, this verse plays a particularly important role in exegetical attempts to construct a qur'anic doctrine on the covenant.

The more literalist exegetes took this verse to mean that God gathered all of Adam's descendants before him in a single primordial moment, a time of preexistence, and that he addressed them verbally in that moment just as they replied to him verbally. Within kalam circles, the verse was interpreted metaphorically. God uses the powers of reasoning that he has implanted within the mind of every human being to bring humans into an encounter with him. He does not literally address them with the words "Am I not your Lord?" but impresses the question upon their minds nonetheless. He does so when they reach the point of full maturity. As they become aware of the question, the answer wells up within them: "Yes, verily." The question clearly has a Socratic purpose, namely that of quickening in the human mind an awareness of something the truth of which cannot, on reflection, be denied. In other words, God, having ushered humans into his presence through the instrumentality of the rational powers he himself created in them, immediately impresses his sovereignty upon their consciousness, thus leaving them no recourse but to acknowledge that sovereignty. There are consequently two primary moments in the development of the primitive human religious consciousness: a moment of realization that the Creator exists as a living presence before whom all humankind stands and a moment of realization that the Creator alone is sovereign and humans are his subordinates.

The encounter between God and humans, whether conceived as a discrete primordial event or as a stage in the development of the human psyche, is covenantal inasmuch as it entails two parties, a superior who lays down terms of a relationship and an inferior who accepts those terms. The literature of commentary on the Qur'an accordingly sometimes speaks of the encounter as "the covenant of sovereignty and subordination" (*'ahd al-rubūbiyya wa'l-'ubūdiyya*). This covenant adheres to the general pattern of divine-human covenanting found in the Bible, although important differences obviously exist between the biblical and Muslim conceptions. Unlike covenants between human beings, the divine-human covenant is a covenant between unequals. The overarching term of the covenantal relationship is the obedience that humans are to render to God as Lord. From that term all other terms—that is to say, specific commandments—derive.

The law is thus rooted in a covenant relationship between God and human beings. A covenanting Creator-Lord hands down to his creature-slave a body of commandments, of rules, that define the obligations that the creature incurs as a result of the covenantal encounter. The law is the totality of specific terms that the creature must fulfill as party to the covenant. The covenant is the bedrock of legal obligation and responsibility. Because humans have said yes to God's question, "Am I not your Lord?" they cannot, as the qur'anic verse states, on the Day of Judgment say, "Of this [i.e., of your lordship and our obligation to obey you] we were unaware." For the human yes pronounced in the covenantal moment will be held as testimony against those who make excuses in the Day of Judgment.

Fakhr al-Din al-Razi (d. 1209), a late twelfth-century jurist-theologian, makes the relationship between covenant and legal obligation clear in his explication of the concept of covenant. "A covenant [*mī-*

*thāq*] occurs through the doing of those things that render obedience obligatory" (*iʿlam anna'l-mīthāqa innamā yakūn bi-fiʿl al-umūr allatī tūjib al-inqiyād wa'l-ṭāʿa*).[9] The things that render obedience obligatory are the Creator's ushering his creatures into an encounter with him and impressing upon them his lordship and the creatures' responding with an acknowledgment of that lordship. The doing of these things constitutes the covenant-*making* process. The covenant itself is, clearly, a state of affairs in which one of two parties is under an obligation to obey—to conform to the will of—the other party. The covenant thus has to do primarily with obligation.

Although Muslim discussion of the covenant occurs mainly in commentaries on the Qur'an and seldom in the literature of jurisprudence as such, there does occur in the latter literature discussion of a closely related concept, that of the divine address (*khiṭāb allāh*). The pervasiveness of this concept cannot be exaggerated. The law always, for Muslim jurists without exception, has its primary original setting in the encounter between a divine addressor (*mukhāṭib*) and a human addressee (*mukhāṭab*). God addresses humans in the role of Lord, and humans are addressed in the role of subordinates. The *mukhāṭib-mukhāṭab* relationship on which all Muslim jurisprudential thought turns thus presupposes the terms of the covenant discussed in the qur'anic commentaries.

The Divine Lord's addressing of his creatures entails both an angelic and a human intermediary. The angel Gabriel receives the divine words from on high and brings them down to the mundane world, where he imparts them to the Prophet, who in turn conveys them to his fellow human beings. The Prophet's experience of hearing the divine words upon the lips of the Angel is unique to the prophetic mind and is known in Arabic as *waḥy*, which may be translated as "inspiration." In the inspired state, the Prophet is easily able to recognize his heavenly visitor and identify the words upon his lips as divine words. The general human experience of hearing the words of God upon the lips of the Prophet or upon the lips of reciters who repeat down through the generations what was originally heard upon the lips of the Prophet entails, not waḥy, but the active working of the human reason. Just as human beings of uncorrupted fiṭra are led by their rational powers into a covenantal encounter with their Lord, so they are led by their rational powers into an encounter with the Lord's Messenger, his prophet. One can be in the presence of a prophet and not know it. This is not a true encounter. Only when one knows that the one before whom one stands is a prophet is one in a situation of genuine encounter with the Prophet.

The encounter with the Prophet is a necessary part of the ongoing covenantal relationship between God and humans. The initial covenantal moment, when the divine sovereignty and human subordination are established and recognized as the fundamental terms of the covenant, does not entail a prophetic intermediary. But subsequent to this moment the covenantal addressor-addressee relationship continues thanks to the faithful conveying of God's words to humans by the Prophet. In this continuing phase of the relationship the law unfolds.

Implicit in Muslim thinking about the covenant and the addressor-addressee relationship is the notion that the law is an expression of the will of the Creator and is known from the commands and prohibitions that the Creator conveys to his creatures through his prophetic mouthpiece. A large segment of Muslim thought carries this notion to the point of an extreme voluntarism that makes the law utterly contingent upon a sovereign and unbound divine will and refuses to acknowledge any rational element in the law that the human mind is capable of comprehending on its own without the help of revelation. This attitude found its classical expression in the literature of the Ash'ari school of theology, to which many outstanding jurists belonged. Reflecting a point of view described centuries earlier in Plato's *Euthyphro,* these jurists equated "good" with "commanded by God." God did not command acts because they were good; rather, acts were good because God commanded them. This made any reversals of divine commands theoretically possible.[10] Quite obviously, this way of thinking was inhospitable to the development of any notion of natural law in Islam.

But not all Muslim jurists embraced the Ash'ari point of view. Among the Shi'is and within a sizable segment of the Hanafi school of law (largely those who identified themselves as followers of Maturidi rather than Ash'ari), a more positive view of the role of reason prevailed. The human reason *could*, on this view, discern on its own what the law required and forbade and the good that the law served. A recent study of A. Kevin Reinhart has called into question the commonly held belief that such a view was distinctive of the Muʿtazilis, a theological school that flourished in the ninth and tenth centuries and was ultimately branded as adhering to erroneous doctrine by later Muslim orthodoxy.[11] No longer may we regard the question of the reason's ability to know the law as simply pitting Muʿtazilis (and with them the Shiʿis) against "orthodox" Sunnis. Shiʿi jurisprudence, it should be noted, singles out *ʿaql* (reason) as a fourth source of law (after the Qur'an, the Sunna, and the consensus) unlike any Sunni school of law, but as Reinhart has shown, the Hanafi jurists could be just as sanguine as the Muʿtazilis or the Shiʿis about the role of reason.

Neither the Shiʿis nor the Maturidi-Hanafis went so far as to regard the human reason as the author or ultimate source of the law. Despite their rationalism, the law remained God's law, not a human law, and the divine will remained its true determinant. The phrases *lā ḥukma illā min allāh* ("Every rule of law is from God") and *al-ḥākim huwa allāh* ("God is the lawgiver") appear throughout the writings of Muslim jurisprudence. As ʿAbd al-ʿAli Muhammad al-Ansari, an early nineteenth-century Hanafi jurist, put it, "No one who professes Islam would be so brazen as to regard the human reason as lawgiver."[12] The role of reason is strictly instrumental. Because God himself is a rational being, and because he has endowed his human creatures with rationality, the human reason provides a link between the divine mind and the human mind. Through reason, humans have some degree of access to the divine law apart from revelation. A famous dictum of Shiʿi jurisprudence has it that "whatever judgment the reason makes [regarding a human act] is also the judgment of the Sharīʿa" (*kullumā ḥakama bihi al-ʿaqlu ḥakama bihi alsharʿu*).[13] The judgments of human reason are the judgments that prevail among rational persons (*ʿuqalāʾ*), for example, the judgment that lying is blameworthy (and therefore something the law prohibits) and the judgment that justice is praiseworthy (and therefore something the law commands). Since God is a rational being, his law will never conflict with sound rational judgments of this sort. This anchorage of the divine law in the human mind gives the jurist the ability to scrutinize his own interpretive efforts critically. If any rule of law that he formulates is in clear conflict with any confident judgment of the human reason, the jurist may conclude that an interpretive error has been made.

Despite the spread of this rationalist way of thinking among the Hanafi jurists, the dominant position among the jurists of Sunni Islam remained that of the Ashʿari school. Although Ashʿari theology is as thoroughly rationalistic as is Shiʿi and Maturidi in its dealing with major issues such as the existence and attributes of God and the prophethood of Muhammad, its rationalism stops short of entering the domain of law. It should not be supposed, however, that the Ashʿari jurists regard humans as devoid of all natural appreciation for what the law requires. The law does indeed, for these jurists, accord to a very large extent with the judgments of human reason; but this agreement is in the final analysis a pure coincidence, for which humans have every reason to be grateful. Ashʿari thought was unwilling to take the next step and say that the human sense of the praiseworthy and blameworthy, of good and evil, is itself a reliable indicator of the divine law. Between human reason and the law of God there stretched an essentially unbridgeable gap.

# 3 The Textualist/Intentionalist Bent

The universal insistence of Muslim jurists upon the divine authorship of the law and their refusal to accord to human reason any role in the creation of law accounts in large part for the features of Muslim juristic thought that will form the subject of this chapter: textualism and intentionalism. By "textualism" I mean an approach to the formulation of the law that seeks to ground all law in a closed canon of foundational texts and refuses to accord validity to law that is formulated independently of these texts. Among Muslim jurists the foundational texts are known collectively as *naṣṣ*, the two subcategories of naṣṣ texts being the Qur'an and the Sunna. They are not, it must be kept in mind, the only texts in which the law may be found. The larger corpus of texts of Islamic law is immense. It includes, for example, texts containing reports of sayings and deeds of eminent Muslims, especially those of the early generations, from which may be gleaned evidence of occurrences of consensus on points of law. The formulations of the law by the great pioneering jurists also came to be embodied in school texts of enormous authority for later generations of jurists, as was noted in Chapter 1. But none of these texts has the foundational character of the naṣṣ texts.

That the Ashʿari jurists should have embraced the textualist point of view is quite understandable, given their extreme voluntarism and refusal to grant reason a role in the discernment of the law. If the divine will is not accessible through rational means, then the texts stand as the *sole* point of contact between humans and the Lawgiver. The jurist literally hangs on the words of the texts, for the divine will must be discovered by human beings in those words or not at all. Although the Lawgiver does reveal his will in part through one important nonverbal medium, namely the actions of the prophet Muhammad, those actions must be reported in words that can be transmitted from generation to generation, in other words, in texts. Texts, then, are the indispensable medium for all that the Lord wishes to communicate of his will.

But those jurists who repudiate Ash'ari voluntarism by no means place themselves outside the pale of textualism. They are after all voluntarists of sorts inasmuch as they identify the law with the will of its divine author. The fact that the divine will is to some extent accessible through the working of human reason does not, for them, undermine in any way the centrality of the foundational texts to the enterprise of formulating the law. Had God so chosen, he could have let humans depend entirely on reason as the instrument of access to the law. But this in fact has not been the divine plan. Rather, God has chosen to reveal his law through the Prophet (and, for Shi'is, through the Imams). This being the case, it is the first responsibility of every jurist seeking to formulate the law to explore the foundational texts to the best of his ability. To the extent that human reason has a role, it is a strictly subordinate one. Muhammad Baqir al-Sadr, a Shi'i jurist of recent times, has in fact gone so far as to say that reason is a potential source of the law rather than an actual one. Sadr claimed that while reason has in principle the ability to discover the law on its own, this has never actually happened nor need ever happen, given the existence of the Qur'an and the Sunna, for whatever reason might discover would in any case be found in these foundational texts.[1]

Shi'i thought emphasizes the role of correlations (*mulāzamāt*) in the operation of human reason.[2] Reason operates entirely in the context of revelation. Where it sees correlations between the law found in the foundational texts and conceptions of right and wrong that prevail among rational persons it is able to validate those conceptions and use them in the formulation of the law whenever it is helpful to do so. The notion that reason is able to operate entirely on its own, apart from revelation, is absent from Shi'i thought. Another modern Shi'i jurist makes this point clear: "Without the help of correlations [of the sort just mentioned] there is no way for the reason to know the status of a given human act in the eyes of the Lawgiver . . . for the divine rules [which are the basis of all such correlations] are revealed (*tawqīfiyya*) rules, and there is no way to know them except by way of what has been transmitted from the one who communicated those rules which God ordained to be communicated."[3] This is as clear an endorsement of the textualist position as one could hope to find anywhere in the literature of Muslim jurisprudence.

Just what this textualism entails in actual practice is a question on which the Muslim jurists have differed. Among Sunnis, some jurists of earlier times regarded the textualist methodology as incompatible with the use of analogical reasoning in the formulation of the law. Those who defended analogical reasoning were obliged to do so in a manner that left the fundamental convictions of textualism basically intact. The opponents of analogical reasoning adopted a rigorous and highly restrictive textualism which insisted that rules of law must be located within the meaning of the texts. Defenders of analogical reasoning, who eventually prevailed in Sunni circles, acknowledged that the rules they established through this method lay outside the realm of the texts' actual meaning but insisted that these rules were nonetheless justified on the basis of considerations firmly anchored in the texts. We will take a closer look at the textualist presuppositions of their arguments in Chapter 4. The point to be noted here is that they saw reasoning by analogy not as a way of formulating the law independently of the texts but rather as a method of extrapolating law from a textual foundation. In other words, they shared with their opponents the core conviction behind the textualist stance, namely, that no law that was formulated independently of the texts could be regarded as God's law.

How is one able to identify these foundational texts of the law? The world is, after all, filled with texts. Every human community has its own texts. What are the grounds for singling out certain texts from this plethora of texts as naṣṣ? The initial answer to this question is that the texts in question must be texts that emanate from the Prophet (as well as, for the Shiʿis, the infallible Imams), for it is the Prophet (and Imams) who mediate the will of the Creator to the creature. But this is only half an answer. The question still remains, how does one know who the true Prophet of God is, and how does one identify the texts that emanate from him? (The same question arises, for Shiʿis, with respect to the Imams.)

The answer to this most crucial question entails consideration of the special role and unique character of the Qur'an. Islam incorporates into its prophetology the ancient notion of signs of prophethood. Since there are both genuine and false prophets in the world, the claim of any person to be a prophet must be accompanied by signs that verify the claim. Such a claim cannot simply be taken at face value. The signs of prophethood must be in the nature of miracles that exceed the abilities of ordinary mortals. A true miracle is a divine intervention into the natural course of events. When a miracle occurs, the beholders recognize that an act of God has occurred, not an act of a human prophet. The miracle will, however, occur "at the hand" of the Prophet, that is to say, in a manner that constitutes a clear attestation of the Prophet's claim to prophethood. The gushing forth of water from a rock in the middle of a desert, for example, is clearly a miracle but not necessarily a sign of prophethood. When it occurs in response to the Prophet's tapping the rock with his staff, then it is linked to the Prophet in such a way as to give it the status of a sign.

The miracle that constitutes the supreme attestation of the prophethood of Muhammad is, for all Muslim jurists and theologians, the Qur'an itself. The Qur'an is in fact a sign of Muhammad's prophethood by its own declaration. It portrays the skeptics among Muhammad's contemporaries as demanding from him a sign. To this demand it responds: "Has it not sufficed them that we have sent down to you [Muhammad] the book to be recited to them?" This response suggests that the book—the Qur'an—is the sign of Muhammad's prophethood. Muslim commentators read this passage in conjunction with certain other qur'anic passages to form a foundation for the conviction that the Qur'an is, among various signs that accompanied Muhammad's claim to prophethood, the supreme sign.

These other passages speak of the Qur'an as something the likes of which humans would be unable to produce on their own. One passage declares, "If humankind and the unseen spirits (*jinn*) came together to produce the like of this Qur'an, they could not produce it, even if they helped each other" (17:88). The underlying point is brought home in 10:37: "This Qur'an is not such as can be produced by other than God." Several passages contain the well-known challenge (*taḥaddī*) to skeptics among Muhammad's contemporaries to produce the likes of even a part of the Qur'an. For example: "Do they say: he forged it? Say: Bring then a chapter (*sūra*) like unto it and call upon whomever you can [for help], besides God, if you speak the truth" (10:38; cf. 2:23–24; 11:13; 52:34).

These passages form the foundation of all Muslim thinking about the miraculous character of the Qur'an. "Miracle" is the standard translation of the Arabic word *muʿjiza,* which is derived from a verb (*aʿjaza*) meaning "to render unable." A miracle "renders people unable" in the sense that it exposes their inability to produce the likes of it. This debilitating character of a miracle comes into play when the miracle is proffered as a challenge, as in the Qur'an. Humans are impressed with miracles precisely because the miraculous event lies beyond their own finite powers. The challenge to produce a like miracle evokes in humans an awareness of their inability to do so, and this in turn impresses the miracle indelibly on their minds. Miracle and challenge, muʿjiza and taḥaddī, are thus correlates in Muslim usage, which derives its inspiration from the Qur'an.

Classical Muslim thinking about the miracle of the Qur'an begins with a confident historical affirmation. God, speaking through his prophet Muhammad, challenged Muhammad's skeptics to produce the likes of so much as a single chapter (sūra) of the Qur'an, and the skeptics did not respond to the challenge. Had they responded, this information would surely have been passed down to us. The fact that we have no such information can only mean that they did not respond. Taking this solid historical fact as a starting point, one may then reason as follows. The skeptics did not respond to the challenge because they were unable to do so; for had they been able, they surely would have responded. Their social and political position in Mecca and throughout Arabia was, after all, severely threatened by Muhammad. By demonstrating that they were capable of producing the likes of a chapter from the Qur'an, they would have effectively silenced Muhammad and rid themselves of the threat. That they did not avail themselves of this opportunity is sure evidence that Muhammad's challenge was effective and that the Qur'an showed itself to be a true "disabler," a miracle, and thus a sign of Muhammad's prophethood.

That the Qur'an proved itself to be a miracle is thus beyond dispute among Muslims. Exactly how the nature of this miracle is to be understood is, however, a question on which various views have emerged over the centuries. Does the miracle have to do with the form of the Qur'an or its content or both? Those who emphasize form make the Qur'an a literary miracle appropriate among a people—the Arabs—for whom literary excellence was especially highly valued. Anyone experienced in the literary arts of the Arabs is, it is argued, bound to discover in the Qur'an an arrangement of words and phrases the likes of which are not to be found in the literary productions of even the most accomplished Arab litterateurs. In respect to eloquence and conciseness, the literary qualities most highly prized by the Arab, the Qur'an represents a marvel far beyond the highest possible human achievement. It compresses a wealth of apposite meaning into parsimoniously constructed phrases and balances abstract and concrete language, clear and obscure, in a manner that is truly unique and without parallel in Arabic literature, not to mention non-Arab.

Those who emphasize content, on the other hand, place the qur'anic miracle in the realm of information. The Qur'an, they argue, contains information about bygone peoples and events that lay beyond Muhammad's reach and the reach of his Arabian contemporaries. As Muhammad, being unlettered (*ummī*), was not versed in the literature of the ancient world, the information had to have a divine source; and his fellow Arabs, too, lacking access to this literature, would have been unable to produce lines containing like information. Furthermore, the Qur'an contains information about future events—that is to say, events that had not yet taken place in the time the information was given but that subsequently did take place—that Muhammad could only have gotten from his divine source and that his contemporaries could hardly have matched.[4]

Historically, the literary interpretation of the miracle has come to have pride of place in Muslim literature on this subject. Both in special treatises on the miracle of the Qur'an[5] and in sections of the larger theological works in which this subject is discussed the lion's share of space is devoted to the literary aspect of the miracle. That this is so has much to do with the heightened literary sensibilities that have marked Muslim culture since the time of its Arab beginnings. The ancient Arabs were a people for whom the literary arts were the primary and almost the only vehicle of aesthetic expression. Tribal propagandists and soothsayers had since time immemorial employed special styles and forms to dazzle and mystify their audiences, and Arab emotions had come to be easily aroused by the elegantly constructed phrase. In a setting dominated by such artistry of the word, it was only fitting that the miracle attesting the prophethood of the bearer of the divine Word should be a literary miracle.

Since appreciation of the literary aspect of the miracle of the Qur'an required that these sensibilities be kept alive within the world of Islam, certain scholars devoted their energies to the cultivation of the discipline of Arabic rhetoric and literary criticism (*'ilm al-balāgha*). This discipline became a mainstay of Arabic philology, and every scholar worth his salt, including the jurist, was expected to master it. In addition to enhancing appreciation of the qur'anic miracle, it also became a useful tool in the interpretation of legal texts.

It is through his appreciation of the qur'anic miracle that the jurist knows the Qur'an to be a foundational text, a naṣṣ text, for the miracle signifies not only that the Qur'an's original bearer is a prophet of God but also that the words that make up the Qur'an are the actual words of God. Reflection upon the signs of God in nature has already brought the creature into a covenantal encounter with his or her Lord. Now, through exposure to the miracle of the Qur'an the creature comes to the realization that the speaker of the words in the Qur'an is none other than the sovereign Lord, the source of all law, for the miracle of the Qur'an is the sign or signature of the divine speech. The covenantal relationship thus moves to a stage in which the creature becomes aware of being addressed by God through the words of the Qur'an.

But God also addresses the creature through the Sunna. In this case God is not addressing the creature directly through his own speech but indirectly through the sayings and deeds of the Prophet, which are the material of which the Sunna is (in part for Shi'is, exclusively for Sunnis) made. This form of address is also part of the covenantal relationship. Whether God speaks through his own words or through the words and deeds of his Prophet, he is always speaking, always addressing. Only through the Qur'an do humans other than the Prophet have a direct encounter with the divine speech. The Prophet's encounter with the divine speech is not, however, limited to the Qur'an. He is privileged to hear words of God beyond those that constitute the Qur'an.

Muslim juristic and theological thought eventually, after generations of reflection upon the provenance of the foundational texts, came to view both the Qur'an and the prophetic Sunna as having emerged out of the Prophet's experience of waḥy. Waḥy came to be defined as the special experience of direct contact with the angel Gabriel that only prophets enjoy. The Angel was primarily a conduit of the divine speech. Through him God "sent down" his speech from on high. The Sunna, as much as the Qur'an, was "sent down" (*munazzal*). The difference between the two repositories of revelation is that the Qur'an is the divine speech recited verbatim (*matlūw*), while the Sunna is the divine speech mediated through the words and deeds of the Prophet.[6] The divine speech is the object of all revelation—the primary thing revealed. It is revealed in two ways: through verbatim recitation and through prophetic word and action. When revealed through the latter channel, the divine speech undergoes a transformation, but its meaning is not lost. Rather it is a source of instruction for the Prophet, and the Prophet, endowed as he is with the special grace of infallibility, is able to convey the divine message to humans without an iota of error.

Closely related to this difference between the Qur'an and the prophetic Sunna is another difference. As the very speech of God recited verbatim, the Qur'an displays the miraculous character discussed above. The Sunna does not. This is no loss for the Sunna, however, since the miracle of the Qur'an is sufficient to establish the entire edifice of revelation of which the Sunna is a part. The miracle attests both that the Qur'an is what it claims to be, the very word of God, and that Muhammad is who he claims to be, the Prophet of God. Furthermore, the miracle-attested Qur'an repeatedly enjoins humans to obey both God and his Prophet, thus signifying that what the Prophet says and does is an expression of God's will, since no merely human will can on its own rightfully demand obedience.

What has been said in the previous paragraphs holds true of the Shiʿi thinking about the Sunna with certain qualifications. Shiʿis share with Sunnis the confinement of the experience of waḥy to the Prophet. For them the Sunna is linked to a related but distinct concept, that of infallibility (*ʿiṣma*). Unlike the Sunnis, Shiʿis regard the Sunna as embracing the words and deeds of "the infallible one" (*maʿṣūm*), a broad category that includes both the Prophet and the Twelve Imams.[7] Only the Prophet is privileged to have a direct encounter with the divine speech, but the Sunna is not limited to what emerges out of that encounter in the way of prophetic words and deeds. Those words and deeds constitute the revelational elements in the Sunna. Also to be included in the Sunna are the infallible interpretations and elaborations of divine revelation provided by the Imams. The infallibility of the Imams is confirmed by the dictum of the infallible Prophet.

The Qur'an and the Sunna are thus the foundational texts of Islamic law by virtue of a process of attestation in which the miraculous character of the Qur'an plays the central role. But there is more to the textualism of the Muslim jurists than the mere identification of the two principal categories of foundational texts. All texts must be transmitted through time and are, in the course of this transmission, subject to the possibility of corruption over time. The Muslim jurist must be able to work with foundational texts whose authenticity is subject to no doubt whatsoever. It is not a requirement of his textualism that every text with which he works must be of undoubted authenticity; in some cases probable authenticity may suffice. But the jurist must have at least some textual material with which to work whose authenticity cannot be questioned.

This requirement is grounded in systematic considerations. If a text whose authenticity is merely probable is to have authority for the jurist, this authority must be grounded in some other text or body of texts whose authenticity lies securely within the realm of the certain. The Muslim jurist cannot abide a law grounded entirely in texts of probable authenticity. What is probable in the law must be validated with reference to what is certain. Furthermore, while the details of the law may lie within the realm of the probable thus validated, the most fundamental principles of the law may not. For such principles nothing less than complete certainty is demanded.

As we will see in Chapter 5, the Muslim jurists have differed with respect to where the line between certain text and probable text, certain law and probable law, should be drawn. Here we will explore a point on which all agree, which is that some part of the body of foundational texts must lie securely within the realm of the certain.

The agreement of the jurists can be further narrowed down. All agree that the text of the Qur'an is of certain authenticity. Their disagreement thus pertains only to sunnaic texts. The certainty of the Qur'an's authenticity assures not only the jurists but also the entire Muslim community of the possibility of a direct encounter, from generation to generation, with the very words of God himself. This assurance undergirds the validity of Muslim worship, in which the recitation of the Qur'an plays a central role. For the jurist in particular, the certainty of the Qur'an's authenticity makes possible a firm and unshakable confidence in the truth of the law's most fundamental principles.[8]

But the authenticity of any text must be demonstrated in some way. In seeking to provide this demonstration, Muslim thought has in the course of its long history given rise to two principles, one of which eventually became universally accepted, or nearly so, and the other of which has been the subject of perennial controversy. The universally accepted principle is referred to in Arabic by the term *tawātur*. Since this term has a technical meaning that cannot be conveyed by means of the standard translation ("recurrence"), I will refer to this principle as the tawātur principle. The other principle may be called the "truthful transmitter" principle. Here we will confine our attention to the tawātur principle, since it forms a bedrock of Muslim textualism. We will consider the disputed "truthful transmitter" principle in a later chapter.

The tawātur principle, it must first be noted, relates to the *oral transmission* of texts. We moderns are conditioned in our thinking about texts by the existence of the printing press and of the more technologically advanced techniques of reproduction that have been developed in recent times. We think of a text as something that can be replicated with complete precision from a single plate or other type of original in any number of copies. For the great jurists of Islam, a text could be reproduced in one of two ways: through writing or through oral recitation. They favored the latter as the more reliable method. Although written texts abounded in premodern Islam and scribes flourished in every major city of the Muslim world, preference was always given to the recited text. A written text was a dead object that existed outside human persons, though it was the product of a human scribe. A recited text was a text stored in the memory of a reciter. Although a reciter could be forgetful, the well-memorized text was believed to be most secure against corruption. When listening to a recited text, one was always in the presence of a living reciter whose reputation for a sound memory one could hope to know. Written texts often bore the names of their copyists, but the copyist was hardly a living presence for the majority of readers.

Scribal copying, like oral recitation, could of course be based on memory, but this could not be counted upon, and in any case copying was a laborious task in which the likelihood of error—due to a slip of the pen, momentary drowsiness or weariness on the part of the copyist, or a defective or dripping pen—was much greater than in oral recitation.

The preference for the recited text can further be explained by the fact that the foundational texts—both the Qur'an and the Sunna—originated as oral texts and were only subsequently committed to writing. The Qur'an in fact presents itself as an intrinsically oral text—as a text originally recited by the Angel to the Prophet and then, with the Angel's command *iqra'* ("Recite!" in Qur'an 96:1), by the Prophet to his contemporaries. The very word Qur'an means "recitation" in Arabic. Through the reciting of countless reciters down through the ages, the Qur'an retained its character as a recitation. Islamic tradition has the writing down of the Qur'an beginning during the lifetime of the Prophet himself and reaching its final phase during the decades following his death; but it carefully distinguished the written text—which it calls *muṣḥaf*—from the Qur'an per se.[9] In the case of the Sunna, a much longer period of oral transmission elapsed before the text was committed to writing, and Islamic tradition attributes this delay to an overt reluctance to write down sunnaic material. Despite the preference for oral recitation, the written copies of the Qur'an acquired symbolic and ceremonial importance that was not to be accorded to any such written representations of the Sunna.

A further point should be noted. The script in use during the earliest stages of the writing down of the foundational texts was a scriptio defectiva, a script devoid of diacritical marks whereby certain consonants could be distinguished from one another and of vowel markings. The consonants *b, y, t, th,* and *n,* when occurring at the beginning or middle of a word, were thus all represented by one and the same written symbol, to mention only one example. And without vowel markings a written word could be vocalized in a variety of ways: a verb, for example, could be active or passive. Given this deficiency, no written text could be an adequate vehicle of textual transmission. When a scriptio plena was developed—one replete with diacritical marks and vowel signs—the preference for the oral text was still maintained but with less urgency. The reasons now had to do with misgivings about the copying process.

The term *tawātur* came to refer, in the technical usage of Muslim jurisprudence, to the recurrence of recitation of a text on a scale sufficient to give rise to the knowledge that the text recited is fully authentic. According to the theory that informed the use of this term, if one is repeatedly exposed to the recitation of a text, one will eventually reach the point where one will "discover" (*yajid*) within oneself a knowledge that the text is authentic. This way of thinking makes sense only within a culture that places a high premium on the memorization of texts. We must bear in mind that the memorization of the entire Qur'an and of large portions of the Sunna was an essential ingredient in the education of a Muslim jurist. In Muslim religious literature in general it is common for an author, in referring to a qur'anic verse, to cite only the first few words and leave it to the learned reader to supply the rest of the verse from memory, even when the missing part plays a key role in the discussion. The tawātur principle presupposed a Muslim world in which the Qur'an at the very least was repeatedly recited from one end of that world to the other by a vast multitude of reciters.

It is difficult for a modern person to imagine such a world. On a limited scale, however, we do transmit oral texts through recitation, despite the pervasiveness of the printed text. A good example of such a text is the pledge of allegiance to the American flag, which schoolchildren recite daily in their classrooms. Most children have seldom, if ever, seen the pledge of allegiance on paper. They learn it by hearing other children or a teacher recite it. With repetition it becomes drilled into them as a fixed and unalterable text never to be forgotten. If one wishes to test a schoolchild's knowledge of the "authentic" text, one may recite it with an error: for example, "I pledge allegiance to the flag of the United States of America and to the nation for which it stands . . ." The schoolchild will readily, with conviction, object, "But you're supposed to say: and to the *republic* for which it stands." The lyrics of popular songs, well-known Bible passages, and other such famous texts have this same character of orality and transmissibility through recitation.

The theory of tawātur affirms that widespread recitation of a text, if established among the original recipients of the text and maintained throughout all subsequent generations of transmitters, assures the foolproof transmission of the text from generation to generation. It thus assures that the text recited in the present generation is the very same text, down to the last jot and tittle, that was recited originally at the time of its first appearance. As one hears, for example, the words of the Qur'an recited over and over again, one experiences, according to the theory, a growing conviction that the words are indeed the very words recited by the prophet Muhammad to his contemporaries centuries ago, and eventually one reaches the point where the conviction has become unshakable knowledge. At this point, the authenticity of the text is raised above all shadow of doubt.

The fact that traditional qur'anic recitation embraces seven variant systems (*al-qirā'āt al-sab'*) does not, for the Muslim jurists, invalidate the tawātur principle, since all seven systems are believed to have been recited on a scale sufficient to engender confidence in their authenticity. The authentic Qur'an is thus not a monolithic text; it comprises all seven systems, which is to say that all seven originated with the Prophet himself. The differences between the seven systems are on the whole minuscule and seldom have implications of any importance for the law.

If the variability of the authentic oral text of the Qur'an did not pose a problem for the tawātur principle, something else did, namely the fact that within non-Muslim religious communities, scriptures whose authenticity Muslim scholars did not acknowledge enjoyed widespread distribution on a scale sufficient to suppose that the tawātur principle was at work. A case in point is the New Testament, which reports not merely that Jesus died on the cross but also that he predicted such a death. Since the Qur'an, the clearly authentic word of God, denies that Jesus died by crucifixion, the New Testament passages in question could not be regarded as part of the authentic Gospel. Yet those passages are widely known and recited within Christian communities. How could this anomaly be explained? The answer could be only that the widespread character of Christian transmission of these passages did not extend back to the original Gospel. Where the Qur'an was in conflict with another scripture, its authenticity took precedence over all other considerations, negating the authenticity of the other scripture. The rationale for this approach entailed complex argumentation that is laid out with great care in the pages of the great works of Muslim jurisprudence.[10]

Whatever the problems encountered in the defense of the tawātur principle, its application to the Qur'an seemed to all the jurists to yield positive results. The entire Qur'an in all seven of its variant readings was universally considered to be of unassailable authenticity. Just how far the tawātur principle could be applied to the Sunna, and with what results, was more of an open question, although virtually all the jurists were convinced that tawātur undergirded the authenticity of at least some sunnaic material. We find no agreement among them, however, on particular sunnaic passages. Some frankly acknowledged the impossibility of identifying particular passages whose authenticity was assured by the working of the tawātur principle. For them, all sunnaic texts were for all practical purposes probable, not certain, texts. A probable text could, after all, be decisive for the law, a point to which we shall return later.

But the probability of a sunnaic text did not necessarily entail a probability of the meaning of the text. The jurists were careful to distinguish between the text per se—by which they meant a particular sequence of words—and its meaning. A group of texts that differed in their wording could share a common meaning. Could not the common meaning be certain even if the precise wording contained in each text was not? And could one not regard the meaning as meeting the requirement of widespread dissemination entailed in the tawātur principle? Why could this principle not work for meanings as well as it worked for words? The jurists were convinced that it could and so developed a variant of the tawātur principle that applied to meaning (*maʿnā*) as opposed to wording (*lafẓ*). This application of the principle to meaning was especially useful with respect to the Sunna, for it made possible the elevation of important aspects of the Sunna above the realm of the merely probable to the realm of the certain.[11] Authenticity of meaning mattered in the final analysis much more than authenticity of wording.

Given the importance of the tawātur principle to the textualism of Muslim jurisprudence, it is not surprising that the lengthiest and most thorough discussions of this principle in Islamic literature are to be found in the literature of jurisprudence, not theology or any other Muslim discipline.[12] Tawātur was very much a topic for jurists. It undergirded their textualism. The law, more than anything else in Islam, was dependent upon revelation, upon foundational texts. Theology could explore vast regions without recourse to revelation. Its method of inquiry was not essentially textualist. Not so jurisprudence. But if the knowledge of the law was to be in any degree sure and confident, it had to rest upon a body of foundational texts whose authenticity was beyond doubt. The principle of tawātur made this possible and thus brought closure to the textualism of the jurists.

Closely bound up with this textualism is intentionalism, the other feature of Muslim juristic thought to be explored in this chapter. The Muslim jurists always thought of texts as carriers of meanings intended by their authors. The decisive author of the foundational texts of the law is, of course, God, the only true Legislator. In the case of the Sunna, it is possible to speak of the Prophet or (among Shiʿis) of the Imams as authors but only in a very qualified sense. What they say carries authority only because it represents with perfect transparency the mind of God. Through their speaking God speaks; the meanings that they intend are the meanings that he intends. He is thus more truly the author than are they. They are conduits of the divine intent.

To speak of the Muslim jurists as intentionalists is, perhaps, to run the risk of sounding anachronistic. They did not engage in anything like the intentionalist versus nonintentionalist (or originalist versus nonoriginalist) debates common in modern legal hermeneutics. There was in fact nothing for them to debate. They were for all practical purposes all intentionalists, even though it would not have occurred to them to call themselves that. The widely accepted contemporary notion that a text has a life of its own apart from its author, that its meaning may continually evolve and change over time and will always be what the community of readers/interpreters want it to be was far from their thinking. For them the only meaning that could matter for those who formulated the law was the meaning intended by the divine author.

In using the term "intentionalism" in these pages, I am concerned less with establishing affinities between the Muslim point of view and that of contemporary intentionalists (though I believe such affinities exist) than with describing as aptly as possible a very real and salient feature of Muslim juristic thought. A contemporary participant in the intentionalist versus nonintentionalist debate might be inclined to say that virtually all premodern thinking about texts is naively and simplistically intentionalist and that it is not particularly insightful to speak of the Muslim jurists as intentionalists. What else could they be? How does this make them different from any other juristic community in the ancient or medieval world? Given their lack of familiarity with the issues raised in modern legal hermeneutics, what use is there in calling them intentionalists?

My own inclination to use this term comes from reflection upon what I perceive in the literature of Muslim jurisprudence to be a conscious effort to demonstrate the viability of a hermeneutics that focuses on authorial intent as the object of all interpretation. The Muslim jurists believed strongly in the discoverability of authorial intent but did not take it for granted. They knew it entailed various problems and had to be supported by arguments that addressed these problems. They may not have been aware of many of the issues that are raised in modern hermeneutics, but they were far from simplistic in their envisioning of the interpretive process. In particular, they had a highly sophisticated understanding of the workings of language as a vehicle of communication and of the impediments to effective communication that language itself created. The deliberateness with which they endeavored to demonstrate the discoverability of authorial intent—their awareness of the problems that this entailed and their conscious struggling with these problems—justifies our calling their approach to the interpretation of texts intentionalism. We are indeed confronted here with a movement of thought, a methodological posturing, an ism.

One need not spend a great deal of time reading the great classical writings of Muslim jurisprudence to discover how central the three Arabic terms *murād, maqṣūd,* and the already mentioned *khiṭāb* are to Muslim thinking about the interpretation of texts. All three terms are indicative of the intentionalism of which I am speaking. The first two of these terms may in fact be translated as "intent" or "intended." The term *khiṭāb* refers to speech in relational terms that entail intention on the part of the speaker. In a khiṭāb situation, an addressor seeks to communicate a meaning to an addressee.

Another term that one frequently encounters in the classical literature is the term *maʿnā,* which is usually translated as "meaning." Frequently the jurists use this term as a synonym of *murād* or *maqṣūd. Maʿnā* can, in their usage, refer to the meaning of an expression or passage considered as the meaning intended by the author. The related verb *yaʿnī* usually has a speaker or author as its subject. *Maʿnā,* however, is also frequently used without any implication of intention. It has, in fact, the same ambiguity as the English word "meaning." A speaker of English can, in speaking of the meaning of a word, have in mind the meaning that the word has in the English language. In this case, the meaning of the word is understood to be a lexical datum that exists entirely outside the context of usage by any particular speaker. Alternatively, the speaker in question may have in mind the meaning that a speaker/author wishes to communicate to his audience. The meaning in this case is not merely something that the word "has" in the language but something that the speaker has in mind, something intended by the speaker. The word *maʿnā* can likewise be used in either way. It thus does not necessarily entail intentionality in the way *murād* and *maqṣūd* do.

Considered as a lexical datum, *maʿnā* is synonymous with *madlūl,* "signified" (or "significatum"). The subject of the related verb *yadullu* ("signify") is almost always, in the classical literature, the sign, that is to say, the expression, the word. Words signify, not people. We will explore the importance of the sign-signified relationship presently.

A word or expression may have several meanings (*maʿānī, madlūlāt*) in the language. In this case the intending of a meaning entails a singling out of that meaning from other lexically possible meanings. But intending need not entail this singling out. Even when a word admits of only one meaning in the language, an intending of that meaning must still take place. A speaker always intends a meaning and subsequently chooses an expression that will convey that meaning. Whether he chooses a expression that has that meaning alone in the language or an expression that has other meanings as well, he is in either case intending a meaning. His intending makes a meaning that a word has in the language come alive in an actual speech situation. Through intending, a static lexical datum becomes a living meaning in the mind of a speaker.

Like their textualism, the intentionalism of the Muslim jurists is, as was noted at the beginning of this chapter, rooted in the voluntarist view of law described earlier. Voluntarism is a way of looking at the nature of law. Intentionalism is an approach to the interpretation of the texts upon which the law is based. Voluntarism, it seems, inevitably leads to intentionalism, although an intentionalist need not necessarily be a voluntarist. The intimate connection between voluntarism and intentionalism in Muslim juristic thinking is adumbrated by the term *murād* itself. This term may appropriately be translated as "intended," but it may also with equal appropriateness be translated as "willed." *Murād* is in fact a cognate of *irāda,* which is the term used in classical Muslim theology to refer to the will of God.

An intended meaning is thus a willed meaning. What was said above of intending can also be said of willing. Speakers do not of course will that words have certain meanings. The words already have these meanings in the language they employ. Rather, a speaker wills a meaning, then employs the word that conveys that meaning in the language. If a word has several meanings, this willing of a meaning entails a singling out of one meaning from other meanings. The will of which we are speaking here is authorial will. The voluntarism and intentionalism of the Muslim jurists are opposite sides of the same coin. To say that law is determined by the divine will is to say that law is determined by the divine intent, and vice versa.

In the case of the Sunna, the divine willing/intending merges with the willing/intending of the Prophet (and, for Shiʿis, the Imams), as was noted earlier. It is the divine willing/intending that matters to the jurists, since it is the source of authority of all other willing/intending.

The will of God is, of course, not limited to his authorship of the foundational texts. Everything in the creation exists or occurs by the will of God. When one speaks of law as determined by the will of God, however, it is his authorial will that one necessarily has in mind. Law is to be found in the realm of divinely willed meaning. It is important to understand that meaning—in other words, the law—is here the object of God's will, not human behavior. It is not possible, at least in classical Sunni theology, to speak of the law as representing God's will as to how humans should behave. The will of God considered as the determinant of the law must be distinguished from the will of God considered as the determinant of human behavior. These workings of the divine will are independent of each other. The law is exactly what God wills it to be, but God may or may not will that a particular human being be obedient to the law. If humans are disobedient, they are disobedient by the will of God, since the will of God cannot be frustrated. This is not to say that God is at cross-purposes with himself. There is no logical contradiction between willing what the law should be and willing that particular humans should disobey the law.[13]

The term *maqṣūd* is not quite as suggestive of the voluntarist outlook as *murād*, although its usage in the literature is certainly grounded in voluntarism. It is, however, clearly an intentionalist term. One readily translates it as "intended" or "intent" but not as "willed." It has no cognate meaning "will," much less one used to designate the will of God. *Qaṣd,* for example, is not such a cognate.

Like *murād, maqṣūd* can be applied to the meanings of particular words, phrases, sentences, or passages. The classical writers do, however, when speaking of the meanings of whole statements or passages tend to prefer the term *maqṣūd* over *murād* and to favor *murād* when dealing with the meanings of smaller units. Frequently *maqṣūd* refers to what may be called the main drift of a passage, another term for which in Arabic is *siyāq al-kalām.* Occasionally, one encounters in the literature discussions of meanings that are not part of the main drift of a passage but may nonetheless be considered as adumbrating the law, as part of the divine intent (*murād*).

An example of law that is not part of the main drift of the passages on which it is based but is nonetheless part of the divine intent is the legal doctrine that states that the smallest possible term for a full gestation is six months. This is important for the purpose of establishing paternity. No passage in the Qur'an or Sunna states this doctrine outright, but there are two passages in the Qur'an from which it can be extrapolated: one passage that says "and the bearing of him and the weaning of him is thirty months" and another passage that says "and his weaning is two years" (in other words, twenty-four months). In order to determine what the minimum term for a full gestation is, we need only subtract twenty-four months (the period of nursing mentioned in one passage) from thirty months (the period of gestation plus nursing mentioned in the other passages) to arrive at the figure of six months.[14] No jurist would wish to deny that this legal doctrine is willed by God, even though it lies outside the bounds of the main drift of each of the two qur'anic passages.

The use of *maqṣūd* to refer to the main drift of a passage is only one of several uses of this term found in the literature, and one should not assume that the legal doctrine mentioned in the previous paragraph cannot be regarded as *maqṣūd* in some sense of that term. Occasionally, one finds the term used to refer not to meanings of particular expressions or passages but to the larger "intentions" of the law taken as a whole. The intender is still, ultimately, God, but what the term in this case designates is the grand purposes or objectives that he wills to see realized through the law. We will have occasion to consider this subject in a later chapter.

The fact that God dwells in the realm of mystery, that we do not have the same direct encounter with him that we have with our fellow human beings (in Islamic belief even prophets with the exception of Moses do not have a face-to-face encounter with God), does not undermine the intentionalism of the Muslim jurists. The divine intent is, in their thinking, no less discoverable than the intent of a human author or speaker. Humans after all, though capable of face-to-face encounter with each other, do not have direct access to each other's minds. With God as with humans, what is initially inaccessible becomes accessible through the medium of language.

It is therefore necessary, in trying to understand the jurists' case for the discoverability of the divine intent, to consider their view of language and its workings. Perhaps in no premodern civilization were the nature and workings of language explored in such depth and with such sophistication as in the Islamic. The refinement of the linguistic sciences of the Muslims—lexicography, syntax, morphology, phonology, and etymology, not to mention the rhetorical sciences—is an oft-mentioned feature of their civilization. To a large extent these sciences were developed to equip the jurist to carry on the interpretive tasks that went into the formulation of the law.

It is significant that while syntax, morphology, phonology, and etymology were given their own distinctive names, lexicography was called "the science of the language." This gives us a degree of insight into how the classical Muslim writers viewed language. It was for them a code before it was anything else. There is in fact good reason to translate *lugha,* which normally one translates as "language," as "lexical code." Language was seen primarily as a system of signs that a speaker employed to communicate with others. The dichotomy of signifier and signified, which has become central to much modern discussion of semiotics and literary theory, has an exact parallel in the Arabic of the classical writers: *adilla* (or *dallāt*) and *madlūlāt.*

The signs or signifiers that make up language are the patterned vocal sounds that speakers emit. In Arabic these patterned sounds are called *alfāẓ* (singular *lafẓ*), which may be translated as "vocables." Vocables include all meaning-bearing elements of language: simple words (that is, words that cannot be broken down into morphemes or other types of meaning-bearing components), meaning-bearing components of words, syntactic structures (*murakkabāt:* meaning-bearing structures made up of words).[15] Every vocable signifies a meaning or meanings by virtue of an established correlation between vocable and meaning.

It is this vocable-meaning (lafẓ-maʿnā) correlation that gives language its character as a code. Speakers communicate meanings by means of vocable-meaning correlations that already exist prior to their use of the words. They do not give meanings to vocables as they communicate but rather employ vocables that have already *been given* meanings. Speakers appropriate these preexistent meanings, transforming them into intended meanings. We have already noted the distinction between meanings that words *have* in a language and meanings that speakers intend. In the act of speaking, the former are transformed into the latter.

Appropriation of meaning is a key concept in the Muslim understanding of the communication process. Individual speakers do not, strictly speaking, produce meaning de novo. They may perhaps be said to create ideas or particular arrangements of meanings, but they do not produce meanings considered as meanings (maʿānī) signified by vocables. Such meanings exist apart from the deliberations of speakers. They are the data that constitute the code, and as such they belong to the public arena. They are available to all speakers as well as to all to whom they are speaking. Meaning qua meaning intended by a speaker (murād, maqṣūd) is preexistent public meaning that a speaker appropriates for the purpose of communication with others.

The public, appropriated character of meaning, in the thinking of the Muslim jurists, constitutes the core of the argument for the discoverability of the original intent of the author of the texts upon which the law is founded, or, for that matter, of the author of any text. By appropriating public meaning, a speaker/author objectifies what is in his mind; his intent enters the public arena, where it is available to all who know the code, the lugha. As long as the text of what he has said—the orally transmitted replica of his words—remains intact, his intent is there for all to consider.

The classical writers, of course, were not exposed to some of the dilemmas that contemporary writers in the fields of hermeneutics and literary theory have raised. Intentionalism has in this century fallen onto bad times as those who theorize about the law and about the interpretation of texts have become skeptical about the ascertainability of original intent and about its relevance. Considering that the law emerges from complex legislative and judicial processes involving a multitude of human beings with diverse and often conflicting thoughts and passions, how, it is asked, can one ever identify a single consistent intent behind all this complexity? But even if a single author of the texts one is working with can be identified—as the Muslim jurists would have claimed is the case—what difference would this make? A common contemporary view is that legislators give rise to texts that have a life of their own quite apart from original legislative intent. And the reason is that language has a life of its own. Legal texts enter into the domain of what Gadamer called linguisticality (*Sprachlichkeit*). That is to say, they are subject to the play of forces that constitute our experience as human beings caught up in the inexorable flow of language. Among recent writers a favorite way of proving that texts have a life of their own quite apart from authorial intent is to refer to computer-written texts, behind which there is presumably no authorial intent. At least one writer has invited us to ponder hypothetical texts etched upon sandy beaches over millennia of time by natural forces—in other words, texts that are formed purely accidentally.

On the other hand, we cannot regard intentionalism as having been utterly defeated even in these times of skepticism about original intent. One well-known contemporary argues the case of intentionalism in words that could well have been written by a Muslim jurist and for that reason are worth quoting:

> There is only one style of interpretation, the intentional style. . . . In order to hear sense in arbitrarily produced sounds or marks we

> have to hear those sounds and marks within the assumption that they have been produced by some purposeful agent; that is, we have to hear them *as not arbitrarily produced,* even if to do so we must attribute purpose and intention to the waves or to the wind or to the great spirit that rolls through all things. Computer poems are read *as* poems (as opposed to random marks) only because we read them as issuing from intentional beings, only because we grant them—*in* the act of construing, not in addition to it—a mind. . . . The act of construing will begin by assuming an agent endowed with purposes, and *then* the words will be read as issuing from that agent; and in the (certain) event of a dispute between the construers, pointing to the words as a way of adjudicating the dispute will be futile because the words will mean differently in the light of differently assumed intentions. . . . Originalism is not the name of a distinct style of interpretation but the name of interpretation as practiced by anyone. . . . Everyone who is an interpreter is in the intention business, and there is no methodological cash value to declaring yourself (or even thinking yourself) to be an intentionalist because you couldn't be anything else.[16]

For the Muslim jurists, speaking is by definition intentional. For this reason, in talking about the speaking that is behind the foundational texts, they favor the term *khiṭāb,* which denotes speech as something that a speaker addresses to others. Speech always has communication (*tafhīm*) as its purpose: the addressor communicates, and the addressee seeks to understand (*fahm*) what is communicated. Words can, of course, be haphazardly thrown together to form babble, but this is not true speech. Speech is an ordering of words, called in Arabic *naẓm.* Whenever one is confronted with a flow of words that exhibits such ordering, one immediately endeavors to make sense of the words, in which case one is presuming that behind the words there is a purposeful agent, a speaker-addressor. In the case of a scripture said to be the product of a divine author, one may choose to be skeptical about the identity of the author, especially if one is an unbeliever, but one may not be skeptical about the intentionality and communicative purpose—the authorial presence—that is apparent in the ordered lines of the scriptural text.

The classical jurists all lived centuries after the original coming into existence of the foundational texts and were therefore necessarily concerned with the question of how the lugha, the code, is preserved through time. It mattered to them not simply that the code be preserved but that it be preserved intact, for only if it was preserved intact could future generations be assured, right up to the final Day of Judgment and end of history, that the divine intent was accessible to them. It is a central conviction of Islam that the foundational texts upon which the law is based—the Qur'an and Sunna—represent the final revelation of God to humankind. God's law would therefore have to be formulated on the basis of these texts throughout the rest of history.

Thus we have the same question with regard to the code that we had with regard to the texts themselves. All effort to show that the texts have been transmitted intact through time is pointless unless it can be shown that the code—the language employed in the texts—has also been transmitted intact through time, for a text, even one whose authenticity cannot be doubted, is useless without the code. And just as the classical writers employed the concept of tawātur (widespread inerrant transmission) in developing their arguments for foolproof transmission of the Qur'an and portions of the Sunna, so they employed the same concept in developing their arguments for foolproof transmission of the code.

The notion of transmission of language (considered throughout these pages, let us remember, as a code) through time embroiled the classical writers in speculation about the origin of language.[17] Preoccupation with the origin of language is not likely to occur among thinkers who see language as constantly in flux, as ever changing. It may be a matter of some interest, but it will not be a matter demanding attention. On the other hand, if a language is seen to be not a continually evolving phenomenon, but a constant that is moved through time as one moves an object through space, then the subject of origins is much more compelling. The notion of transmission of a thing through time irresistibly arouses interest in the starting point of the transmission. A thing that has been transmitted intact through time must logically be capable of being projected back to a point of origin, since it cannot be projected back ad infinitum.

Muslim thinkers of the Middle Ages seem to have been familiar with the discussions of the Greek philosophers of the origin of language and, in particular, with the two views that had arisen among them: the view that language originated in human attempts to imitate the sounds of nature and the view that it originated in an entirely arbitrary assignment of vocal sounds to meanings. According to the first view, the vocable-meaning correlation was rooted in *physis* (nature); according to the second, it was rooted in *thesis* (arbitrary assignment). In Arabic physis became *ṭabʿ* and thesis became *waḍʿ*.

But the Muslims did not simply repeat the debates that had taken place among the Greeks. In fact, the upholders of ṭabʿ were few among them and belonged to an early period in the development of Muslim thought. By the tenth century there seem no longer to have been any serious advocates of their position. The physis/thesis debate was thus short-lived among the Muslims. The notion that language originated in waḍʿ became universally accepted. But there was still a question that could be debated: by whom were vocables originally assigned to their meanings? Some attributed this role to primordial human society, others attributed it to God. There is no need to recount here the arguments that were used on each side of this debate,[18] because there eventually emerged a consensus among the Muslims to the effect that the question could never be resolved with finality and did not need to be resolved. All that mattered, it seems, is that language be understood to have arisen, not from a natural connection between vocables and their meanings, but from a deliberate, conscious assignment of vocables to their meanings. It was not necessary to identify the assigner or assigners or to determine when the assignment—the founding of the code—took place. It was only necessary to postulate the assignment process. The concept of waḍʿ took on the character of an orthodoxy, both among Sunnis and Shiʿis.

This primordial assignment of vocables to meanings was considered to be final and irrevocable. Once a code has been established, it has, in its original form, a normative character among the people who use it. New words may be coined and new meanings attached to old words, but only for specialized needs and purposes. These new accretions are an addendum to the basic language of the people; they are merely grafted onto it as a technical idiom, suitable for the various crafts and sciences that may develop over time. The basic language is all-sufficient as far as fundamental human needs are concerned and requires no alteration or amending. The original code becomes a given, an unchanging tool, for countless generations.

Among the accretions is the special terminology (*iṣṭilāḥāt*) of the law, much of which originates in the foundational texts themselves. But once established, this legal idiom has the same staying power as the original basic language, assuring that the Legislator's intent, even when couched in the idiom, will always be accessible.

Despite their firm belief in the discoverability of the divine intent and the thoroughness of the arguments they endeavored to make for it, the Muslim jurists were realistic enough to acknowledge that no amount of argument on behalf of this principle could guarantee that efforts to discover the divine intent—the law—would be easy or successful in every case. The code contained, after all, ambiguous expressions, and furthermore a speaker might always, even when employing a relatively unambiguous expression, have a metaphorical meaning in mind or a rare meaning that escaped the interpreter's attention or a specialized idiomatic meaning of which he was unaware. This is not to say that the jurists thought of language as anything but a perfect instrument of communication. A speaker/author—including the divine speaker/author—was expected to rely on contextual factors to impart meaning when expressions were ambiguous or diverted from their standard lexical meaning. The interpreter was also expected to rely on contextual factors in seeking to grasp the divine intent. The working of the code always depended on a cofunctioning of word and context. This being so, the jurists adhered steadfastly to the view that the divine intent was always discover*able* in principle, even when it was not discover*ed* in fact. Nondiscovery did not invalidate the notion of discoverability. We will consider at greater length the obstacles to discovery and their implications in a later chapter. We will also at that point consider the implications of failure to establish with full certainty the authenticity of a given text.

To sum up: the textualist/intentionalist bent of classical Muslim jurisprudence is firmly grounded in a rich legacy of reflection and argumentation. The voluntarism of the jurists requires that they always turn to foundational texts as the ultimate substantive source of all law. The theory of tawātur provides grounds for confidence in the authenticity of the qur'anic text in its present form as well as some parts of the Sunna; and it also assures that common themes found throughout a wide spectrum of sunnaic texts are authentic. The discoverability of original legislative intent—that is to say, divine intent—behind the foundational texts is assured by a view of language that makes language an entirely serviceable tool of communication through which a speaker/author is able to objectify what he has in mind, using a realm of public meaning to which all who are conversant with the language have access. The preservation of the language—that is to say, the code—through time, making it possible for generations down to the Day of Judgment to have access to the divine intent, is assured by resort, again, to the theory of tawātur.

# 4 The Venture Beyond the Texts

In the previous chapter we have concentrated on points on which the classical jurists of Islam were in basic agreement. The identification of the Qur'an and Sunna as the foundational texts of the law became a universal hallmark of Muslim jurisprudence. The use of the tawātur principle to demonstrate the authenticity of the foundational texts also in time became universal, as did the intentionalist approach to the interpretation of the texts and the view of language that it entailed. In this chapter we turn to a subject on which there was no such unanimity, although a majoritarian position did emerge. This subject is the use of analogy as a means of developing new rules. As was indicated in the previous chapter, some of the jurists considered this procedure to be incompatible with the textualist stance. Those who favored the use of analogy—I will call them, following Aron Zysow, the analogists—were therefore obliged to show that this was not the case.

The basic contention of the analogists was that the law found in the foundational texts covered only situations that had arisen during the period of revelation. The development of law within these texts was seen as essentially casuistic, as proceeding case by case. The divine Legislator did not establish rules in a vacuum. No matter how numerous or how common to human experience were the situations that the foundational texts addressed, it was unreasonable to expect to find in those texts a body of rules that sufficed for all time, that covered all future situations. In order to enable the law to keep up with the inexorable flow of new facts, the jurist therefore had to venture beyond the foundational texts. If the texts did not supply a rule for the case at hand, the jurist had to supply the rule. But he had to do so in a manner consistent with the essential demands of textualism. Extratextual rules had to have firm textual grounds. Analogy seemed to be the appropriate instrument for this purpose.

The classical example of the use of analogy, the one that appears throughout the literature, has to do with the prohibition of the beverages *khamr* (wine) and *nabīdh* (fermented date juice). The Qur'an explicitly states that khamr is forbidden but says nothing about nabīdh. Assuming that there is no sunnaic text that clearly forbids nabīdh, we are left with a legal problem: how to determine the legal status of nabīdh. The analogist program offers a solution based on a consideration of the "cause" (ʿilla) of the prohibition of khamr: khamr is prohibited because it is intoxicating. Since nabīdh is intoxicating, it too is forbidden. Thus from a rule found in the texts—the rule pertaining to khamr—has been derived a new, extratextual rule. This movement from rule to rule is based on an assimilation of cases, a respect in which the two beverages resemble each other, which is that they both intoxicate.

As this example indicates, an analogy requires the presence of four basic factors, called "pillars of analogy": an original case (the drinking of khamr), an original rule (the rule forbidding the drinking of khamr), a novel case (the drinking of nabīdh), and a feature common to both cases (*waṣf jāmiʿ*) that by virtue of its constituting the cause (ʿilla) of the original rule may be considered a cause or ground of a new rule. In contrast to these four prerequisites of an analogy, the new rule is its product or outcome (*farʿ*).[1]

It is important to emphasize that the term "cause" must here be understood somewhat loosely and not in terms of strict necessity or determinism. The intoxicating quality of wine does not in itself necessitate its being prohibited. Rather it is always the will of God that is the true necessitating factor, the real determinant of rules. The intoxicating quality of wine is a cause of its being prohibited only insofar as one can say that wine is prohibited *because* it is intoxicating. To say that wine is prohibited because it is intoxicating is to imply that were it not intoxicating it would not be prohibited. The prohibition is thus in some way connected with intoxication, and the word "cause" designates this connection. Other possible translations of *ʿilla* are "ground," "reason," or even *ratio* (as in *ratio legis* and *ratio decidendi*). I have elsewhere translated it as "occasioning factor."[2] Just what was involved in the functioning of the cause of a rule was a topic on which the analogists themselves differed. We will explore their differences later in this chapter.

The use of analogy can, it was recognized, lead to the formulation of more general rules and categories. One may be inclined, for example, once it has been determined that khamr is forbidden because it is intoxicating, to formulate the general rule: all intoxicants are forbidden. With this general rule, one then proceeds by way of mere subsumption—subsuming the particular under the general—not by way of analogy. The classical analogists were, however, careful not to move in this direction. Once one embarked on the formulation of extratextual rules, one proceeded as cautiously as possible. The extratextual rules were best kept at the same level of particularity as the textual rules to which they were analogous. General rules found within the texts were one thing; general rules formulated extratextually were quite another thing, an expression of human initiative that was difficult to justify within a textualist framework.

Analogical reasoning has a long history in Islam, going back to the very beginnings of the development of legal thought, as Joseph Schacht noted and as Norman Calder has demonstrated in even greater detail. But the earliest use of analogy did give rise to generalization and was part of the process of systematizing the law. Calder gives a number of examples of how early Muslim legal speculation worked.[3] If one had, for instance, a rule stating that the water at which a dog had lapped could be used for ritual purification, one had something to work with in determining the legal status of water from which other animals had drunk. How should one regard, for example, water from which a donkey or mule had drunk or a cat or bird of prey or wild beast? One naturally sought categories. If it was as a *domestic* animal that the dog by its drinking left the water ritually pure, then the drinking of a donkey, mule, or cat should also be regarded as ritually innocuous but not that of a bird of prey or wild animal. On the other hand, if the drinking of a *predatory* bird or animal qua predatory bird or animal left water unclean, then the drinking of the dog had to be seen in a different light. But perhaps it was the drinking of carrion-eating animals that left water unclean, in which case the drinking of a dog could be regarded as noncontaminating. All of this speculation could easily lead to related questions, for example: what effect does the drinking of these animals have upon milk? May milk from which they have drunk be drunk by humans? Can any correlations be made between the effects on water used for ablution and the effects on milk intended for consumption?

Deliberation over particular cases led irresistibly to the formulation of general concepts and principles, and through such generalizing activity the law became more systematic. Schacht has shown how the concepts and principles reached in this way were frequently expressed in the form of legal maxims,[4] which by virtue of their pithiness and in some cases their rhyme lent themselves to easy memorization, an important consideration during the preliterary stage in the development of the law.

Textualism of the more rigorous sort that rejected the use of analogy is, like the use of analogy itself, a fairly early development in Islam. For the rigorists, all analogism allowed an unjustified intrusion of human judgment and speculation into the formulation of the law. The foundational texts, they reasoned, were quite sufficient as a source of rules for all time. Their attitude amounted to something on the order of a textual positivism. Only what was clearly and decisively stated in the texts could be accorded the status of divine law. All else was the product of unacceptable human innovation.

Textualism eventually triumphed over the freer speculation of the early jurists but did not in the course of its triumph undo the analogist program altogether. The textualism that ultimately prevailed was of the sort that made its peace with analogism, a peace made possible by modifications in the use of analogy that did not threaten the basic textualist commitment. Thus modified, the use of analogy proved to be of great service to textualism. All analogical reasoning now began exclusively with rules found within the foundational texts. Furthermore, such reasoning stopped short of generalizing rules. The analogous rule must always be on the same level of particularity as the original rule. The purpose of analogical reasoning was to decide new cases, to produce rules that governed those cases, and not to raise rules of law to a higher level of generality than pertained to real down-to-earth cases.

This is not to say that the analogists would not seek to develop general principles. The point to be made is that these principles would guide the jurists in the formulation of rules but would not constitute rules in their own right. A rule was concrete. Every rule began as a ruling in response to a particular situation. Islamicists who write on Islamic law in fact, in translating *ḥukm*, ambivalently vacillate between "rule" and "ruling" as translations. General principles—even normative ones—thus lie beyond or above the realm of rules as such. It was by virtue of their use of such principles that the analogists were vulnerable to criticism from their opponents.

Although analogical reasoning was eventually accepted as a valid method of rule formulation within all four of the extant Sunni schools of law, opposition remained strong in certain circles. During the formative and classical periods of Islamic law the opposition constituted in fact a sizable segment of the Islamic community, comprising virtually all Shiʿis, most Kharijis (a branch of the Muslim community not dealt with in these pages), many adherents of the Muʿtazili movement, and an entire Sunni school of law, the Zahiri school, which, though extinct, has in its history counted some illustrious jurists among its members.[5]

The most thorough and penetrating study that has thus far been done on the disputes between the analogists and their opponents and on the various ways in which the analogists themselves conceived of the method of legal argumentation to which they were committed is that of Aron Zysow, which appears in the pages of his unpublished doctoral dissertation.[6] In what follows I rely largely on Zysow's work together with my own previous work on the analogical method as elaborated by Sayf al-Din al-Amidi.[7] Zysow's work is broadly based, taking in not only the major Hanafi writings of Central Asia—his stated focus is on Hanafi jurisprudence—but a wide array of other Muslim jurisprudential works as well.

In order to justify the use of analogy in terms acceptable within a textualist jurisprudence, the analogists sought to demonstrate two things: first, that the validity of the analogical method could be sustained by convincing argument; and second, that the results actually achieved—the rules arrived at—through the use of analogy satisfied the essential requirements of textualism.

The most widely employed argument for the validity of the analogical method consisted of an appeal to the consensus of the earliest generation of Muslims. Many of them, it was contended, had made use of analogy in the formulation of rules, and the others, by voicing no objection, had given tacit consent to this practice. Such consensus could only mean that this procedure was valid, since the early Muslims would not have agreed on following it had it been invalid or erroneous. The other type of argument attempted to draw upon direct textual proof, of which there was not a great abundance. This proof consisted in fact of one qur'anic passage and a few sunnaic passages. The key qur'anic statement was brief: "Reflect, O you who have understanding." The strongest sunnaic proof was generally thought to consist of the Prophet's commendation of an early judge named Muʿadh who, upon being questioned by the Prophet, said that if he did not find a solution to a case brought before him in the Qur'an or the Sunna, he would exercise discretion (*ajtahidu ra'yī*).[8]

None of these arguments convinced the opposition. That the first Muslims really made use of analogy was less than certain, since the evidence could be variously interpreted. Furthermore, the absence of objection was not a sure indication of agreement. (We will have occasion to look at the problems relating to argument from consensus in the following chapter.) As for the qur'anic command to reflect, it seemed too vague to constitute a clear sanction for analogical reasoning. And the story about Muʿadh was of doubtful authenticity and in any case also made no direct reference to analogical reasoning. Even the analogists for the most part felt constrained to admit that in the final analysis their arguments were not entirely conclusive. But at least these arguments, it was thought, constituted grounds of sorts for holding the opinion that the validity of analogical reasoning was textually sanctioned. If the sanction was not certain, it was at least probable.

At this point we come to the crux of the dispute between the analogists and their opponents. The dispute was really an encounter between, on the one hand, a rigorous textualism that demanded full certainty regarding the validity of analogical reasoning and would settle for nothing less and, on the other hand, a more liberal textualism that was willing to proceed with the business of analogizing on the basis of its probable validity. Otherwise stated, it was an encounter between a dogmatic jurisprudence whose textualism could tolerate no use of a methodology whose validity was tinged with uncertainty and a probabilistic jurisprudence anxious to make this methodology central to the formulation of the law. Here we touch on a topic that will be explored at greater length in the next chapter, namely the tension between the demand for certainty and the acceptance of the probable in Islamic jurisprudence.

The difference between the two points of view can be stated in yet another way. As we have noted, the analogists were convinced that the foundational texts did not cover all the cases with which the law would have to deal over time and that if the law was to deal with these cases new rules would have to be formulated. The only means by which such rules could be fashioned, so it seemed, was analogy. The opponents of analogy were equally convinced that the foundational texts were quite sufficient for all time. The texts potentially covered all the cases that truly mattered for Muslim society until the Day of Judgment, and the rules discoverable within the texts therefore constituted the whole law. This is not to say, however, that the law might not unfold gradually in the consciousness of jurists who worked with the texts. There was often more in the texts than met the eye.

The remaining pages of this chapter will consider how the analogists understood the workings of analogy as an instrument of legal construction and how they demonstrated its compatibility with the textualist way of thinking. On two crucial questions they were themselves not entirely in agreement, and their differences on these questions form a lively chapter in Muslim juristic debate. First: how was the concept of a "cause of a rule of law" (*ʿillat al-ḥukm*) to be understood? What was the true nature and function of such a cause? Second: when considering a case to which a rule was known to apply, how was one to identify the particular feature of the case that constituted the cause of the rule? We know, for example, that the Legislator has ruled that the drinking of khamr is forbidden, since this is clearly stated in the Qur'an. What is it about wine that makes it subject to this rule? Wine displays a variety of features: it is red, liquid, of a certain taste and smell, and it intoxicates. Which of these features explains why khamr (and perhaps nabīdh as well) is forbidden? What method do we use to identify that feature?

With respect to the first question, Zysow has shown that two different models of the cause of a rule were in competition with each other among the classical jurists: the pure sign (*amāra mujaddara*) model and the motive (*bāʿith*) model.[9] The qualifier "pure" was necessary, since the cause was always in some sense a sign of a rule. One can always say, for example, that since khamr is forbidden because it is intoxicating (meaning that it would not be forbidden if it were not intoxicating), the power to intoxicate functions as a sign of forbiddenness wherever it may be found. Therefore, if the sign is present in some other beverage such as nabīdh, we can know that that beverage, too, is forbidden. We know, of course, that khamr is forbidden from the words of the Qur'an quite apart from any knowledge we may have of its cause. But when we become familiar with its cause, our knowledge that khamr is forbidden acquires an added dimension. We are now acquainted with the sign of its forbiddenness so that we would know that it is forbidden even if we did not have the qur'anic words that expressly forbid it. The sign is thus a potential means of knowing rules.

What the adherents of the pure sign model maintained was that this sign function of the cause is what defines the cause and nothing more. Adherents of the motive model insisted that a further function enters into the definition, namely the motive function and that without this function a cause of a law is not truly a cause. On the pure sign model of the cause, a particular feature of the case—in the case of khamr, the power to intoxicate—was all-sufficient as the cause of a rule. On the motive model, the particular feature was not sufficient but rather had to be linked to some higher purpose or rationale in the mind of the Legislator in order to be reckoned a cause. The intoxicating quality of khamr was thus a cause of forbiddenness only insofar as it could be linked to a higher purpose, namely the preservation of human rationality. Considered entirely on its own merits, apart from any consideration of a higher purpose, it did not constitute a true cause.

Closely related to the two models were two different ways of identifying the feature of a case that constituted the cause of the rule.[10] If one adopted the motive model, one looked for a feature that could be associated with a known higher purpose of the law. In the case of khamr, one knew that features such as redness, liquidity, taste, and smell had no connection with any known higher purpose. But on considering the power to intoxicate, one familiar with the higher purposes of the law soon came to the realization that this feature of khamr is closely linked with one of these purposes, namely the preservation of human rationality. By forbidding the drinking of khamr, the Legislator achieves the higher purpose. This constitutes the motive element in the function of the feature in question as a cause. By taking the motive into consideration, one knows that the power to intoxicate is truly the cause of the forbiddenness of khamr.

On the other hand, if one adopted the sign model, one was likely to take a very different approach to the task of determining which feature was the cause. Instead of scrutinizing the various features of khamr in the light of higher purposes of the law, one scrutinized them in the light of what one knew about causes of rules from the foundational texts. It is here that causes stated in the texts became useful. The rule under consideration—the prohibition of khamr—is, of course, not a rule for which the texts supply a cause; but in seeking to determine which feature of khamr is the cause of the rule, one can learn from the *known* causes of other rules, causes that *are* indicated in the texts. By studying these causes, one can get a sense of the sorts of things that constitute causes in the mind of the Legislator. That is to say, one can get a sense of the typology of causes. With this typology in mind, one can, in reviewing the features of khamr, look for a feature that can be subsumed under one of the types of causes. As Zysow puts it, "What was required was that a candidate for recognition as a valid cause be of the same *type* as one already known to be a cause."[11]

With this approach to identifying the cause of a rule, we are back in the realm of legal reasoning encountered among the earliest jurists of

Islam. The concept of motives related to higher purposes of the law was a later development. The early jurists used what was known to arrive at categories or types that would enable them to deal with the unknown. They did not attempt to explore the mind of the Legislator but rather were content to explore the givens of previously established law. These givens were publicly available to all and did not entail subjective criteria that might be vulnerable to criticism. Thus in pondering the causes of rules permitting the ritual use of water from which donkey, mule, or dog has drunk, one might extrapolate a generic cause, namely domesticity, which could apply to a wider range of cases.

We are of course concerned here with a task that could arise only after the body of foundational texts had become well defined. This task has to do with rules found in the texts for which the texts supply no causes. The Qur'an explicitly forbids khamr but supplies no cause. The method under consideration entails scrutiny of causes supplied by the texts for other rules, the purpose being to extract from these textually verified causes a typology of revealed causes that will enable one to determine the cause of the forbiddenness of khamr. Once this has been accomplished, it is then possible to move on to cases not covered in the texts, such as the case of nabīdh.

We can easily discern the textualist preoccupations of this approach. Unlike the freer, more open-ended reasoning of the early jurists, the reasoning entailed in this approach works entirely with textual givens. It sees the causes behind the divine law as finite but sufficient for all future cases by virtue of the typology that they exhibit. In dealing with cases not covered in the texts, one does not seek hitherto undiscovered causes but works entirely with previously revealed causes. The causes are not the purposes of the law; they do not take us into the realm of motives, of the subjectively perceived divine psyche. Rather they are raw textual data that exist within the public arena. As will be readily noted, the primary movement in this approach is from textually indicated causes to textually indicated rules for which causes are not supplied in the texts. The movement from textually indicated rules whose cause has been determined by this method to new rules is strictly secondary and almost incidental. If one has a typology that enables one to determine the cause of the textually stated forbiddenness of khamr one will have no difficulty determining the cause of the forbiddenness of other beverages such as nabīdh. In this method the determination of the cause of the forbiddenness of khamr and the determination of the cause of the forbiddenness of nabīdh are virtually a single operation.

The insistence upon grounding all analogies in textually indicated causes required that the search for causes in the texts employ every reasonable interpretive strategy. Two types of textually indicated causes were postulated: explicitly mentioned causes and implied causes.[12] No jurist seriously hoped to find statements as explicit as "The cause of the rule forbidding khamr is khamr's power to intoxicate." The category "explicitly mentioned" applied rather to causes that were indicated by various Arabic expressions meaning "because," "on account of," or "for the reason that." The classical literature often provides lists of such expressions. Important as these were in the search for textually indicated causes, however, the analogist did not depend entirely on them but could, if need be, decipher causes from the broader import of a passage. In this case the cause was deemed to be implied. If, for example, the Prophet upon seeing a man inebriated by khamr were to say, "That drink has been forbidden," an interpreter might with reason assume that the inebriation was the cause of the rule expressed by the statement.

The opponents of analogy were fully aware that the foundational texts contained references to causes of certain rules but were nonetheless unwilling to accept the analogizing procedures just described. In their view, the existence of textually indicated causes did not warrant the kind of typologizing that this method of identifying causes entailed. The texts, after all, referred to specific causes, not to types. The postulating of types was an extratextual work of the human mind, an intrusion into the law's own proper self-revelation. But even if one refrained from typologizing and based one's analogy on a specific cause (as opposed to a type that it represented), one was still, according to many opponents of analogy, building the law on a foundation of sand. If one were to discover, for example, a text that explicitly stated that khamr is forbidden because it is intoxicating, this would not justify using intoxication as a reason for forbidding other beverages. If the Legislator wished to forbid all intoxicating beverages, he would have said so in plain words that would have left no doubt about the matter. Without such explicit language, who are we to say that the Legislator might not forbid intoxication in one case and countenance it in another?

In the final analysis, then, the dispute between the analogists who made textually indicated causes the sole basis of their analogizing and their opponents was a dispute over how the references to causes in the texts should be interpreted. What for one party in the dispute was an unwarranted intrusion of human judgment was for the other party a reasonable ascertainment of the Legislator's intention. Why would the Legislator mention a cause if he did not intend for it to be applied to all cases where it—or its type—could be found? Without such an intention, would not the mention of the cause be a wasting of words? Not so, was the answer. The Legislator may have had a reason for mentioning the cause that we have simply not been able to fathom.

For adherents of the motive model of causes of rules, the method of determining causes we have been considering lacked a vital ingredient, namely rationality. In their view a cause should make sense within the framework of some purpose that the Legislator had in mind in laying down a rule. The proper way to go about determining the cause of the rule, therefore, was to examine the various features of the situation or object to which it applied with a view to identifying a feature that could be linked to a legislative purpose or rationale. That feature would then constitute the cause. Of the various features of khamr, for example, its power to intoxicate could be linked to a definite purpose, the preservation of human rationality. That is to say, it made sense, given this purpose, to say that khamr was forbidden on account of its being an intoxicant, whereas it did not make sense to say that it was forbidden on account of its being red, or liquid, or the product of the vine, or of a certain taste, since no purpose of the law could be associated with any of these features. The power to intoxicate alone, among the various features of khamr, satisfied what was known as the criterion of "suitability" (*munāsaba*). It alone, in other words, was suited, in the light of a known purpose of the law, to be regarded as the cause of the forbiddenness of khamr. This method of determining causes was in fact commonly called the method of suitability (*maslak al-munāsaba*). For our purposes it will be helpful to use a somewhat more elucidative designation: the method of linkage with a legislative purpose. The method discussed in the previous paragraphs may, by way of contrast, be called the method of assimilation to known (textually indicated) causes.[13]

The purposes of the law in the light of which causes were thus identified related to vital human interests (*maṣāliḥ*). Human beings, it was thought, know very well what these human interests are. It is a knowledge that arises out of experience and reflection upon the human condition. Five interests are paramount and universal: religion, life, offspring (lineage), property, and rationality. Through experience humans discover that when these interests are well served they enjoy maximal happiness; otherwise, unhappiness and hardship follow. Alongside these universal interests are a multitude of lesser, nonuniversal interests that vary in importance from situation to situation and from time to time. One may or may not, therefore, take them into account in particular instances. It is clearly the universal interests that will have the greatest overall impact on the determination of causes.

Examples readily present themselves. Homicide, as a physical act, shares several features with accidental killing or justified killing. One feature it does not share, however, namely the intent to kill without legal justification, and this feature constitutes the cause of the forbiddenness of homicide and of the right of the victim's family to demand retribution, for it makes sense, in the light of a purpose of the law (the preservation of life), to say that homicide is forbidden and punishable on account of its entailing the intent to kill without legal justification. It does not make sense, in the light of this same purpose, to say this of any other feature. Similarly, it makes sense, in the light of the law's intent to preserve the patrilineal family unit, to say that a certain type of sexual activity (fornication) is forbidden on account of its being extramarital, or, in the light of the law's intent to preserve property, to say that a certain type of transaction (gambling) is unlawful because of the indefiniteness of the consideration received for money paid. We have already referred to the example of the forbiddenness of khamr.

The inclusion of religion among the vital interests of humans reflects the grounding of Muslim jurisprudence in a natural theology that makes the knowledge of God's existence the result of rational reflection. If humans can naturally know that God exists, then they can naturally know that it is in their interests to render to God any service that he may require. The Lord-subject relationship is, let us remember, built into human consciousness prior to the reception of revelation. The institutionalization of this relationship through the institutions of the ritual law is thus a prerequisite of human happiness.

The practice of referring to human interests as a way of identifying the causes of rules was, quite naturally, a ready target of criticism. Within a jurisprudence dominated by textualism, it could seem to many to give too much license to mere human judgment. On one point all were agreed: the law is not of man's making. God is its sole ultimate author, and independent judgment concerning right and wrong in no way enters into the shaping of the law. The only acceptable kind of human judgment is a strictly exegetical judgment as to what constitutes the intention of the Legislator. Any judgment about the law made independently of the texts amounts to an arrogation of a prerogative that belongs only to God; it is thus a form of disobedience. These were the core convictions of textualism, and any jurists who proposed to build analogies on the basis of humanly perceived vital interests would have to do so in a manner that did not challenge these convictions. It would be necessary to demonstrate that this method of formulating the law fell safely within the domain of bona fide exegesis.

What this entailed, to begin with, was demonstration from the texts that God took human interests into account when ordaining rules of law, that the safeguarding of these interests did indeed constitute the purpose of the law. Human interests, no matter how universal or vital, could be of no relevance to the formulation of the law unless this were done. The task, however, required that certain methodological issues be addressed. How were the purposes of God to be known?

Admittedly, the texts provided no precise delineations of those purposes. One could not know the purposes of God from any passages in particular. Careful and sustained reflection on the entire body of foundational texts, however—and especially on the rules of law contained in those texts—would, it was believed, reveal that the law of God, as known from the texts, does indeed serve the vital interests of human beings. On reflecting upon family and inheritance law, for example, one could not but conclude that the safeguarding of the patrilineal family unit was a major concern of the law, just as one could not but conclude, on reflecting on contract law, that the safeguarding of property was also a major concern of the law. Similar evidence could easily be found for the other purposes of the law.

It should be noted that the Arabic term normally used to designate the purposes of the law is *maqāṣid* (singular *maqṣūd*). In the preceding chapter we observed that *maqṣūd* is one of the terms used for authorial intent of particular words, phrases, or whole passages and that it is in respect to this usage interchangeable with the more common term *murād*. But we also observed that unlike *murād*, this term is also sometimes used for the larger intentions of the law taken as a whole. In the present context we are concerned with this latter usage. Purposes, after all, entail intentionality. The search for the purposes of the law, insofar as it entails investigation of texts, is an exegetical undertaking and belongs within the domain of intentionalist interpretation.

The type of exegesis to be employed in the search for purposes was essentially inductive (*istiqrā'*). Wael Hallaq, who has done the principal work on this subject in recent times, aptly calls it "inductive corroboration."[14] As the interpreter begins exploring passages dealing with contract law, for example, he observes that the provisions contained in these passages are of the sort that contribute to the safeguarding of property. In his continuing journey from passage to passage, he finds this initial observation corroborated again and again until finally he is able to assert with a high degree of confidence that the safeguarding of property is indeed an intention, a purpose, of the law as a whole. Once he has reached this conviction, he is then in a position to refer to that purpose in his attempts to identify the causes of rules.

Along with this inductively reached awareness that the law serves purposes relating to vital human interests went formal argumentation, which was also firmly grounded in the foundational texts. God describes himself in the Qur'an as *ḥakīm*, a rational being. A rational being is one whose actions are purposive, who takes ends into account in all he does. The ends that God takes into account entail either harm or benefit. Since he himself is above harm and benefit, they must entail harm or benefit to his creatures. That they entail benefit rather than harm is something we learn from the texts, not only through the inductive investigation noted in the previous paragraph, but also from explicit statements such as "We sent you only as a mercy for all creatures" (Qur'an 21:107), "My mercy embraces all things" (Qur'an 7:156), "God does not intend to cause hardship for you" (Qur'an 5:6), "O people! An exhortation has come to you from your Lord and a balm for what troubles your breasts" (Qur'an 10:58), and "Do not inflict injury nor repay one injury with another" (*lā ḍarār wa lā ḍirār*, a prophetic saying). One could hardly speak of God as merciful or as a giver of balm and reliever from hardship if the rules he ordained for his creatures were devoid of objectives relating to their well-being, for in this case the rules would constitute a blight upon the creatures, not a mercy. Conformity to rules that were not conducive to well-being constitutes affliction and adversity, the very things God's religion is not.[15]

Such passages as those cited above did not, however, warrant the conclusion that God inevitably takes any given human interest into account, that he *must* take it into account. That was a Muʿtazili view, one that classical Sunni thought roundly rejected. The Muʿtazilis had affirmed that God's ordaining of the rules of law in conformity with purposes having to do with human interests was a rational necessity, not something known solely from the texts. God was bound to do what was best (*aṣlaḥ*) for the creature and could not be conceived as doing otherwise. The classical view preferred to leave God's sovereignty and freedom unfettered by notions of rational necessity. God takes human interests into account, not because he must, but because he sovereignly chooses to do so. Grace, not rational necessity, was the foundation of the divine purposes. That God in fact takes human interests into account is something we discover as a result of reflection upon the foundational texts, not something we already know in advance.

Inductive investigation of the texts revealed, according to the classical view, the divine custom (*ʿāda*). We know from the texts that it has been God's general practice in establishing rules of law to take human interests into account. This does not entitle us, however, to predict that God always or inevitably takes any given interest into account. The sovereign Lord is always free to take it into account in some cases and not in others. Again, it is important to remember that the Muslim jurists saw the law as having developed, during the period of revelation, casuistically. What we know from the inductive study of the texts, therefore, is God's practice as it relates to cases covered in the texts.[16]

It is by virtue of this textual evidence of the bearing of human interests upon divine legislation that these interests acquire relevance to the process of determining the causes of rules. Some jurists could see no reason not to treat the interests themselves as causes. If it can be established that the law seeks to safeguard human reason, why treat intoxication as the cause of the forbiddenness of khamr? If the justification for singling out intoxication as the cause depends on a linkage between intoxication and a higher purpose of the law, why not just settle for the higher purpose as the cause? If one must rationalize the statement "khamr is forbidden on account of its being an intoxicant" with reference to the law's intention to safeguard human reason, why not simplify matters by saying that khamr is forbidden on account of its being detrimental to human reason? One could then, just as easily, go on to make the judgment that nabīdh is forbidden because it is likewise detrimental to human reason.

This approach had an undeniable attraction. One who adopted it could ascend to the highest imaginable level of interpretive judgment in the formulation of the law. Once one had been able, through careful inductive study of the texts, to identify the law's purposes, one could base rules directly on these purposes. Whatever in one's judgment served any one of these purposes would then constitute a valid rule of law. Since the purposes were relatively few in number, especially as compared with the vast body of rules and of lower-level causes that might be postulated for them, the work of formulating the law at this point became less arduous and the scope of its results much broader.

But there were problems with this approach that most jurists were quick to see. If one treated a purpose of the law as the cause of a rule, one opened the door to almost unlimited and certainly uncontrolled analogizing, to an outpouring of virtually endless analogous rules. We may refer again to the classic example. If the cause of the forbiddenness of khamr is the capacity of khamr to diminish human rationality, and not just its power to intoxicate, then the door is wide open to all sorts of rules, and one must face certain perplexing questions. Are all acts that entail a diminishing of human rationality, however slight, to be counted as forbidden? If not, where does one draw the line? Without specific guidance from revelation, one of two things follows: either the jurist will rely upon his own wholly independent judgment or he will refrain altogether from attempting to analogize. Since independent human judgment (as opposed to a truly interpretive or exegetical judgment) is forbidden, the latter would seem to be the inevitable outcome.

Problems of this sort prompted most analogists who worked with the purposes of the law to insist that constancy (*inḍibāṭ*) should be a requirement of a cause of a rule. Since the purposes of the law entailed factors—the diminishing of human rationality, for example—that were highly variable from case to case, it was necessary to look for something more stable, something that did not require the jurist to draw subjective lines between cases. The power to intoxicate was just such a factor. A person might drink varying amounts of an intoxicating beverage—might get intoxicated in varying degrees—but the power to intoxicate as such was a constant present in the beverage; it allowed a jurist to make a completely objective judgment based on its sheer presence or absence.

Though lacking this constancy, the purpose behind a rule could still function as the basis for selecting the power to intoxicate, as opposed to some other feature of khamr, as the cause of forbiddenness. Purpose and cause were in fact seen as interdependent factors. A purpose gave the cause its motive character. Without the purpose, the cause was not a true cause but only a mere sign, as far as the adherents of the motive model were concerned. At the same time, a purpose had no legislative import on its own; it required a cause in order to have any bearing upon the formulation of the law. What the cause did for the purpose was to supply the constancy and determinacy that the purpose lacked. Thus, in the case of khamr and nabīdh or other intoxicating drinks, it was not the diminishing of rationality in general that became decisive for the jurist but rather the more specific kind of diminishing of rationality that results from intoxication. Intoxication is thus the operative factor in determining whether other cases are to be treated as analogous.

To state the interdependence of purpose and cause in terms of our classic example: intoxication considered entirely in and of itself without reference to a purpose of the law cannot be a cause of a rule. Only when considered in regard to its diminishing of human rationality can intoxication function as a true cause. On the other hand, the diminishing of human rationality by virtue of its variability can never be considered as the cause in its own right. It acquires relevance to the process of formulating the law only when linked to a constant, namely intoxication.[17]

The concern with constancy can be readily appreciated. The whole enterprise of formulating the law on the basis of analogies had faced stiff criticism from early times, especially from Zahiri and Shiʿi circles. The demand for constancy—for objectivity and precision—reflects sensitivity to this criticism and a wish to demonstrate to critics that analogizing was not as slippery a method of formulating the law as they had imagined. By insisting on constancy, one hoped to eliminate human subjectivity from the analogizing enterprise and convince the critics that this method of formulating the law entailed strict controls.

The primary substantive role of human judgment in the formulation of the law through analogical reasoning was thus the positing of a linkage between cause and purpose. But was this not a dangerous compromise of textualist convictions? Could not a jurist be mistaken about such linkages? Was not this type of judgment too much an extratextual, nonexegetical deliberation? How could the jurist be positive that a given purpose of the law was operative in the particular case under consideration? Was not God as sovereign Lord in the final analysis free to ignore or definitely rule out any given human interest? How was one to know that an interest under consideration was not in fact ignored or ruled out? And if in a given case the interest was in fact ignored or ruled out, how could any feature of the case associated with it be regarded as a cause? Would it not be necessary to say that God had ignored or ruled out the feature as well?

To these questions those jurists who advocated the method of identifying the causes of rules through association with human interests had a ready answer. The original rule in an analogy must always be a rule found in the texts. The rule forbidding khamr, for example, is clearly stated in the Qur'an. It is therefore undeniably a rule that the divine Legislator had laid down. Given that the Legislator is a rational being, he may be presumed to have laid down this rule, not haphazardly, but on account of something and for some purpose. There is no known purpose of the law that better fits this case than the safeguarding of human reason, and there is no feature of khamr that is more connected with this purpose and therefore more suited to be regarded as the cause of forbiddenness than intoxication. Therefore, there is good reason to conclude that the Legislator did take a human interest as well as a particular feature of khamr into account in laying down the rule. And the reason has a solid textual grounding.

Despite the opposition that the analogizing enterprise faced in the course of its struggle for acceptance within Muslim jurisprudence, this approach to the formulation of law gained the support of the great majority of the jurists of Islam and became part of the official methodology of all four Sunni schools. However convinced the critics may have been that the texts supplied a body of rules sufficient for all time, their way of thinking was not to be that of the mainstream. In the view of the majority it was necessary to establish rules beyond the confines of the texts. But this venture beyond the texts could enjoy legitimacy only to the extent that it entailed use of textual givens. The end product of the use of analogy—the rules established thereby—might lie beyond the confines of the text, but the means did not. Both the all-important original rule and the criteria for determining its cause were supplied by the texts.

The theory of law that came to prevail in all four Sunni schools included analogy, along with the Qur'an and the Sunna, among the four sources (uṣūl) of the law. (The remaining source, the consensus of jurists, will be discussed in the next chapter.) Opposition to the use of analogy among Sunnis thus in time virtually disappeared. Only among Shiʿis did it ultimately find a permanent foothold, and Shiʿi books of jurisprudence preserve to this day a wide array of arguments inherited from earlier opponents of analogy.

Among Sunnis, the use of analogy gained acceptability, as we have seen, only because it was shown not to conflict with the conviction that no law should be formulated apart from the foundational texts. In principle, therefore, textualism retained its supremacy in Sunni legal theory. The tenacity of the textualist outlook is evident in the great care that Sunni jurists took to avoid all appearances of formulating the law entirely independently of the texts. We see this concern at work in the discussions of a controversial procedure known as *istiḥsān,* a term best translated as "preference." Frequently regarded as a distinctively Hanafi concept, istiḥsān seems to have originally represented a vestige of the free use of judicial discretion (ra'y) of earlier times. In the literature of uṣūl al-fiqh, it is given a broad spectrum of definitions, some of which are suggestive of the earlier ra'y and some of which denote a procedure entirely consistent with later textualist convictions.

In all cases, istiḥsān was seen as a procedure to be adopted when the use of analogy produced an undesirable result. One definition made istiḥsān the setting aside of a rule based on analogy in favor of a rule based on "that which arises spontaneously in the mind" (*alladhī yasbiq ila'l-fahm*),[18] that is, the jurist's own intuition. Another definition made it the setting aside of an analogy-based rule in favor of a rule based on local custom (*ʿurf*). These definitions suggest something on the order of equity, a principle of justice to which one could turn in the event that formal law was in some way wanting. As John Makdisi has made clear, however, Muslim legal thought steered decidedly clear of all intimations of the notion of equity. Makdisi has used passages from a number of leading classical Muslim jurists to show how they astutely avoided understandings of istiḥsān that entailed a formulation of the law independent of the divinely ordained foundational texts.[19]

The definitions of istiḥsān that rendered this procedure acceptable within Sunni, and especially Hanafi, circles made it the setting aside of a rule reached through a rather straightforward, facile use of analogy in favor of a rule based on a more subtle and somewhat obscure, although in the end more convincing, process of analogical reasoning. Such definitions presupposed that reasoning by analogy could lead to various results and made istiḥsān simply a method of giving one result precedence over the others.

Within Maliki circles, a technique of legal reasoning similar to istiḥsān and known as *istiṣlāḥ* ("consideration of a human interest, or *maṣlaḥa*") gained prominence. The Maliki jurist al-Shatibi in fact places it under the rubric of istiḥsān and describes it as the distinctly Maliki form of istiḥsān. He explains that for the school of Malik, istiḥsān is a method of reasoning in which the jurist allows a particular human interest to take precedence over the results of strict analogical reasoning. Here the assumption is that in some cases a rule based on analogy might give rise to some sort of harmful consequence for human beings. In such cases the jurist is allowed to offer a solution that he deems more consonant with a human interest whose realization he knows is among the purposes of the law. In this instance the jurist turns from analogical reasoning to something quite different, his understanding of the purposes of the law. We have already noted the problems associated with this approach to the formulation of the law. But Shatibi is convinced that it can be undertaken with absolute faithfulness to the foundational texts and without any intrusion of merely human proclivities (*dhawq*).[20] Not all jurists were so sanguine. The point that matters for us, however, is that even at this furthest limit of juristic interpretive endeavor, the textualist outlook reigned supreme.

# 5 Probabilism and the Limits of Certainty

Despite their steadfast commitment to the textualist approach to the formulation of the law and to the authority of authorial intent, and despite their confidence in the adequacy of language as a vehicle for the communication of authorial intent, the Muslim jurists were not blind to problems involved in the actual work of determining authorial intent. As astute observers of the text-critical and interpretive processes involved in the formulation of the law, they were everything but naive idealists. They were in fact realists who understood perfectly well that certainty in the understanding of the law often lay beyond the reach of the interpreter and that probable constructions of the law were often the most the interpreter could hope to attain.

This is not to say that certainty could never be achieved. The jurists were all sure that in principle it could, but they differed among themselves as to how much of the law was certain and how much merely probable and as to which parts of the law—which rules and which principles—were certain and which probable. They also differed as to how to assess the probable formulations of the law. Were such formulations to be regarded as correct or incorrect, and if incorrect, how was their authority to be rationalized? This latter issue arose from the fact that probable formulations of the law were expressions of jurists' fallible opinions, and opinion could vary from one jurist to another, giving rise to pluralism in the law.

Given the difficulties encountered in the work of formulating the law, the jurists saw this work as a kind of toil and customarily called it *ijtihād* ("toil," "arduous effort," "striving"). The workers themselves, the formulators of the law, were accordingly called *mujtahids*, "toilers." In Chapter 1 we noted that the jurists also applied to the formulation of the law the metaphors of cultivation. The law was the fruit or crop; the formulator of the law was the husbandman who facilitated the appearance of the crop (*istithmār, istikhrāj*). For people living in an agrarian society, this agricultural language conjured up the image of the cultivator toiling daily under the sun, struggling against the adversities of climate, weed, and sometimes intractable soil.

That the work was hard and toilsome was part of the divine plan. A law sent down from heaven in the form of a finished product would leave no room for human effort and for the rewarding of that effort. The law was not something to be passively received and applied; it was rather something to be actively constructed by human toilers eager to gain the approval of their Lord for their effort. The soil with which they worked was the canon of foundational texts, the tools that they used the philological methods required for the "harvesting" of authorial intent, to which may be added, for Sunnis at least, the principles of analogical reasoning.

In order to appreciate why the formulation of the law was seen as toil, as hard work, we need only to review the principal tasks that it entailed. Strictly speaking, the interpretation of texts is only part of the work. There is an important preinterpretive part, which includes what we may call the text-critical task. Before the toiler, the mujtahid, begins the process of interpreting a text he must be sure that he has an authoritative text to work with. At this stage the Qur'an constitutes a kind of bedrock, a sure starting point for what lies ahead. The qur'anic text is, by virtue of its miraculous character, the self-attesting authoritative word of the Divine Legislator; and, thanks to an error-free transmission process (tawātur), the mujtahid can be sure that the qur'anic text that lies before him is fully authentic.

On pondering the qur'anic text, the mujtahid becomes aware of the Sunna as a complementary authoritative source of law. With respect to the hadith, those texts in which the Sunna is to be found, however, he faces problems that do not beset the qur'anic text, problems having to do, not with authority (which is established by the unassailable qur'anic text), but with authenticity. By general agreement among the jurists, the tawātur principle did not serve the actual text of the Sunna very well, although it might serve thematic content common to many sunnaic passages. Consequently, with respect to the text the mujtahid had to employ criteria other than tawātur to evaluate authenticity. We will consider these criteria shortly and also various juristic views as to how well they worked. In contrast to the unanimity surrounding the authenticity of the Qur'an, we encounter among the jurists profound differences of opinion regarding the authenticity of sunnaic texts. For most jurists, this latter authenticity could never be more than probable—in other words, never certain. An uncertain text meant that the law drawn from it would inevitably be in some degree uncertain, however high the degree of probability.

But authenticity of texts is not the only issue with which the mujtahid must deal at the preinterpretive stage of his toil. A given passage in the texts may be of undoubted authenticity and yet inoperative by virtue of having been abrogated or superseded by another passage. The development of the law during the period of revelation had, according to the generally accepted theory of abrogation, been progressive because of the transitional character of the earliest Muslim community, which was caught up in gradual unfolding of the kind of social order that the Legislator intended for all time to come. Earlier rules were therefore sometimes designed for situations that became outmoded as the new order unfolded and had to be abrogated or replaced by more progressive rules. Even though the number of abrogated passages was judged by most jurists to be small, a mujtahid nonetheless had to consider the possibility of abrogation in the case of any text, whether qur'anic or sunnaic. Not infrequently, differences of opinion regarding the abrogation of a particular passage would emerge, giving the abrogated (or nonabrogated) status of a passage an aura of uncertainty.[1]

At the level of interpretation one encountered further realms of potential uncertainty and disagreement among the jurists as to how far this uncertainty could be allowed to go. The jurists never ceased to regard language as a perfect vehicle of communication (tafhīm), but its perfection did not rule out a struggle to understand or the possibility that understanding might often be imperfect. Perfection was safeguarded by the insistence that authorial intent was *in principle* always discoverable, even if in fact it remained undiscovered in particular instances despite efforts to discover it. The principal obstacle to its discovery was the ambiguity of language, though there were other obstacles as well. Ambiguity was not in itself an imperfection. The fact that a word or phrase had more than one meaning in the lexical code (lugha) enhanced its value as a tool of communication. Communication always occurred, after all, through the cofunctioning of word and context. Any mujtahid who tried to determine authorial intent on the basis of a word or phrase taken in isolation from a larger context was necessarily doomed to failure, through no fault of language as such.

The context in the light of which ambiguous expressions were to be understood included, for the Muslim jurists, the entire body of foundational texts, not just the immediate context (that is, the larger passage within which the ambiguous expression was located). These were, after all, texts of law that proceeded from the all-embracing eternal mind of the divine Legislator; as such their authority was characterized by simultaneity. *Any* text (with the exception of abrogated texts) could impinge on any other text. The mujtahid thus worked in a vast and (because of the authenticity problem) indeterminate sea of intertextuality.[2]

Just how much ambiguity was to be found in the foundational texts was another question on which jurists disagreed, and we can see in the classical literature two different tendencies: a tendency to reduce ambiguity as much as possible and a tendency toward a realistic openness to wide-scale ambiguity.

These two tendencies are related to a bipolarity of postures that is discernible throughout the discussions in the classical literature of issues relating to the different stages in the work of formulating the law. On the one hand, we have what I would call a rigorist posture, one that attempts to maximize certainty through any means possible, that is willing to settle for probability only reluctantly, if at all, and only in regard to peripheral areas of the law. On the other hand, we have what I would call a liberal posture, one that sees itself as having a more realistic view of the vagaries of the texts and of the difficulties in determining authorial intent and is content with a law that is probable in large part or even in the greater part. The difference between the two postures is not a simple difference between acceptance and rejection of probability in the law. With few exceptions, both camps recognized a place for the probable. What they differed on was the degree to which the probable could be admitted into the law. Differently stated, the issue had to do with the limits of certainty. How far could the certainty of the law be convincingly pushed?

It now remains to consider each stage of the work of the mujtahid in greater detail. Problems relating to authenticity, we have noted, bear entirely upon the Sunna, since by common agreement very little, if any, of the Sunna enjoyed the widespread transmission that guaranteed the authenticity of the Qur'an. If there were any sunnaic passages that did, the jurists were seldom able to reach agreement on which passages these might be. For all practical purposes, therefore, the authenticity of the sunnaic texts had to rest upon something other than tawātur. This need gave rise to a method of text criticism known as *al-jarḥ wa'l-ta'dīl*, "impugning and verifying integrity." Strictly speaking, this method focused on transmitters rather than texts, since its main concern was with the assessment of the character of transmitters. But since its goal was to establish the reliability of the text, it can be said to fall under the heading of text criticism broadly conceived.[3]

We must remind ourselves once again that the foundational texts of Islamic law were all understood to be, in their essence, oral texts. Written texts occupied a strictly secondary position vis-à-vis oral texts; they were written records of the "real" text, which consisted of words heard upon the lips of reciters, memorized, and then recited to others. The written record could be a convenient aid to those of poor memory or to nonscholars who did not aspire to the memorizing of great amounts of text. As a means of transmission through time, it was far inferior to the recitation of texts by reliable transmitters. The reliability of a text thus became inseparable from the reliability of the transmitter. In fact, it was impossible to make a judgment about the reliability of a text on the basis of the text as such. The ultimate speaker/author behind all the texts was, after all, the sovereign Lord who was free to say whatever he chose to say. Even when texts seemed contradictory, one should not use the contradiction as a way of determining the authenticity of one text vis-à-vis the other. Contradiction had to be handled through interpretation, if not through resort to the notion of abrogation.

In order to receive serious consideration, every sunnaic text had to have an accompanying chain of transmitters, called in Arabic *sanad*, "support." The following hadith narrative displays a fairly typical sanad: "Muhammad ibn Khalid related to us ["us" being the final compiler], saying: Muhammad ibn Aʿyan related to us, saying: My father related to us from [or, on the authority of] ʿAmr ibn al-Harith, from ʿUbayd Allah ibn Abi Jaʿfar, that Muhammad ibn Jaʿfar related to him, from ʿUrwa, from ʿA'isha, that the Prophet of God—may God bless him and grant him peace—said: If any one should die with days of fasting still to make up, let his heir fast in his stead."[4] A chain of this sort met two important criteria: it traced a saying of the Prophet from the final compiler ("us") all the way back to the Prophet with no links missing from the transmissional chain, and it indicated that each transmitter got the information directly from the previous transmitter and that the first transmitter heard the saying directly from the Prophet himself. The transmissional formula "related to us/me" (*ḥaddathanā/nī* or *akhbaranā/nī*) was considered stronger evidence than "from" (ʿan) of direct transmission from transmitter to transmitter, but very few if any chains one finds in hadith collections have "related to us/me" from beginning to end. Most commonly, the more recent stages in the transmission process are represented by "related to us/me" and the earlier stages by "from." Other formulas of transmission not found in our example are also used.

But even if one had a chain that met both of the above-mentioned criteria, one could still doubt the authenticity of the text (the saying of the Prophet). As further criteria, one needed to consider the religion, maturity, strength of memory, and character of the transmitters. Since virtually all transmitters were Muslim adults, religion was not normally a pressing issue. In regard to memory, one needed only to be satisfied that a transmitter did not have a reputation for poor memory or that he was not senile or mentally ill at the time of transmission. By far, it was character that most occupied the attention of those engaged in text criticism.

The presumption underlying the assessment of the character of transmitters as a means of determining authenticity was that a truly trustworthy person does not lie. If one has for a particular sunnaic text a chain of transmitters made up entirely of transmitters of trustworthy character, then one has a transmissional chain that is secure against fabrication. This means that the text has come through the transmission process free of corruption and may be considered in its present form as fully authentic. The logic of this way of thinking seemed to those who espoused it to be airtight. Trustworthy Muslims of sound mind report what they have heard directly from other trustworthy Muslims of sound mind. They are in other words reporting a fact, something heard with their ears. If they were not sure of what they were reporting, they would not report it, or they would qualify their report as mere opinion. If they had misgivings about their memory, they would let these be known. Trustworthy people do not report facts with an air of certainty unless the certainty is genuine.[5]

In order to understand this logic, we must take into account the extraordinarily superlative assessment of character that was entailed in the concept of trustworthiness in the thinking of most of the jurists, particularly when this concept was applied to the early generations of Muslims, those believed to have been responsible for the transmission of sunnaic hadith until the time of the great written compilations. The process of screening hadith narratives that led to the great compilations had focused upon the trustworthiness of the transmitters as the principal criterion for accepting or rejecting narratives, and the hadith specialists who engaged in this screening went to enormous lengths to determine which transmitters possessed this quality and which did not.

The whole enterprise required that information about transmitters be gathered and preserved. This activity was in fact a major impetus to the development of a biographical literature among Muslims, one known for its richness and massiveness.[6] The biographical information served as a tool not only in the process of screening of hadith narratives but also in the intelligent use of the compilations that were the product of the screening. The reliability of a given sunnaic text was assured, after all, not by its mere inclusion in a compilation, but only by the chain of transmitters that accompanied it. Intelligent scholarship did not place unquestioning trust in the compilations as such but rather assured itself of the reliability of the material through direct familiarity with the biographical information relating to the transmitters. Biography remained an important tool of Muslim scholarship throughout its history. The viability of the compilations depended in principle upon the preservation and continuing active use of the biographical literature.

The airtightness of the logic surrounding the notion of trustworthiness did not in itself guarantee the authenticity of a sunnaic text. This logic represented only what *followed from* trustworthiness. The process of assessing the character of transmitters required that issues beyond this logic be addressed. How was trustworthiness—the principal premise upon which the logic depended—to be ascertained? A minimalist answer taken by some jurists was that a transmitter should be judged as trustworthy as long as he was to all outward appearances a Muslim and free of iniquity.[7] The principal criterion used in this approach was a transmitter's general reputation among peers in his own generation. The appearance of being trustworthy was thus a function of a transmitter's standing in society. If he was accepted as trustworthy among his peers and untarnished by public accusations of iniquity, he should be judged as trustworthy.

Quite obviously, trustworthiness as thus determined could hardly be more than probable. This approach amounted to giving the benefit of the doubt. As was widely acknowledged, a person could fool his peers and hypocritically give the appearance of being trustworthy while in fact inwardly harboring deceitful thoughts and motivations. However unlikely this scenario might be with respect to persons of high standing in Muslim society, it still had to be counted as a possibility and therefore as ground for a margin of doubt. And if the trustworthiness of a transmitter was in any degree uncertain, the logic of trustworthiness would necessarily lead to uncertain authenticity of the text. This approach to determining trustworthiness could obviously be used only by jurists who leaned toward probabilism in the formulation of the law.

The maximalist approach insisted that the trustworthiness of a transmitter must be determined on the basis of an intimate knowledge of his character and innermost attitudes and dispositions. This approach required a more careful use of the biographical material. One needed to base one's assessment of a transmitter's character on the testimony of those who were in direct and close contact with him and whose familiarity with him went beyond the level of outward demeanor or public profile. Only in this way could one have a premise that could lead to a conclusion about authenticity that was certain and free of doubt. This was obviously the approach taken by those who wished to extend the certainty of the law as far as possible.

The quest for certainty about the authenticity of sunnaic texts was clearly rooted in the activities of the hadith specialists (ahl al-ḥadīth) in the first two centuries of the Islamic era. Those who traveled throughout the lands of Islam in search of information about the Prophet called their effort "the search for knowledge" (*ṭalab al-ʿilm*).[8] To a large extent this search was expressly undertaken as an alternative to the legal scholarship of the early juristic schools, which was viewed as too speculative and as productive of mere opinion. The hadith seekers consciously sought to distance themselves from all speculation. They yearned for a law spelled out for them in unassailable texts. The knowledge they sought was knowledge of the Sunna. Opinion as to what constituted the Sunna would not do.

The maximalist approach to the determination of the trustworthiness of transmitters, however, proved to be fraught with problems. If one must rely solely on the testimony of those who knew a transmitter intimately in order to get a reliable assessment of the transmitter's true character, what criteria does one use to determine what constitutes intimate knowledge? How long must the source have known the transmitter, and how close must his relationship to the transmitter have been? And since biographical information about transmitters was itself orally transmitted, must not the same standards of transmission be met? Must one not also take into consideration the trustworthiness of the transmitters of biographical information? And if indeed we must, do we not have to repeat the whole process of character assessment? And does this not embroil us in an infinite regression?

And is the biographical material not also a corpus of texts that require interpretation? Must we demand from biographical sources explicit affirmations of a transmitter's trustworthiness, or will implications and innuendos do?

Questions of this sort prompted many scholars of the law, and ultimately the majority of them, to acknowledge that the process of assessing the character of transmitters could seldom produce absolute certainty regarding the authenticity of sunnaic texts. But this realism did not necessarily mean the abandonment of the notion of trustworthiness altogether as a useful tool, for it could still serve as a way of establishing probable authenticity. Here again probabilism becomes the decisive posture. Whether one judged character on the basis of outward demeanor or insisted upon information relating to the inner traits of a transmitter, the result was the same—a probable text, not a certain one.

Once a mujtahid had judged a text to be authentic or likely to be authentic, he was then obliged, before proceeding to endeavor to interpret the text, to determine whether or not the text was actually in force as a source of law. Since a text was always subject to the possibility of abrogation, however slight, it could never be assumed from the outset to be in force. Before the business of interpretation could begin, therefore, the possibility of abrogation had to be ruled out. The judgment that a text was abrogated required a number of determinations. First, two texts had to be shown to be in genuine contradiction. If one text in fact merely placed a qualification upon the other text, the mujtahid could not posit an abrogation. Second, the text judged to be the abrogated one had to be shown to have preceded the other text chronologically. Third, the mujtahid had to be sure that the categories of texts were such as to allow a judgment of abrogation to be made. To satisfy this requirement, the mujtahid had to consider and take a position on the question of whether a qur'anic text could abrogate a sunnaic text or vice versa. Complications abounded throughout these deliberations, and the result might very well be tinged with uncertainty. Again, many jurists considered probability to be the most one could hope for, while others aspired, despite the difficulties, to certainty.

In the realm of interpretation the work of the mujtahid reached new heights of toilsomeness. In keeping with the intentionalist spirit, the mujtahid could settle for nothing less than authorial intent as the object of his striving, since anything else would represent an unwanted intrusion of an alien element into the law of God. The divine intent was always in principle discoverable, although in practice it could often be difficult to discover. The greatest obstacle to its discovery was, as noted before, the ambiguity that one occasionally encountered in the texts. It was, however, an obstacle that the mujtahid should always seek to overcome, and the jurists were sure that there were ways to overcome it. The same was true of other obstacles.

Ambiguity was a simple lexical fact; a given word had two or more literal meanings. An example in Arabic is the word *ʿayn,* which means in the lugha (the lexical code) both "eye" and "spring." In English the word "bank" is a good example. It signifies in the code used by English speakers both a certain kind of financial institution and the side of a river. If one says, "I am going to the bank today," the listener will not be able to determine from these words alone what the speaker intends. Is he going to the financial institution, or is he going to the riverside? Generally, the speaker in such a case will (consciously or unconsciously) depend on contextual factors to communicate his intended meaning, and the listener will look for contextual clues to determine the intent. Speakers succeed in communicating, and listeners succeed in understanding through the cofunctioning of ambiguous expression and context.

Without a contextual clue the mujtahid is stymied in the presence of an ambiguous expression and may not attempt to formulate the law. Literal meanings considered apart from the context all have an equal chance of being the intended meaning. The mujtahid has no reason to regard one meaning as more likely to represent authorial intent than the other. If he did, he could attempt at least a tentative formulation of the law; he would have something to start with, something to test through further exploration of the texts. But with ambiguity no such starting point exists, and he remains without a starting point as long as he is unable to discover something in the context that will break the deadlock of multiple meanings. The law has not even begun to unfold for him.

In contrast to the ambiguous expression (*mujmal*) stands a type of expression to which the Muslim jurists applied the term *ẓāhir*, which I shall call the univocal expression. This is the expression that has in the lexical code only one literal meaning. When a speaker uses such an expression, one meaning alone arises immediately in the mind of the listener, not two, and the listener is able to make a judgment as to the speaker's intent. If a speaker says, for example, "Yesterday I saw a lion," the hearer will immediately understand the intended meaning of "lion" to be the particular kind of predatory feline that speakers usually have in mind when using the word. *Ẓāhir* means "apparent" and is sometimes used of meanings, in which case it has the sense of "apparent intent." When applied by extension to expressions, it refers to expressions whose intended meaning in speech situations is apparent. An ambiguous expression, on the other hand, is an expression whose intended meaning in a speech situation is obscure.[9]

Univocal expressions play a key role in the interpretation process. The contextual clues that a mujtahid seeks in attempting to determine the intent behind an ambiguous expression must ultimately consist of or contain univocal expressions, since ambiguity cannot be overcome with ambiguity. As an interpreter of a closed canon of foundational texts who does not have the advantage of direct contact with the author/speaker, the mujtahid depends totally upon the presence somewhere in the texts of illuminative univocal language.

A univocal expression allows the mujtahid to make an immediate judgment as to the author's intent and thus to launch the process of formulating the law. But this immediate judgment nonetheless has a degree of tentativeness about it and must be tested through further exploration of the texts. The reason is that speakers/authors sometimes "divert" (*ṣarafa, awwala*) expressions from their literal meanings to other, nonliteral meanings, in which case the expressions are said to be functioning as figures of speech (majāz). If a speaker says, "Yesterday I saw a lion," the listener immediately understands him to mean the feline predator but on subsequent reflection will recognize that there is a possibility that he could intend "lion" figuratively to denote a particularly ferocious or fearless man.

Many univocal expressions thus have multiple possible meanings, but in contrast to the meanings of an ambiguous expression, these meanings do not all have an equal chance of being the intended meaning. One meaning in particular, the literal meaning, is the likely intended meaning, while the nonliteral meanings are unlikely intended meanings. When confronted with an ambiguous expression, the mujtahid is stymied (*muʿaṭṭal*)[10] and cannot proceed with the formulation of the law. When confronted with a univocal expression, the mujtahid is not stymied but rather may embark on a tentative formulation of the law. He then subsequently looks to the context for clues of figurative usage. If he finds such clues, he abandons his formulation in favor of a new one that takes the figurative usage into account. If he finds no such clues—and he is likely not to—he may adhere to his original formulation.

It is worth noting that the context functions in contrasting ways in these two cases. In the case of the ambiguous expression the mujtahid must search through the texts until he finds a clue that resolves the ambiguity. If he does not find a clue, he remains stymied and may not proceed to formulate the law. In the case of the univocal expression, he must search the texts for a clue indicating figurative usage, but he need not actually find one and is in fact likely not to. In the event that he does not find a clue, he proceeds to formulate the law on the basis of the sole literal meaning. The univocal expression clearly has an inherent communicative power that the ambiguous expression lacks; it communicates a degree of probability.

It should be noted that the Arabic term here translated as "figure," the term *majāz,* has a much broader application in the literature of Muslim jurisprudence than does the English term. Not only may words such as "lion" be classified as majāz, so also may conjunctions, prepositions, and word forms. When one uses the conjunction *wa-* (usually equivalent to "and"), for example, to signify sequence rather than mere connection, one is said to be using it as a majāz. Other examples that English speakers would not normally consider to be figurative usage will emerge later in this chapter. The reader should therefore understand that in these pages the term "figure"—which will be retained as a translation of majāz in the want of a more suitable translation—will sometimes be used in a manner that is atypical for English speakers.

So that we may gain a fuller picture of how the interpretive process, as conceived by the Muslim jurists, worked it will be useful at this point to consider how it worked in relation to a particular passage. Qur'an 5:38 is especially illustrative for our purposes.[11] It reads: "As for the male thief (*al-sāriq*) and the female thief (*al-sāriqa*), cut off the hands of the two of them." This statement is generally understood by the jurists to impose an obligation on the head of the Muslim government or his appointed representative to inflict the penalty of amputation of a hand upon a thief. Interpretive issues surround virtually every part of the statement.

We may begin with the terms "cut off" and "hand." These are the standard translations of the Arabic terms *iqṭaʿū* and *yad*. They represent, however, only possible meanings, which the Muslim jurists considered along with other possible meanings. For *yad* three possible meanings had to be taken into account: this term, it was thought, could signify the part of an upper limb that extends upward (from fingertips) to the wrist, or the part that extends to the elbow, or the entire limb up to the shoulder. As unlikely as it may seem to Arabists accustomed to translating *yad* as "hand," the word could, in other words, mean "hand," "forearm," or "arm." ("Forearm" and "arm" must here be understood to include the hand.) We must suppose that the jurists who posited these multiple meanings offered some sort of lexicographical or other kind of evidence. Whatever the evidence, the question that the mujtahid had to face was whether to regard all three meanings as literal and accordingly treat *yad* as ambiguous or to regard only one of the meanings as literal and accordingly treat *yad* as univocal with respect to that meaning and as figurative with respect to the others.

In attempting to decide which course to follow, the mujtahid was to be guided by his sense of the language, which would usually be based on familiarity with the "high" literary tradition. Upon hearing the word *yad*, did one familiar with the tradition and thus conversant with the code (lugha) find that all three meanings rushed immediately to his mind as equal possibilities, or did one only rush to his mind, leaving the other meanings in the realm of secondary meanings likely to arise in the mind only after subsequent reflection? Answers would inevitably vary from mujtahid to mujtahid, all with momentous implications for the interpretative process. If he chose to treat *yad* as ambiguous, then he created a situation in which the work of formulating the law would remain at a complete standstill (*taʿṭīl, tawaqquf*) until a contextual clue as to the Legislator's intent was located. If he chose to treat it as univocal, he created a situation in which the work of formulating the law could be said to have already begun. He had a probability to work with.

It is curious that those jurists who regarded *yad* as univocal did not necessarily regard "hand" as the literal meaning. One opinion regarded "arm" as the literal meaning on the basis of a linguistic claim that speakers may with propriety say with respect to any part of the arm, "That is part of the yad, not the whole yad." The literal meaning, in other words, had to be that anatomic unit of which it could never be said, "This is part of the yad." On this logic, anyone claiming that the Legislator had in mind the hand only had to have contextual evidence apart from which it would be proper to assume that he had in mind the arm and to formulate the law accordingly.

The term *iqṭaʿū* conjured up similar problems for the mujtahid. Not only could it mean "cut off," "amputate" (the common English translation); it could also mean "cut into," "lacerate." Were these both to be regarded as literal meanings such that *iqṭaʿū* should be treated as ambiguous, or was one meaning alone the literal one such that the word should be treated as univocal with respect to that meaning and figurative with respect to the other two? Both possibilities had their adherents among the jurists, with amputation as the favored literal meaning among the adherents of univocality. The consequences of the position that one chose for the interpretation were the same as those mentioned in connection with *yad*.

But unlike *yad, iqṭaʿū* required two stages of deliberation. Once the mujtahid had achieved some sort of closure on the question of whether the Legislator intended amputation or merely laceration of the hand of the thief, he had yet more work to do relating to this word, for the word had a formal component that carried meaning beyond the meaning conveyed by the word considered solely as an individual word distinct from all other words. To be more precise: *iqṭaʿū* was a verb in the imperative mood, a mood conveyed by its form. At the level of form, the mujtahid had to face a question that pertained not only to *iqṭaʿū* but to any verb in the imperative mood: what does the form convey?[12]

Since verbs in the imperative mood are omnipresent in the foundational texts, they constitute a subject of special interest in the literature of Muslim jurisprudence, and lengthy chapters in the major works of that literature are in fact devoted to them. The form exhibited by these verbs was called in the literature *ṣīghat al-amr,* and I shall accordingly refer to it by way of direct translation as the imperative form. In Arabic grammatical works, this form is frequently denoted by its morphological designation, *ifʿal.*

Muslim jurists and philologists universally agreed that the imperative form had multiple meanings. It could signify an imposition of a duty, an exhortation, a permission (as in "Take my cloak if you wish"), an invitation (e.g., "Come to my house for dinner"), a supplication (e.g., "Have mercy on me"), an admonition (e.g., "Stay in this place and see what will happen to you"), a disparagement (e.g., "Go ahead and make a fool of yourself if you wish"), or an expression of indifference ("Stay or go as you please"), to mention only some of the possibilities. On all the above meanings except the first two there was further widespread agreement. These meanings, it was believed, were nonliteral, and the imperative form was to be counted a figure when used to convey any of them. Here, it should be noted, we encounter an instance where our use of the term "figure"—though justifiable, I think, as a translation of *majāz*—is from the point of view of English usage atypical.

With respect to the first two meanings—imposition of obligation and exhortation—the jurists differed, and here we come to one of the most important debates in Muslim jurisprudence. These two meanings correspond, as will be readily noted, to two of the categories of the Shariʿa discussed in Chapter 1: obligatory and recommended. The Arabic term I am translating as "exhortation" is, in fact, *nadb,* a cognate of *mandūb* ("recommended"); it may just as appropriately be translated as "recommendation." Thus the debate we are presently considering was in reality a debate over how far the imperative could take the mujtahid in his quest for specific categories of the Shariʿa.

Some jurists regarded both imposition of obligation and exhortation as literal meanings and accordingly treated the imperative form as ambiguous. Most jurists, however, preferred to treat this form as univocal but differed on the question of what constituted the sole literal meaning. Each of the two meanings had its partisans, while some jurists, seeking to find common ground between the two meanings, posited a more general meaning—that of calling for or summoning to an act—as the sole literal meaning.

One can readily understand why the majority of jurists resisted the attribution of ambiguity to the imperative form. A form as ubiquitous as this in the texts was bound to be seen by jurists as a major vehicle of revelation of the Shariʿa. Furthermore, imperatives by their very nature demand the attention of those engaged in the formulation of the law. However variously they may be interpreted, they simply cannot be ignored. Muslim religious literature in fact frequently calls prophets "bearers of divine imperatives" (*mubligh al-awāmir*), which suggests that the imperatives constitute the very core of the revelation that prophets bring to their fellow humans. Thus if anything in the language of the texts would be spared the status of an obstacle to the understanding of the law, it should be the imperative form.

The position a mujtahid took in this debate would determine how he would handle *iqṭaʿū* in Qurʾan 5:38. If he espoused the view that the imperative is a univocal signifier of imposition of obligation, then he would be able immediately to make a tentative judgment to the effect that the cutting off of the hand of the thief was an obligation. (I shall assume that our mujtahid has interpreted *qaṭʿ* and *yad* as meaning "cut off" and "hand.") Once he had scanned the texts and found to his satisfaction that they contained no indication of figurative usage in this case, he would then transform his tentative judgment into a final opinion. If, on the other hand, our mujtahid regarded the imperative as a univocal signifier of exhortation, he would again have a tentative judgment to start with, but in this case it would be a judgment to the effect that the cutting off of the hand of the thief was recommended. That judgment would then become his final opinion once he had ruled out figurative usage.

If the mujtahid was convinced that the imperative was ambiguous, he would then be unable to begin his deliberations with any kind of tentative judgment as to whether the cutting off of the hand of the thief was obligatory or recommended. Both would be equally likely representations of the divine intent. The imperative *iqṭaʿū* would in this case only have the value of having evoked awareness of possibilities that had to be explored. Without an initial tentative judgment to work with, he would now be more dependent on the context inasmuch as he would need the context to bring him to the point of being able to make an initial judgment. One thing he might look for in the context would be an indication that failure to cut off the hand of a thief either is or is not subject to a penal sanction. If such a sanction is indicated, then the cutting off of the hand of the thief may be judged as obligatory; if not, then as recommended.

If our mujtahid decided that imperatives were univocal signifiers after all but that what they signified as their sole literal meaning was the more general idea of a calling for an act—an idea present in both the idea of imposition of obligation and the idea of exhortation—he would not have improved his situation very much from the standpoint of interpretive procedure. In fact, his situation would be much like that created by the decision to treat imperatives as ambiguous, for he would still be unable to form an initial judgment on the crucial question of whether the cutting off of the hand of the thief was obligatory or recommended. The knowledge that this action was called for would not be a sufficient basis on which to formulate the law.

An important aspect of this debate over interpretive procedure should not be allowed to go unnoticed. In Chapter 1 we noted that while the category "obligatory" lends itself to being subsumed under the heading of law, the category "recommended" does not. To declare an act to be obligatory is to establish a rule that is capable of being judicially applied and enforced, that is to say, capable of becoming a rule of law. It is in the nature of rules of law to categorize acts as obligatory. It is not, however, in the nature of rules of law to categorize acts as recommended, for the recommended cannot be judicially applied and enforced. To recommend is to exhort, not to demand with the threat of a sanction.

The foundational texts, let us remember, are abundantly populated with imperatives, and these, therefore, constitute a major preoccupation of Muslim jurisprudence. Those jurists who treat the imperative as a univocal signifier of imposition of obligation are in effect erecting a principle of interpretation that favors law over mere exhortation, a principle that is bound to produce an understanding of the Shariʿa heavily weighted on the side of those categorizations of human acts that admit of being enforced by the state and its tribunals as opposed to those categorizations that do not. Those who treat the imperative as a univocal signifier of recommendation are, in contrast, favoring an approach that is bound to produce a more exhortation-oriented understanding of the Shariʿa, one that reduces the strictly legal part of the Shariʿa to less demanding proportions. Those who treat the imperative as ambiguous or as a univocal signifier of the general idea of a calling for an act are in effect making the heaviness or lightness of the legal part of the Shariʿa more dependent on the deliberations of mujtahids. The imperative, in their view, plays a more neutral role.

A last issue pertaining to *iqṭaʿū* in Qur'an 5:38 relates to the audience addressed. To whom is this imperative addressed—to humans in general, to Muslims at large, to the head of the Muslim government and his delegates? And if addressed to any one of these categories, is it addressed only to persons living at the time the verse was revealed or to all generations? Or is it perhaps addressed to certain individuals living at the time of revelation? Here again we clearly have questions that can be answered only through exploration of the larger context.

Turning to the phrase "the male thief and the female thief," we may first note that in this instance the Qur'an, in employing both the masculine and feminine forms of the Arabic word for "thief" (*sāriq* and *sāriqa*), circumvents an issue that emerges with respect to many other passages, which is whether or not masculine forms are intended to be inclusive or male-specific. Given the predominance of male forms in the foundational texts, it would not have been surprising to encounter in this passage the masculine form alone, in which case the mujtahid would have had to deliberate over the question of whether female thieves were included. But as the passage stands, the mujtahid is spared such toil.

To facilitate the present discussion I will focus in what follows on the expression "the thief" (*al-sāriq*). As with "cut off" (*iqṭaʿū*), this expression, according to the interpretation theory of the jurists, also comprised two distinct meaning-laden components: "thief" considered as an individual word and the combination of definite article and singular noun considered as a form common to many words ("the thief," "the soldier," "the scholar," etc.). As an individual word, "thief" was not, to my knowledge, considered by any jurist to be ambiguous. It was therefore treated in the manner of a univocal expression. With the formal component of "the thief," however, we again find ourselves in the arena of juristic debate; and, again, the question is whether to treat the expression as univocal or ambiguous.

To begin with, "the thief" considered as a form could signify either a particular thief or thieves collectively. Since no jurist proposed the former as the divine intent in the case of Qurʾan 5 : 38, juristic debate pertained entirely to the latter. Here the question was whether "the thief" embraced all thieves or certain thieves in particular (but not a single individual thief). Modern linguistic analysis that distinguishes meaning from reference would see this as a question of reference, not meaning. The theory the Muslim jurists relied on, however, made no such distinction. In their analysis, the form in question had two possible meanings: generality (or inclusivity) and specificity. Given that this was so, it made sense to them to raise the question whether both meanings were literal or just one, whether "the thief" was in respect to these meanings ambiguous or univocal.

In this debate we find the same spectrum of positions as in the debate over the imperative. Some jurists considered "the thief" to be a univocal signifier of generality ("all thieves"), while others considered it to be a univocal signifier of specificity ("certain thieves"). Accordingly, in their view, the mujtahid could begin with a tentative judgment regarding the divine intent and then proceed in the manner required of univocal expressions, as described above. For some the tentative judgment would be to the effect that the intended meaning was "all thieves," for others it would be to the effect that the intended meaning was "certain thieves." A third group regarded "the thief" as ambiguous, as having both generality and specificity as literal meanings. Accordingly, these jurists allowed a judgment to be formed only after a mujtahid had found contextual evidence indicating generality or specificity as the divine intent.[13]

The concept of specificity warrants a word of explanation. To say that "the thief" signifies "certain thieves" and that this is the meaning intended by the Legislator is not to say that it does so in a manner that identifies precisely which thieves are meant. In order to have this information, the mujtahid had to turn to the context. A commonly used passage for this purpose was the Prophet's saying, "There is to be no amputation except where an amount worth a quarter of a dinar or more has been stolen." From this saying the mujtahid could know who the "certain thieves" signified by "the thief" were. They were the thieves who had stolen an object worth a quarter of a dinar or more. But this further information was not part of the meaning of "the thief" as such. All one knew from "the thief," once specificity had been established as its intended meaning, was that it embraced a specific (but unidentified) group of thieves, not all thieves. Muslim interpretation of Qur'an 5:38 would use additional contextual information to narrow down the identity of the thieves who were subject to the penalty of amputation even further.

It should be noted that the position a jurist took with respect to "the thief" informed his interpretation of this form (definite article plus singular noun) wherever it occurred in the texts as well as his interpretation of similar forms (for example, definite article plus plural noun as in "the thieves," or plural noun without definite article as in "thieves"). In other words, his adopting of a particular position on "the thief" entailed the adopting of a principle of interpretation that applied broadly to all types of expressions in the text that might be seen as either general or specific. Those jurists who took these expressions to be univocal signifiers of generality fostered what in modern jurisprudence would be called broad or liberal construction, while those who took them to be univocal signifiers of specificity fostered what would be called strict construction. Those who treated these expressions as ambiguous gave greater flexibility to the mujtahid, allowing him to adopt a broad or strict style of construction in accordance with his reading of the texts on a case-by-case basis.

This survey of the various interpretive issues pertaining to Qur'an

5:38 has underscored an important point. Certainty regarding the Legislator's intent could never be attained through the consideration of particular passages taken in isolation from the larger context. Rather, such certainty lay at the end of a long journey through a vast landscape of texts. Whether the language he had to deal with in a particular passage was univocal or ambiguous, the mujtahid could never make a final judgment about the Legislator's intent without the help of contextual clues. There is reason to believe that during the early period in the development of Muslim thinking about legal interpretation, some may have seen in univocal language a refuge from uncertainty and may for that reason have held out persistently for univocality in the univocality versus ambiguity debates. After all, when asked, for example, how one knew that the ritual prayer constituted a duty for Muslims, could one not reply, "God says plainly in the Qur'an: perform the ritual prayer (Qur'an 17:78, etc.). What more do we need?" Imperatives such as "perform the ritual prayer" could seem to the unreflective to be a crystal clear expression of the divine law.

For the more reflective, however, the matter could not be so simple. As juristic debate intensified and deepened with the passing of time, it became obvious to all that the univocal expression did not give rise to instant certainty about the Legislator's intent, for one had always to take into account the possibility of figurative usage. When we recall the wide array of usages that the concept of figure of speech (majāz) was made to cover, we can appreciate why the possibility of figurative usage took on such importance for Muslim juristic thought. Until a mujtahid had scanned the textual landscape and had either found or not found an indication of figurative usage, he could not possibly make a viable claim to certainty.

In fact, the univocal expression offered no advantage over the ambiguous expression as far as certainty was concerned. The only advantage it offered lay in the realm of probability. A univocal expression afforded instant probability; an ambiguous expression did not. With the ambiguous expression, the sense of probability was more difficult to achieve, for it could arise only out of recourse to the context, the textual landscape.

With both the univocal expression and the ambiguous expression, certainty about the Legislator's intent could be had only by way of a route leading through realms of probability. Whether the sense of probability came before or after the plunge into the context, the mujtahid had to go through a process of probability building before reaching the point where probability transformed itself into certainty.

How likely was the mujtahid to reach that point? It is hard to get an accurate reading of Muslim juristic opinion on this question. There is no doubt that most jurists regarded the attainment of certainty as always possible, but certain considerations, I think, suggest that they saw it as unlikely in most instances. For one thing, the textual landscape that the mujtahid had to explore in search of contextual clues was vast, and no matter how great one's mastery of it, modesty required that one always admit that an important clue might have escaped one's attention. But the textual landscape was not only vast but indeterminate. Islam, we must remember, never produced anything on the order of church councils capable of authoritatively defining and setting the boundaries of a sacred canon. The boundaries of the Qur'an were believed to be self-evident. Whatever constituted the very words of God transmitted reliably from the Prophet by way of tawātur was part of the Qur'an; all else was not. The boundaries of the Sunna, by virtue of which the Sunna along with the Qur'an constituted a closed canon, were harder to discern, and one mujtahid's perception could differ from another's. It is true that the major collections were widely used and treated as authoritative, but in principal a mujtahid was not limited by what he found within any particular collections. A sunnaic text was not authoritative because it was found within any given collection but only by virtue of its authenticity as determined by an evaluation of its chain of transmitters.

Finally, most jurists eventually acknowledged that the authenticity of the sunnaic texts, which made up the greater part of the corpus of foundational texts, was for the most part merely probable. A probable text is a text that is in some degree uncertain. If either the principal passage a mujtahid was working with or other passages from which he was extracting contextual clues were of uncertain authenticity, the final product of his interpretive efforts had always to be itself uncertain, no matter how decisively the contextual clues may have seemed to illuminate the principal passage. Thus only if there was certainty both in regard to text and in regard to meaning as contextually determined could there be certainty in the final formulation of the law.

Uncertainty also reigned in other realms of interpretive endeavor that we have not considered in this chapter. In these pages we have focused on the mujtahid's efforts to determine the Legislator's intent within the realm of what the jurists called "explicit" (*ṣarīḥ*) meaning. But beyond this realm lay the realm of implication and nuance wherein also the Legislator's intent might possibly be found. In pondering the Prophet's statement "Alms-tax is due upon free-grazing animals," for example, a mujtahid had to struggle with a question: was it the Legislator's intent that the alms-tax *not* be due on other animals, that is to say, on stall-fed animals? How much could the mujtahid reasonably read between the lines? How far could he venture beyond the realm of explicit meaning? Once implication was admitted as an acceptable basis for the law, where was one to draw limits? The realm of implication was potentially vast. Here again there were few sure guidelines, and the mujtahid could hope to achieve little certainty.

If certainty was rare in the realm of implication, it was likely also to be rare in the realm of analogy. The crucial step in analogy building was, let us remember, the determination of the cause of an existing rule. As was noted in the previous chapter, this entailed for some jurists exploration of known causes of other rules and the setting up of a typology of causes, while for others it entailed referral to the purposes of the law. Both approaches required investigation of the entire corpus of foundation texts and grappling with the kinds of issues of interpretation and authenticity that we have already considered. Most jurists who accepted the use of analogy in the formulation of the law readily admitted that the results would almost always be less than certain.

But uncertainty in the law was seen by the jurists as no loss to the jurisprudential enterprise, as no setback for the cause of regulating human life in accordance with the will of God. Thanks to a carefully argued probabilism, the law did not need to be certain in order to be authoritative. Probable law could have an authority equal to that of certain law.

This probabilism was enshrined in the dictum, "Opinion is binding in matters of law" (*al-ẓann wājib al-ittibāʿ fi'l-sharʿ*). Opinion was understood to be the sense of the probable that a mujtahid attained as a result of his study of the texts. In describing the working of opinion, the jurists frequently made use of the metaphor of the scale or balance. As the mujtahid worked his way through the texts, he placed evidence for a particular rule of law on the scale, causing the scale to tip in its favor. The Arabic term that I have been translating as probable is in fact *rājiḥ*, which can be more literally translated as "preponderant." The related term *tarjīḥ* means "determining preponderance," or, more loosely, "weighing."

Once the scale has been tipped, the mujtahid has begun the process of probability building. As he continues his journey through the texts, he adds more and more evidence to the scale, thus tipping it further. Occasionally, he may encounter textual evidence that works against the rule he is testing. If the counterevidence accumulates and proves to be preponderant, he will desist from holding an opinion in favor of the rule. What matters in the end, when all his interpretive endeavors have been completed, is how the scale tips. If it tips—even ever so slightly—in favor of the rule, he will be justified in embracing the rule as the probable law of God and in declaring this opinion to others.

A mujtahid must always, however, at the beginning of his endeavors aspire to attain certainty. Probable law can enjoy the same authority as certain law only when certain law has been proven to be unattainable. Probable law, in other words, is law that acquires authority in default of certain law. Proof of the unattainability of certain law occurs by way of the actual experience of the mujtahid. Once he reaches the point where he can say with a clear conscience that he has investigated the texts to the best of his ability, then, if he has not attained certainty, he may rightfully regard it as, for him, unattainable. It is at this point that the dictum "Opinion is binding in matters of law" becomes operative. But this leads us to a topic that falls within the scope of the following chapter.

# 6 Juristic Authority and the Diversity of Schools

Joseph Schacht spoke of Islamic law as representing "an extreme case of a 'jurists' law.'"[1] The term "jurists' law" he borrowed from the field of Roman law studies, where it had come to be used to designate a body of law developed by private specialists who labored outside the hierarchy of government-appointed officials. The authority of these specialists—the *auctoritas prudentium*—derived from the respect accorded them by the rest of society, including both those within and those outside the circles of officialdom. The statement that Islamic law represents an extreme case of a jurists' law apparently meant for Schacht that the authority of the private specialists was far more pervasive in the Islamic system than in the Roman or any other system that comprised a jurists' law. Great as it was, juristic authority never monopolized Roman law. Law among the Romans emanated not only from auctoritas prudentium but also, according to A. A. Schiller, from "statutes, plebiscites, resolutions of the Senate, enactments of the emperors."[2] The Muslim auctoritas prudentium was virtually supreme and always vigilant in maintaining its independence from officialdom.

Schacht also referred to Islamic law as a type of sacred law.[3] It was thus for him both a jurists' law and a sacred law, a law that emanated from jurists and at the same time a law that originated with God. In order to understand how Islamic law could be both of these, it is important that we understand that the authority of jurists in Islam is an exclusively declarative authority, an authority to declare God's law on the basis of an intentionalist interpretation of foundational texts. The Roman jurist depended, in his exposition of the law, on intuition as much as on substantive legal doctrine, and this intuition, according to Schiller, derived from the social and psychological forces of the age.

In Roman eyes, a jurist was a person possessed of legal wisdom; it was his sound judgment and insight more than any specific philological or hermeneutical skills that elicited the respect of his contemporaries and provided the basis for his authority.

The Muslim jurist, on the other hand, was much more bound to formal sources, to sacred texts. His authority depended more upon his skills as an interpreter of texts than upon any inherent wisdom. His role was to give expression to the wisdom and will of God as revealed in the Qur'an and Sunna. He was thus a spokesman for God and sought to be as faithful to the divine intent as possible. It is true that the earliest Muslim jurists, as was noted in Chapter 1, relied heavily on their own sense of equity and propriety, their *ra'y*, but even then they appear to have been mindful of being in some sense subservient to the divine will. In any case, Islamic jurisprudence eventually set aside the relatively unrestricted, discretionary *ra'y* in favor of a more constrained, text-oriented approach to the exposition of law, and this approach—this textualism, as I have called it—became characteristic of the classical jurisprudence that has been the subject matter of this book.

We may, I think, distinguish between two types of authority in Islamic legal thought: legislative authority, which belongs to God alone and which becomes concretized as the authority of the foundational texts, and interpretive or declarative authority, which belongs to the jurists. Legislative authority is directly operative only in the sphere of what the jurist-interpreters do, which is to formulate the law, that is to say, to articulate rules of law that are not precisely articulated in the texts. Within the sphere of actual human conduct, it is the declarative authority of the jurists that is directly operative. It is the jurists' law that has the actual force of positive law within Muslim society in the sense that it is what Muslim governments in principle seek to apply and enforce and what ordinary people seek to live by.

To describe the authority of the jurists as declarative is to say in effect that it is a derivative authority, that it derives entirely from the legislative authority of God. The jurist bears no authority in his person or status in the sense that his declarations are automatically accepted as valid. Rather the authority of the jurist rests upon the intrinsic validity of what he declares. It is, in other words, an authority that depends upon the methodology that the jurist employs and the skills that he possesses. What the jurist declares is authoritative not because it is he who declares it but because what he declares may be presumed to have been validly derived from the foundational texts and is therefore an acceptable expression of the law of God.

This accounting of juristic authority focuses on its formal or theoretical basis. But it also has a social or sociopsychological basis, as was intimated in the opening paragraph of this chapter. The Muslim jurists enjoyed authority by virtue of the respect accorded to them by the rest of society. This respect was not, however, a function of mere social standing. Although a great many jurists came from commercial families who did enjoy considerable social prestige, on the whole they cannot be characterized as belonging to any particular social class, although few, if any, came from the lowest strata of society, the urban poor and the peasantry. Many came from families engaged in fairly humble trades, such as carpentry. The respect accorded to the jurists was rather born of genuine confidence in the expertise that the jurists possessed, an expertise resulting from years of professional training.[4] The jurists were the ones to whom one could turn when in need of legal advice or assistance. In the eyes of the lay masses, the jurists were indeed what they claimed to be, persons qualified to declare what the law of God was. Thus the social ground of juristic authority meshes with the formal ground.

Not all jurists, it should be noted, undertook the work of deriving law directly from the foundational texts. Those who did were the mujtahids. As the law that the mujtahids produced grew, it became a doctrinal legacy, a tradition, that other jurists then studied, organized, preserved, and communicated to the rest of society. With the passing of time, fewer jurists claimed to be mujtahids, and none claimed the far-reaching authority to formulate the law enjoyed by the great founding mujtahids. The tradition itself came to be seen as a resource for dealing with legal problems, and the areas in which law could still be formulated on the basis of the foundational texts were considerably narrowed down.

The Arabic term generally used to designate the jurists as an entire class, inclusive of both mujtahids and nonmujtahids, is *fuqahā* (sing. *faqīh*). The legal tradition is designated by means of a cognate word, *fiqh,* which means "understanding." The law built up by the mujtahids was always seen as representing their understanding of the law. This way of looking at the law emphasizes the human element in the law. Although the law is of divine provenance, the actual construction of the law is a human activity, and its results represent the law of God *as humanly understood.* Since the law does not descend from heaven ready-made, it is the human understanding of the law—the human fiqh—that must be normative for society. The title of faqīh applies both to the jurists through whom this understanding is first achieved, the mujtahids, and to the jurists who are its bearers and preservers thereafter.

The results of the labors of the great mujtahids—their fiqh—came eventually to be enshrined in texts that themselves became foundational for future generations of jurists. I shall, however, in this book reserve the term "foundational texts" for the Qur'an and Sunna and speak of the texts now under consideration simply as fiqh texts. These included not only organized treatises but also collections of opinions (*fatāwā*) addressing particular legal topics or problems. This body of texts was cumulative over time, as each generation sought to solve problems on the basis of texts of previous generations and in so doing added new texts to the ever-growing store of texts. The interpretive endeavors and methods of the jurists now came to be focused as much on great fiqh texts as upon the foundational texts, if not more so.

The legal doctrine found in the fiqh texts was far from monolithic but rather displayed considerable variation. Not only did each of the schools have its own body of doctrine; within each school jurists held diverse positions. The jurists themselves had a ready explanation for this diversity. Since all understanding of the law was humanly arrived at and therefore fallible, it was inevitable that this understanding would vary from mujtahid to mujtahid and that mujtahids would differ with each other in their formulation of the law. This diversity was, however, perceived to be a sign of God's mercy. Shi'i jurists resisted the fragmentation of their legal doctrine into schools, claiming to belong to a single school, that of the Imams. But once the Imams were no longer present on earth, Shiʿi mujtahids found themselves interpreting the law differently from one another, much like their Sunni counterparts. Their differences may be seen as on the order of differences within each of the Sunni schools.

The notion of fallibility—and with it the concomitant notion of diversity of doctrine—raises important questions. Does not fallibility imply liability to error? When a mujtahid recognizes that the results of his interpretive efforts are merely his opinion—his sense of the probable—and that they are tinged with a degree of uncertainty, is he not admitting that he could be mistaken? Is not error implicit in the very fact of disagreement among mujtahids? When mujtahids disagree, must they not conclude that some—perhaps all—of them have interpreted the foundational texts incorrectly?

Some jurists found the possibility of error in the law to be unpalatable and embraced the famous dictum "Every mujtahid is correct" (*kull mujtahid muṣīb*). This position amounted to a rejection of the very notion of fallibility, and we may accordingly call it, following Aron Zysow's lead,[5] infallibilism. Unlike the ʿiṣma of the Prophet and (for Shiʿis) the Imams, however, this was an infallibilism that posited the possibility of equally correct contradictory formulations of the divine law by individual jurists. The advantage that it offered was that it enabled one to equate error and disobedience and yet allow diversity in the law. It made a certain amount of sense that error was tantamount to disobedience. How could one claim to be obeying the law of God if one's formulation of that law was erroneous? Did not error in the formulation of the law necessarily mean that what the mujtahid declared to be the law was in fact not the actual law of God, and if it was not the actual law of God, how could conformity to it constitute obedience? Infallibilism's solution to this dilemma was simply to eliminate error, to affirm that there was more than one way to be correct about the divine law.

The only condition that the infallibilists imposed on the mujtahid, if his formulation of the law was to be counted as correct, was that he be able to say in truth that he had investigated the foundational texts to the very best of his ability. Any mujtahid whose formulation of the law was not based on a total expenditure of effort, who might have done more than he in fact did, was to be counted as disobedient. This "total expenditure of effort" (*istifrāgh al-wusʿ*) criterion of valid interpretation was in fact accepted both by infallibilists and fallibilists.

The problem with infallibilism was that it relativized the divine law, undermining its objectivity. This was a consequence that had to be borne, and therefore those jurists who accorded correctness to conflicting opinions of mujtahids frankly affirmed that God's law was contingent upon the deliberations of mujtahids (*tābiʿ li-ẓann al-mujtahid*). In other words, God's law was, for each mujtahid, whatever his best interpretive efforts led him to. To state the point in still another way: God's law was in itself indeterminate and waited upon the deliberations of human scholars to attain determinacy. There could thus be, for any given case, no one rule that exclusively represented the law of God.

This way of thinking was understandably disturbing to jurists who founded their entire jurisprudence on the notion of a preexistent singular legislative intent that was "out there," waiting to be discovered by dint of interpretive toil. If the divine law did not reside in an original intent of the divine Legislator, what was the mujtahid striving for in the first place? Was there an original intent that he should seek to understand but that, in case he failed to achieve this understanding, did not much matter in any case, not even as a standard of correctness or as a measure of the success of his interpretive endeavors? How could such an original intent be a genuine object of his search?

At the opposite end of the spectrum of views on this important issue were those who insisted so strongly on the preexistence and singularity of the law of God that they disallowed disagreement altogether among mujtahids. If mujtahids disagreed, then only the one who had successfully discovered the divine law could be counted not only as correct but also as obedient; the others were both mistaken and culpable. This view flew in the face of the probabilism of the majority of jurists, who insisted that the divine law can seldom be known with complete certainty and that where probability reigns, disagreement is inevitable. We have earlier noted that some jurists, in the yearning for maximal certainty, resisted the probabilist trend. It is not surprising that they were few in number.

Most jurists adopted a way of thinking that combined fallibilism and probabilism.[6] God's law was for them preexistent and singular, and the mujtahid was expected to make the discovery of that law the goal of his endeavors. If he did not achieve this goal with complete certainty after having put forth the requisite amount of effort, he could work with what he thought the divine law probably was, his opinion. In doing so, however, he placed himself knowingly in an arena of debate in which nothing was certain and opinions contrary to his had to be tolerated and respected. Given the singularity and preexistence of the divine law, in any disagreement among mujtahids there could be only one correct opinion, but one could not know which opinion, if any, was correct. If one could, one would then be able to brand all other opinions erroneous and unworthy of consideration; but in this event, opinion would give way to knowledge and would cease to be genuine opinion. A climate in which opinion prevailed by its very nature precluded such dogmatism; for opinion was not knowledge. Where knowledge was lacking, error would necessarily go unheeded; where it was present, error would speedily come to light.

Clearly, for those who embraced this way of thinking, correctness (*ṣawāb*) had to be rigorously defined as exegetical correctness, as correctness in the determination of the preexistent divine intent. However much exegetical correctness counted as a goal of the interpretive efforts of mujtahids, it was not a sine qua non of validity. In other words, an opinion could be an erroneous representation of the divine intent—the law considered as an object "out there"—and still be valid as fiqh. Only if the opinion was known to be erroneous was it to be rejected, but in this case, as was just noted, the arena of debate was no longer one in which opinion reigned supreme; knowledge had taken over. As long as error was a mere possibility that hovered equally over every opinion, it could be discounted and validity accorded to all opinions.

But if it was not known which opinion was erroneous, it *was* known that some opinion or opinions were erroneous. This was a corollary of the premise that where mujtahids disagreed, they could not all be right. The presence of error within the arena of debate was thus a certainty, even if the erroneous opinion could not be identified. Necessarily, then, the law formulated by the mujtahid was in some unidentifiable instances other than the preexistent law of God. The fallibilism that granted validity to every opinion thus implicitly affirmed a distinction between two kinds of law: law as an object residing in the being of God and law as a construction of fallible jurists. We may call these Shariʿa law and fiqh law, God's law and jurists' law. Shariʿa law is the product of legislation (*sharʿ*), of which God is the ultimate subject (*shāriʿ*). Fiqh law consists of legal understanding, of which the human jurist is the subject (*faqīh*).

Fiqh law is the positive law of Muslim society, for it is the law that actually regulates human affairs. But fiqh law, in the fallibilist view, enjoys validity only by virtue of the presumption that it represents the closest approximation of which humans are capable to the law of God. God's law is thus, in relation to the positive law, an ideal that human mujtahids seek to capture in their formulations to the best of their ability. It is important that we appreciate the role of "total expenditure of effort" (*istifrāgh al-wusʿ*) in this way of thinking. A mujtahid must be able to say with a clear conscience that he has done all he could possibly do in his investigation of the foundational texts and that he is not aware of any further effort that he might have made. If a mujtahid cannot say this, his formulation of the law is without validity.

The validity that fiqh law enjoys is not a validity that humans presume on their own to accord it. Rather it is a validity that, according to the fallibilists, is solidly grounded in the foundational texts. It is, in other words, a divinely sanctioned validity. A favorite text of the fallibilists is a saying of the Prophet according to which a mujtahid on the Day of Judgment receives a single reward if his formulation of the law turns out to be incorrect and a double reward if it turns out to be correct. Another prophetic saying commonly cited proclaims that diversity of opinion is a mercy (*raḥma*) from God. The principal qur'anic texts used in this connection are the statements "God has imposed on you no affliction in religion" (22:78) and "God does not intend to impose affliction on you" (5:6). These passages are interpreted to mean that God in his mercy has not made knowledge of his law the be-all and end-all of human existence. Had he done so, the human condition would have been one of affliction, which is contrary to the Qur'an. Rather God has given humans another possibility, that of formulating sound, reasoned opinion through the exercise of their utmost energies. Such opinion God mercifully accepts as a measure of human obedience.

We can readily appreciate, in the light of the foregoing, the logic of the infallibilist position. There seems to be a larger sense in which fiqh law is, after all, coterminous with God's law, for if in conforming to fiqh law humans are rendering obedience to God on God's terms, they are in some sense conforming to the law of God. Such being the case, the diverse formulations of the law of mujtahids must all be correct. The fallibilists were not, however, willing to go so far. What we do seem to discern in their position, on the other hand, is a broad interpretation of the will of God that allows his will to extend beyond the limits of the ideal preexistent Shariʿa law and to encompass the fallible law of jurists, including those parts that entail error in interpretation, as attempts at capturing the ideal law.

The fallibilist insistence that correctness must be understood as exegetical correctness reflected an uncompromising intentionalist stance. The law of God could not, properly speaking, be other than authorial intent as determined through normal philological methods, which employed the lexical code as the basic tool and took into account the cofunctioning of word and context as a fundamental principle of communication. What lay outside the boundaries of authorial intent could therefore not be considered part of the ideal law; but, thanks to God's mercy, it could be considered part of a valid positive law as long as the mujtahid had satisfied the "total expenditure of effort" test. The mujtahid must be strongly convinced that his formulation of the law represents the probable intent of the Legislator, in the hope that in the Day of Judgment he will be proven right. But even if he is proven wrong, he will receive a single reward, and in the meantime his formulation will have in the mundane affairs of this world the force of positive law.

The fallibility on which the fallibilists insisted was, it must be noted, a fallibility that characterized the efforts of mujtahids working as individuals. Whenever all living mujtahids at any given time agreed upon a particular formulation of the law, this consensus, according to the commonly accepted doctrine, raised the formulation to the level of an infallible representation of the divine law. Thus the possibility of error hovered over formulations of the law only in the context of disagreement among mujtahids. Where agreement occurred, the fallibility of individual mujtahids was erased through the working of a supervening principle, that of the infallibility of consensus. This infallibility was placed under the heading of ʿiṣma, the same term that designated the infallibility of the Prophet and the Shiʿi Imams.

The principle of consensual infallibility eventually became a hallmark of Muslim legal theory, both among Sunnis and, in a qualified way, among Shiʿis. For all the jurists, the consensus set limits on diversity in the formulation of the law. Whenever the mujtahids are in agreement, the rule of law on which they are agreed becomes written on tablets of stone as an infallible expression of the divine law that may never be set aside by any future mujtahid. Where no agreement exists, mujtahids of the future are free to weigh existing opinions and to undertake fresh formulations of the law, if in their interpretive judgment this step is warranted. The law thus embraces two spheres: the sphere of what is agreed upon (*mujmaʿ ʿalayh*) and the sphere of what is not agreed upon (*mukhtalaf fīh*). Within the former sphere, unity prevails; within the latter, diversity. The existence of multiple schools of law has its justification within the latter sphere.

So widely accepted was the principle of infallibility of consensus that it became incorporated into standard legal theory as a major principle. The consensus of mujtahids was in fact counted among the four foundations of the law, the other three being the Qur'an, the Sunna, and, for most Sunnis, analogy. (The Shiʿi jurists replaced analogy with reason, or *ʿaql*.) The Qur'an and the Sunna were of course textual sources of the law and were collectively called *naṣṣ*, for which I have in this book reserved the term "foundational texts." The consensus for all practical purposes amounted to a textual source, since it had to find expression in quotable words in order to be effective, and these words had to be transmitted from generation to generation in the same manner as the words of the Qur'an and the Sunna. Unlike the

Qur'an and the Sunna, however, the texts in which the consensus was to be found were never gathered into unified compilations.

Despite its prominence in Muslim legal theory, the concept of consensus entailed a number of intractable problems discussions of which form a lengthy chapter in the great classical works of jurisprudence.[7] Since the infallibility of the consensus was not self-evident and could not be proven on strictly rational grounds, it had to have a firm basis in the foundational texts. This entailed a complex and tedious exegesis of certain passages all of which were open to diverse interpretations. A good example is the oft-used saying of the Prophet, "My community will never agree on an error." Was "error" to be taken as a general or a specific term—did it cover all types of error or just certain types? How could one be sure that it was not restricted to error in the realm of fundamental religious belief as opposed to error in the realm of law? And what was the import of the word "community"? Did it include all Muslims or just certain ones? What ground was there for supposing that it included only mujtahids? At least some of the classical jurists, including the eponym of one of the schools, the great Shafiʿi, held that infallibility characterized no less than the consensus of the entire community, including both mujtahids and nonmujtahids, and that no special consideration should be given to the consensus of jurists alone.

The view that eventually prevailed accorded infallibility to the consensus of mujtahids and considered the consensus of the entire community to be infallible by virtue of the inclusion of jurists, but other problems remained to be dealt with—problems relating to the actual working of consensus—and on each of these there was a diversity of viewpoints. How was a consensus constituted? Did it require a verbal statement from every living mujtahid, or did a statement from a single mujtahid to which no other contemporary mujtahid is known to have objected suffice? If a verbal statement from every mujtahid was required, then the task of determining the existence of a consensus became exceedingly difficult, if not impossible; for how was one to know who the mujtahids were at any given moment of time and how was one to go about collecting statements they had made?

Here we are faced with the problem that there was never among

Muslims any identifiable official agency that conferred upon individuals the status of mujtahid so that one could look for a credential as a way of determining who is and who is not a mujtahid. Mujtahids were not card-bearing members of some sort of organized association that kept membership lists. Rather, mujtahids were simply people who claimed to be mujtahids and were judged by others as having made a valid claim. This means that anyone seeking to determine who the mujtahids were at any given time had to rely on his own judgment. Such a judgment would clearly be extremely difficult to make.

But even assuming that one could identify all the mujtahids living throughout the vast reaches of the Islamic world at a given time, how could one ever know their views concerning a particular question of law? If they all were to show up at a gathering or were to send written communications to some agency, one would perhaps have a chance of determining the existence of a consensus. But no such mechanisms as these existed in the world of medieval Islam.

Such considerations explain why many jurists were attracted to the consensus determined by an absence of known objection to the expressed opinion of a single mujtahid. This type of consensus was commonly known as the tacit consensus (*ijmāʿ sukūtī*) because it rested on the principle that silence implies consent. Thus we commonly find in the literature of Muslim jurisprudence quotations from famous Muslims followed by a phrase such as *lā nakīra lahu* ("There was no objection to it"). But how could one be sure that silence indicates consent? And how could one be sure that all living mujtahids were even aware of the expressed opinion of the one mujtahid such that their silence could be construed as an indication of consent? And for those believed to have been aware of the opinion, how long did the period of silence need to be before one could draw a conclusion from it? Must the period of silence extend to the end of the lifetimes of all concerned? In other words, must the entire generation of mujtahids have passed from the scene?

Since the consensus gave finality to the opinions of individual mujtahids, it was in any case not, for the majority of jurists, an independent substantive source of law on a par with the foundational texts. The labors of the mujtahids were after all essentially exegetical, and since the consensus emerged out of those labors, whatever law it undergirded could be said to be grounded in the texts with which they worked.

The consensus had no bearing, let us remember, on the validity of a rule of law. A rule of law duly formulated by a qualified mujtahid was equally valid whether it lay within the realm of law agreed upon or of law not agreed upon. The only real function of the consensus was thus to establish unity in the law and to disallow diversity. It determined whether unity or diversity would prevail in the very moment a question of law first emerged. If in that crucial moment, the mujtahids agreed, their common opinion would be binding on all subsequent generations. If they disagreed, their diverse opinions would become a permanent legacy for subsequent generations to weigh in their own deliberations over the original question, and unity would never be possible.

Given the problems in determining the existence of a consensus, the role of consensus in the actual formulation of the law was something that each individual mujtahid had to assess on a case-by-case basis. The results could vary from mujtahid to mujtahid. One mujtahid might claim to have found evidence of a consensus on a particular point of law, while another mujtahid disputed the claim, perhaps on the basis of a disagreement concerning the method of evaluating evidence. The former would of course refrain from attempting any fresh formulation of the law and would consider other mujtahids to be under this same constraint, but this would merely be his opinion. The latter mujtahid would naturally claim freedom from any such constraint.

On the whole, I think it fair to say that the actual impact of consensus on the formulation of the law was seen by the classical jurists as rather minimal. It was often cited as a foundation for the most fundamental duties, especially in the area of ritual law. That the required number of daily prayers is five was frequently seen as endorsed by consensus, and the unity of Muslim thinking on this subject is undeniable. The same goes for certain other fundamentals. It is in the realm of issues of detail—the kind of issues that humans face in everyday life and turn to the law to solve—that the role of consensus becomes much more reduced.

It is wrong, I think, to suppose that the doctrine common to the four

Sunni schools of law constitutes a consensus of the sort that theory endows with infallibility. For one thing, the theory does not altogether exclude Shiʿis from the process of consensus making. Furthermore, the four Sunni schools originated at a time when there were other schools, for example those founded by Awzaʿi, Sufyan al-Thawri, and Daʾud al-Zahiri. But even if one could ascertain doctrine common to all known schools of the formative period of Islamic law, one would still have to consider, according to the theory, whether one had taken into account all mujtahids. Furthermore, it is only the mujtahids living at any given time who can produce an infallible consensus, and the founders of the various known schools were not all contemporaries. Muslim scholarship, it is true, has produced a special literature that explores differences between the four Sunni schools as well as points on which they agree, but this literature serves scholarly purposes other than the determination of consensus.

We are now in a position to consider certain general points relating to our principal topic in this chapter, juristic authority. We have noted that the authority of mujtahids, of those jurists who take upon themselves the task of formulating the law, was always understood to be strictly declarative and derivative; it rested upon the soundness of the philological and interpretive methods that the mujtahids employed. We must now distinguish between two types of declarative authority: that exercised by the mujtahids collectively whenever they reached a consensus on a point of law and that exercised by mujtahids individually. The former type belongs under a larger heading that may, I think, be called absolute authority, whereas the latter may, in contrast, be described as relative authority. Absolute authority was enjoyed not only by the consensus of mujtahids but also by the foundational texts, although the authority of the latter was of course legislative (originative), whereas that of the consensus was not, according to the majority of jurists.

Absolute authority is what mujtahids are directly subject to. It is undivided and uniform; it does not vary from mujtahid to mujtahid. Every mujtahid is thus subject to the authority of the Qurʾan, the Sunna, and the consensus equally. Nonmujtahids may be said to be subject to this authority also but only indirectly, since they depend upon the mediating role of the mujtahids. Relative authority is the authority that individual mujtahids bear in relation to their followings among the nonmujtahids and not in relation to each other; nonmujtahids are directly subject to it. This authority is divided and inconstant in the sense that it is unevenly distributed among mujtahids each of whom has his own following. There is no single bearer of this authority, no single mujtahid to whose authority all nonmujtahids are equally subject.

Since the consensus of mujtahids is, for reasons discussed earlier, difficult to determine and since it bears in any case only upon a relatively narrow range of fundamental duties, juristic authority may for all practical purposes be placed under the heading of relative authority. In a certain sense, the consensus, though in principle emerging from the labors of individual mujtahids, rises to a level that transcends juristic endeavor, for its authority is established, and its correctness assured, not by the labors of mujtahids but rather by an intervening act of divine grace. Thus from a certain point of view, God may be said to be as much the author of consensus as jurists. Whenever the law enjoyed the endorsement of consensus, it was in principle no longer subject to juristic review or criticism; it was in effect lifted above the arena of acceptable juristic disagreement. There was now an air of finality about it. On the other hand, where nothing beyond juristic endeavor is at work, the results may be said to have relative authority, not absolute. This authority constitutes juristic authority in the truest sense of the word.

A mujtahid's following—the body of nonmujtahids who are subject to his authority—is formed at the initiative, not of the mujtahid himself, but of each individual follower. This initiative is known variously as *istiftā'* and *taqlīd*. The term *istiftā'* designates the act of asking an expert in the law for a fatwā, or legal opinion. In *istiftā'*, one is referring a legal problem to an expert with the intention of complying with or being guided by the expert's opinion. The one asking for the fatwā is called a *mustaftī*, and the one who gives the fatwā, a *muftī*. *Taqlīd* literally means "adornment," and in Muslim jurisprudence it refers to the act of placing oneself under the authority of a mujtahid, an act seen as an adorning of the mujtahid with authority.

The formulation of the law is in reality a partnership. Although only the mujtahid can do the work of formulating the law on the basis of the foundational sources, he cannot single-handedly formulate law that is relevant to the needs of society. For this purpose he must have questions to work with, referrals of real legal problems; and if there are to be questions to work with, there must be people who pose—who formulate—those questions. While a mujtahid might in principle formulate the law with reference to hypothetical cases that he or other mujtahids construct, this is not how the law is normally understood to unfold through ijtihād. That is to say, ijtihād is not normally understood to be a self-contained process. It is, rather, complementary to the process of question posing. It is as mufti, as supplier of responsa, that the mujtahid formulates a law relevant to real human life. Ijtihād is thus essentially altruistic; it is interpretation for others, for society as a whole.

But this working of ijtihād as a social force requires that ordinary people be able to identify mujtahids and that mujtahids accordingly be identifiable. The Muslim theorists, or *uṣūlīs,* discuss at length the qualifications a mujtahid must satisfy in order to be a mujtahid, but these all have to do with the skills and knowledge required to engage in ijtihād, and whether or not a scholar possesses these skills and this knowledge may sometimes be difficult for a nonmujtahid to determine. The discussions of the qualifications for ijtihād all display a total lack of formalism. Nowhere in the literature do we find mention of a process of formal public certification of mujtahids. There was, of course, in medieval Islam a somewhat formalized method of accreditation for study completed under a great master, namely the bestowal of a license known as an *ijāza.* But holding an ijāza did not itself make one a mujtahid.

Given this lack of formalized procedures of certification, the nonmujtahid in search of a mujtahid who might offer an opinion on a particular problem simply had to make a judgment on his own to the best of his ability. His effort in this regard was something like the ijtihād of the mujtahid, except that whereas the mujtahid was trying to arrive at a sound opinion as to what constituted the law, he was trying to arrive at a sound opinion as to who might be truly qualified to interpret the law for him. In this endeavor he was constrained to rely largely on outward appearances. For him, such things as the holding of a teaching appointment in an institution of learning or a high-ranking judgeship might be important clues. Also important might be the respect accorded to him by those under whom he studied or by his peers, or the volume of his scholarly output, or his general reputation within the community at large, or the size of his following. All these factors had to be weighed carefully and a judgment made. No institutionalized procedures could relieve him of the burden of making such a judgment.

But mujtahids, though few in comparison with nonmujtahids, are multiple, and the interpretive endeavors of multiple mujtahids inevitably produce the diversity in the formulation of the law that was noted earlier. Given this diversity, the nonmujtahid is faced with a task beyond that of merely identifying mujtahids.[8] He must choose between mujtahids, especially when their opinions vary. Some of the classical jurists required the nonmujtahid to weigh the qualities of different mujtahids against each other and attempt to select the mujtahid who was the most expert and knowledgeable. Most, however, felt that this task was beyond the capabilities of the nonmujtahid, since it required moving onto the mujtahid's turf to some extent. They therefore allowed the nonmujtahid complete freedom of choice. Once he had identified the mujtahids who were accessible to him, he was free to approach whichever of them he wished.

But if a nonmujtahid could freely choose any mujtahid, could he also, if he wished, freely move from mujtahid to mujtahid? That is, could he seek opinions (*fatwās*) from different mujtahids on a particular problem, and, alternatively, could he adopt the opinion of a particular mujtahid on a given problem and then, on some other problem, adopt the opinion of a different mujtahid? It is remarkable that the majority of the Muslim jurists granted the nonmujtahid freedom in both situations, not, however, without laying down a proviso. A nonmujtahid enjoyed the freedom to move from mujtahid to mujtahid provided he had not bound himself to a particular mujtahid by means of the formal declaration *anā ʿalā madhhab fulān,* "I belong to the school of so-and-so." This declaration amounted to a voluntary sacrifice of freedom in favor of loyalty to a particular school.

This stance—reliance upon the opinion of a particular mujtahid coupled with a declaration of allegiance to his school—constitutes the theoretical justification for the existence of the great schools of law. It is not hard to understand why the Muslim legal theorists should have seen the great schools as originating in the opinion giving of their great mujtahids. To the extent that Malik, Abu Hanifa, Shafiʿi, and Ibn Hanbal produced opinions to guide others—which is what posterity saw them as doing primarily or even exclusively—they were acting as muftis as much as they were acting merely as teachers of legal doctrine. In fact, their activity as muftis *was* their teaching activity. All their doctrine was, in the final analysis, responsum.

The immediate disciples of the great masters were also mujtahids and muftis in their own right and on occasion differed with their masters. It was not uncommon for Abu Yusuf and Muhammad al-Shaybani, for example, to hold views different from those of their master Abu Hanifa. But the eponymic status accorded to Abu Hanifa and the other founding masters implies that certain cardinal doctrines or principles were established by them and had the effect of delimiting the ijtihād of their disciples. His ijtihād was unrestricted and free; theirs was circumscribed. The eighteenth-century encyclopedist Muhammad ibn ʿAli al-Tahanawi, in his entry on ijtihād,[9] speaks of two types of circumscribed mujtahids, *al-mujtahid fi'l-madhhab* and *al-mujtahid fī masʾala,* which translate literally as "mujtahid within a school" and "mujtahid on a particular problem." The latter may be rephrased as "mujtahid within a particular area of the law." A mujtahid within a school is, according to Tahanawi, unrestricted (*muṭlaq*) in the sense that he has the capacity to carry on ijtihād in all areas of the law. Abu Yusuf and Muhammad are good examples of this type of mujtahid. They were free to differ with their master on any question of law whatsoever as long as the methodological principles they used in formulating rules were those they had learned from their master. A mujtahid within a particular area of the law could differ with his master only in the area of his expertise; in all other areas he was an opinion seeker, a follower of his master. Like the mujtahid within a school, he would, of course, always follow the master's methodological principles.

Every school thus has its mujtahids and its nonmujtahid followers.

To be a follower (*mustaftī, muqallid*) within a particular school—that is to say, to be a Hanafi, Maliki, Shafi'i, or Hanbali—is to follow solutions to problems worked out by the mujtahids of that school. Any one within a particular school who claims to be a mujtahid will offer solutions rather than relying on the opinions of other mujtahids within the school. This accounts for the fact that within the Hanafi school, for example, one may have differing opinions originating with Abu Hanifa, Abu Yusuf, or Muhammad, not to mention other Hanafi jurists who engaged in ijtihād. One can as a follower adhere to any one of these opinions while remaining a Hanafi.

It should be noted in passing that the terms that designate the follower, namely *mustaftī* and *muqallid,* as used among the Muslim theorists, denote a status and are not confined to discrete or isolated instances of opinion seeking. The great mujtahids such as the eponyms of the four schools and their more eminent disciples formulated opinions by which individuals conducted their lives generation after generation. All those who follow the legal doctrine of a great master, no matter how long after the master they live, are mustaftīs and muqallids, according to the prevailing usage of this term within Muslim jurisprudence. On the other hand, the legal opinions of the mujtahids were normally presupposed to have been occasioned by questions brought to them, either by their disciples or by others. Even if some questions dealt with hypothetical cases, they were questions nonetheless. The law was always thought to have been shaped through exchange between questioners and answerers. Once an answer had been given, however, it might stand as definitive for those other than the original questioners.

It is important to understand that the relationship of which we have been speaking always entails a nonmujtahid as follower and a mujtahid as opinion giver, or mufti. If the follower and mufti are peers—that is to say, if the two are both mujtahids or both nonmujtahids—the relationship in that case is considered to be unjustified. Situations in which the follower is a mujtahid and the mufti a nonmujtahid are not even discussed. Such situations are clearly regarded as inconceivable and unworthy of scholarly attention.

It is the relationship involving a mujtahid both on the opinion-giving end and on the opinion-seeking end that receives the lion's share of attention among the Muslim theorists. What is especially objectionable about this type of relationship is that it entails a neglect of duty on the part of one of the parties, namely the mujtahid who relies on the opinion of the other. A mujtahid should always work out his own solutions. If one has declared one's self to be a mujtahid, one must accept the consequences. To claim to be a mujtahid is to assume the responsibility of working out solutions on one's own and not deferring to the opinions of others. Ijtihād is hard work, but one who claims to be a mujtahid may never leave this hard work to others. Even if the hard work has been done by other mujtahids and opinions have been formed, the hard work must be done again and a fresh opinion formed. Ijtihād always produces, at best, formulations of the probable intention of the divine Legislator; it never achieves full certainty. A mujtahid must achieve the sense of the probable on his own, for only then will it be a genuine sense of the probable. If he accepts the opinion of another mujtahid, he has no basis on which to sense the probable correctness of the opinion. The opinion will therefore for him have neither probable correctness nor probable incorrectness.

The nonmujtahid is exempt from this requirement. For him the only requirement is the sense of the probable mujtahid status of the one on whose opinion he relies. And this he acquires on the basis of considerations that I have already mentioned.

Returning to our distinction between absolute authority and relative authority, we may here observe that the authority that the opinions of the mujtahids have for their followers belongs entirely to the category of relative authority. The legal doctrine of the great schools as represented in the fiqh texts thus possesses relative authority. Absolute authority is operative for mujtahids, while relative authority is operative for nonmujtahids. If one claims to be a mujtahid, one may not have recourse to fiqh but only to the ultimate sources of the law. Fiqh is there to guide the masses of nonmujtahids. One who claims to be a mujtahid places himself outside the sphere in which the authority of the inherited fiqh is operative. Such a person must produce his own fiqh. If one's ijtihād is of the restricted kind, then this is true only in those areas of the law in which one claims the expertise required of a mujtahid. In all other areas, one places one's self under the relative authority of the fiqh.

Just as a mujtahid may not rely upon the opinion of another mujtahid, so, according to some of the jurists, a nonmujtahid may not rely upon the opinion of another nonmujtahid. Others were not so adamant on this point, however. The classical literature records a controversy among the jurists on the issue of whether it was ever permissible for a nonmujtahid to issue opinions, to act as a mufti.[10] In practice this was done and on a wide scale. Those jurists who opposed the practice feared its implications. If a nonmujtahid could occupy the role of mufti, then the equation between mufti and mujtahid was no longer sustainable. A mufti who was not a mujtahid would have to issue opinions based on the opinions of those who were. In this case, he was not truly the originator of an opinion; his opinions were no longer truly his. How, then, could he rightfully be called mufti?

Those who supported this practice argued that a nonmujtahid may be learned in the legal traditions of his school and be able to impart knowledge of the law to those lacking such learning. As I have already indicated, the ranks of jurists in the broad sense of that term (*fuqahā'*) included both mujtahids and nonmujtahids. A faqih who was not a mujtahid was certainly qualified to advise the general population in matters of law. Why should he not, with respect to this capacity, be called a mufti? Eventually, it was this point of view that prevailed. Although the great muftis of the past—the ones who laid the doctrinal foundations of the schools—were mujtahids, the mufti of the present did not need to be.

A nonmujtahid mufti was, admittedly, something of an anomaly. Insofar as he based his opinion on the opinion of a mujtahid of the past, he was adopting the posture of a follower. Rather than working directly with the foundational texts as a mujtahid would, he was working with an earlier opinion. This could not be called ijtihād; it was clearly istiftā', dependence on the fatwā of a mujtahid. Thus istiftā' operated on two levels: on the level of actual legal advising and on the level of construction of the legal advice. On the first level, a learned nonmujtahid was mufti vis-à-vis an unlearned nonmujtahid. On the second level, the learned nonmujtahid was a follower vis-à-vis an earlier mujtahid, who stood in the position of mufti in relation to him.

Thus the difference between the mufti who was a mujtahid and the mufti who was not had to do with where one looked to find a precedent on which to base a fatwā relevant to the case at hand. The mufti who was a mujtahid looked directly at the foundational texts. If he was a school mujtahid (*mujtahid fi'l-madhhab*) he used the school's methodological principles in dealing with those texts; the point is that he did deal with those texts. The mufti who was not a mujtahid practiced istiftā': that is to say, he looked for his precedent in the school's fiqh literature, which included both summative textbooks and collections of fatwās. He did not work directly with the foundational texts. Rather, he was involved in a process of building fatwā upon fatwā. It was through this process that fiqh law—school law—developed cumulatively over time as a tradition in its own right.

But working with a school's fiqh literature could be just as much an exercise of interpretive effort as working with the foundational texts. A recent study by Sherman Jackson of the legal and constitutional ideas of a thirteenth-century jurist, Shihab al-Din al-Qarafi,[11] has clarified the different degrees of scholarly expertise that this enterprise involved. An important merit of Jackson's study is that it sheds positive light on taqlīd—that is to say, istiftā'—as a more advanced stage of legal development than ijtihād, one entailing an even more complex methodology and requiring a larger spectrum of interpretive skills. His study thus counteracts the hitherto prevailing negative attitude toward taqlīd among modern scholars writing on Islamic law. Taqlīd, he correctly points out, was necessary for maintaining the consistency and continuity of the law from generation to generation. A law developed solely by mujtahids would be a law plagued by excessive diversity and fluctuation.

Jackson finds in Qarafi's writings a distinction between two major types of use of precedent, that is to say, of previous fatwās: the mere transference of an earlier fatwā to the case at hand and the extrapolation (*takhrīj*) of a new fatwā from earlier fatwās and general principles of school doctrine. The first type is possible, obviously, only when the case at hand is identical with one covered by an earlier fatwā. Here the (nonmujtahid) mufti's role is one of merely transmission (*naql*). He is like a hadith scholar in that he is simply relating to his inquirer a previously established fatwā that happens to be applicable to the case at hand without any modification through interpretation. If it happens that he finds in his school's literature conflicting fatwās relating to the case at hand, then he must do more than merely transmit; he must decide which fatwā to adopt. If he decides to favor the one that is most widely accepted (*mashhūr*) within his school, his task is fairly easy to accomplish. Otherwise he must be in a position to evaluate the fatwās against each other, which takes him into a more difficult ijtihādlike critical activity.

On the whole, however, a nonmujtahid mufti's chances of finding a precedent that fits the case at hand exactly are usually slim, and it is more likely that he will have to employ the method of extrapolation rather than that of transmission. At this point his work will be very much like that of a mujtahid except that his texts will be different. Whereas the mujtahid works with foundational texts, he will work with school texts; but interpretation of school texts entails the same methodological considerations as interpretation of the foundational texts. He will have to concern himself with the authenticity of the text he is working with, for example a fatwā or other kind of statement of a school mujtahid. Occasionally he will find contradictory statements from the same mujtahid, in which case he will have to establish the chronology of the statements to be sure he is working with the latest one (mujtahids, it should be noted, are free to change their minds) or use principles of transmission criticism to rule out statements of unlikely authenticity. He must deal with ambiguity and general language, dispelling uncertainty to the best of his ability through reliance on contextual clues and usually settling in the end for what appears to be the probable intent of the mujtahid. Frequently, he will resort to analogical reasoning in order to make his text applicable to the case at hand.

In short, the nonmujtahid jurist who undertakes to issue fatwās must be as thoroughly schooled in the principles of text criticism and intentionalist hermeneutics as the mujtahid. In other words, he must be well versed in the literature of uṣūl al-fiqh, in which these principles are expounded. His intentionalism differs, of course, from that of the mujtahid in that its focus is upon the intent behind a school text rather than upon the intent behind a foundational text. But this difference in no way reduces the importance of his interpretive endeavors. The nonmujtahid jurist remains as devoted to the divine intent as the mujtahid, but he has access to it only through the medium of a master mujtahid. The intent of the master is thus his only avenue to the divine intent. The intentionalism of his hermeneutics derives its validity from an intentionalism of a higher order, that of the master whose words he studies and interprets.

As Jackson insightfully points out, the later jurists of Islam as a rule refrained from claiming the status of mujtahid not because they were unable to perform the exegetical work of mujtahids—if anything, their work was even more demanding—but because of their deference to the principle of school authority. The Muslim jurists appreciated the importance of what I have called relative authority, the authority borne by the mujtahids of the formative period in the development of Islamic law. Once school law, madhhab law, was in place, it enjoyed immense prestige, and jurists accorded it a loyalty of the most profound kind. Interpretive talent abounded in all ages, but the way of the mujtahid became, if anything, a last resort to be attempted only if all else failed. Even the role of "mujtahid within a school" (*mujtahid fi'l-madhhab*), which required only loyalty to the methodological principles of a school, not to its substantive doctrine, was only reluctantly claimed throughout what Jackson has called the "postformative" centuries.

The kinds of deliberations a nonmujtahid mufti had to be capable of undertaking are richly exemplified by recent research on fatwās. David Powers in particular has provided in a number of separate articles a detailed and highly perceptive analysis of a number of fatwās found in the immense multivolume fatwā collection compiled by the fifteenth-century Moroccan jurist Ahmad al-Wansharisi. In the remaining pages of this chapter, we will look at Powers's findings in regard to fatwās dealing with two cases.[12] The telescoping of fatwās that is characteristic of this fascinating literature will readily become apparent.

The first of the two cases involves a certain Fatima and a certain Ahmad who feel wronged over being excluded from what they believe to be their rightful shares in the income from endowment property. The property is under the control of their cousin Abu'l-Qasim, who firmly believes that they are not entitled to shares. Family endowments, it should be noted, allowed an owner of property to arrange for the division of property in such a way that the property would not, upon his death, be subject to the law of inheritance, which divided property among heirs according to a fixed formula (as in modern probate law). According to the original deed of the endowment in question, the endowment property was supposed to have been divided between the mother of Ahmad, the mother of Fatima, and the father of Abu'l-Qasim upon the death of their father (the grandfather of the three cousins). Since Ahmad's mother and Fatima's mother predeceased the grandfather, leaving Abu'l-Qasim's father as the sole survivor, Abu'l-Qasim argued that they had never had opportunity to establish their claim to their share in the endowment (that would have been possible only upon the death of the grandfather) and that the entire endowment therefore had reverted to his father and passed to him on his father's death.

Ahmad and Fatima took their case to a certain mufti named Ahmad al-Qabbab, who dutifully turned to the law books of his school (the Maliki school) in search of a precedent. Finding one proved to be a difficult task, but in a book by Ibn al-Mawwaz, a respected Maliki jurist of the ninth century, he eventually discovered a case that he thought "might possibly" (*yumkin*) serve as a precedent. A man had established an endowment for his four sons and stipulated that if one of them died without leaving a child, his share would revert to his brothers. Two of the sons predeceased their father, leaving children; then, after the death of the father, a third son died, leaving no child. The question was whether the third son's share reverted entirely to the sole surviving son or whether it should be divided between that son and the children of the other sons. In his fatwā on this case, Ibn al-Mawwaz evoked the principle of representation, stating that the children of the two sons who had predeceased the father "occupied the same position as their fathers, had the two of them been alive."

The share of the third son should therefore be divided between them and the surviving son. Accordingly, argued Qabbab in his fatwā addressed to Ahmad and Fatima, when their mothers died, predeceasing their grandfather, they (Ahmad and Fatima) had occupied the position of their mothers with respect to claims to shares in the endowment and upon the death of their grandfather were entitled to advance their claims.

When Ahmad and Fatima are unable on the basis of Qabbab's fatwā to convince their cousin of their entitlement to shares in the endowment, they turn to a consilium made up of six muftis of Fez, who engage in further deliberation on their case and produce in the end a joint fatwā. In this fatwā the muftis support Ahmad and Fatima's claim but with a somewhat different argument. Now an earlier fatwā is evoked that comes, not from Ibn al-Mawwaz, but from an even earlier and higher authority within the Maliki school, the eponym of the school Malik ibn Anas. Malik's fatwā deals with the same case as Ibn al-Mawwaz's (apparently the case dated back to Malik's time but had been discussed periodically by other members of the school), but instead of evoking the principle of representation, it took the approach of nullifying the founder's stipulation that if any of the four sons died without leaving a child, his share would revert to the other sons.

The rationale for Malik's fatwā is found in a statement of a distinguished Maliki jurist of the twelfth century, Abu'l-Walid ibn Rushd (grandfather of the philosopher Averroës), to the effect that one should take into consideration not the sheer words of the deed but the founder's true intention, which must be determined on the basis of something other than literal meaning. Any founder of a family endowment, it is argued, "intends that a child will be included even if his father (or mother) never establishes a claim to entitlement." Thus to rule out a child on the ground that his parent predeceased a grandparent is contrary to our commonsense understanding of a founder's intent. Similarly, according to the six muftis of Fez, one can argue that it could never have been the intention of the founder of the endowment, to a share of which Ahmad and Fatima are laying claim, to exclude them on the ground that their mothers had never been able to establish a claim.

In order to counter the efforts of Ahmad and Fatima, Abu'l-Qasim seeks help from both judges and muftis. I shall not recount here the full history of this complex case except to note that the fatwās supporting Abu'l-Qasim include denials of the relevance of the abovementioned earlier cases to it and attempts to find other precedents. A mufti named Yaznasini, for example, advises Abu'l-Qasim that the fatwā of Qabbab has no relevance on account of Qabbab's statement to the effect that the case discussed in Ibn al-Mawwaz's earlier fatwā "might possibly" serve as a precedent. Qabbab's fatwā is, in other words, lacking in the requisite sense of probability, which is the true mark of juristic opinion. Furthermore, argues Yaznasini, Qabbab did not quote Ibn al-Mawwaz correctly at certain points (here authenticity is the issue), and he was wrong in suggesting that Ibn al-Mawwaz was evoking the principle of representation.

The important feature of the fatwās just considered—those of Qabbab and the six muftis of Fez in particular—is that they entail no attempt to use qur'anic or sunnaic texts in their search for a solution to the case at hand. Both Qabbab and the six muftis are content to let the entire matter rest upon the juristic authority of a respected and rather early Maliki jurist, Ibn al-Mawwaz in the case of Qabbab, Malik ibn Anas and Ibn Rushd in the case of the six muftis. Malik is of course a mujtahid for all members of the Maliki school, and Ibn al-Mawwaz and Ibn Rushd are accorded the status of mujtahid in these fatwās.

In the second case we shall consider, a deceased man's heirs wish to invalidate the man's sale of properties to a religious dignitary on the ground that the sale should be considered *tawlīj*, that is to say, a device intended to prevent their inheriting of the properties. The principal fatwā on this case comes from the pen of Wansharisi himself, the compiler of the fatwā collection studied by Powers. Wansharisi's opinion is that the sale is valid and does not constitute tawlīj. In making his argument, however, he must deal with a problem. The only evidence of the sale is a certification of the sale drawn up some years after it occurred. This document simply recorded attestation by notaries of a man's acknowledgment that he had received the full sale price for the properties. Lacking are eyewitnesses to the actual receipt of the sale price, who would have known its actual amount, and evidence of the conveyance of the properties to the buyer at the time of the sale. These lacunae create a suspicion of tawlīj, but according to Wansharisi, they are not sufficient to establish tawlīj.

From his fatwā it becomes clear that Wansharisi is unable to find an earlier fatwā dealing with an identical case, in which event he would need only to pass the early fatwā on to the disgruntled heirs without creating one of his own, thus confining his role to transmission (*naql*). It is because there is no exact precedent for this case with a ready-made fatwā resolving it that Wansharisi is compelled to enter the domain of *takhrīj* (exegetical extrapolation). He must find a comparable case or cases and show how the opinions of earlier jurists on those cases apply to the case at hand.

Wansharisi, in order to justify his opinion, wants to establish that neither the eyewitness of receipt of the sale price nor conveyance of property sold is requisite to the validity of a sale. To establish the first point, he merely states established doctrine as expressed in the writings of Ibn ʿAbd al-Barr and Matiti, Maliki jurists of the eleventh and twelfth centuries. At this point his own reasoning is at a minimum. He refers to no specific fatwās but merely enunciates school doctrine, which probably falls under the heading of *mashhūr* (widely accepted doctrine), as discussed by Jackson. His role here is purely transmissional. To establish the second point, however, he gets involved in more elaborate argumentation that brings into play the opinion of a late twelfth- or early thirteenth-century Maliki jurist named Ibn ʿAt al-Shatibi on three earlier cases. Wansharisi's reasoning powers at this point must be fully engaged, since the case at hand is in important respects unlike the cases considered by Ibn ʿAt. In order to use Ibn ʿAt's opinion, Wansharisi must be able to show that despite the dissimilarities, the earlier cases are analogous to the case at hand, an interpretive strategy sometimes called *jamʿ* ("linking"). Wansharisi is in fact able to use one dissimilarity to develop an a fortiori argument.

In each of the three earlier cases, a man buys property from himself on behalf of a minor son. By virtue of this sale—if it is to be deemed valid—the property is the son's, not the father's. But the father retains possession of it until his death. The question faced by Ibn ʿAt is whether failure to convey the property—which might be grounds for suspecting tawlīj—invalidates the sale. Ibn ʿAt's reply is that it does not. Failure to convey the property is thus not adequate in itself as a basis either for claiming tawlīj or for invalidating the sale. Wansharisi, reflecting on Ibn ʿAt's pronouncements, sees them as underscoring the principle (*qāʿida*) that there must always be a presumption of an intent to sell (as opposed to an intent to divert property from heirs) without hard proof to the contrary. The earlier cases are different from the present case in that in the present case a man has sold property, not to a son, but to a person unrelated to him by kinship. Wansharisi argues that if a sale to a son without conveyance of the property is to be deemed valid and not to be deemed tawlīj, then surely (a fortiori) a sale to a nonrelative—a person with whom one does not have the natural bond of filial affection—without conveyance of the property is also to be deemed valid and not to be deemed tawlīj.

Whereas Ibn ʿAt's opinion validates a sale of property and invalidates a claim of tawlīj, the other fatwās or opinions cited by Wansharisi take the opposite position regarding the cases they deal with; that is, they invalidate a sale and validate a claim of tawlīj. With these cases Wansharisi must therefore argue that the dissimilarities with the present case are decisive and that the opinions cited do not apply to it. This type of argument is what the jurists sometimes call *farq,* dissociation of the present case from an earlier case or cases. The fatwās of Ibn al-Makwi, Ibn al-Hajj, and Ibn ʿAttab (Maliki jurists of the eleventh and early twelfth centuries) have to do with a sale that was attested by a deathbed acknowledgment of receipt of the price. In the present case, the acknowledgment occurs inter vivos. This difference is taken by Wansharisi to be decisive. The opinions of the three earlier jurists do not apply to cases where the acknowledgment occurs inter vivos.

Perhaps the most important of all juristic opinions in the Maliki tradition to which Wansharisi must apply the technique of dissociation of cases is the opinion of Ibn al-Qasim (d. 806) regarding the sale of a house. The seller had certified the sale by summoning witnesses to attest to his acknowledgment of receipt of the sale. He had acknowledged the sale while in a state of health, not on his deathbed.

Deathbed illness is therefore not a possible basis for dissociation. The two irregularities mentioned earlier are both present: no eyewitnesses to the receipt of the sale price are available, and conveyance of the property to the buyer has not occurred. The buyer is a close relative (a wife, a son, or some other heir). Ibn al-Qasim declares that tawlīj has occurred and that the sale is invalid. The importance of this precedent is heightened by the fact that it has already been used by eminent Maliki jurists in the twelfth century to invalidate sales and to validate a claim of tawlīj. The applicability to the present case seems on the surface to be quite undeniable.

But Wansharisi insists upon nonapplicability. He wants the opinion of Ibn ʿAt to override the opinion of the illustrious Ibn al-Qasim and the eminent eleventh- or twelfth-century Maliki authorities. He must therefore be able to refer to specific features of the original case that are not present in the case under consideration. This he is able to do in short order. In the original case, he points out, the claim of tawlīj was made by the seller's brother, and witnesses attested that the two brothers hated one another and that the seller had often said that he would not allow his brother to inherit any property from him. Thus there was evidence of an intent to disinherit that is absent from the present case. Wansharisi has already established that, in the absence of such evidence, a presumption must be made in favor of an intent to sell, despite the presence of irregularities.

It must be kept in mind that these two cases—which I have presented in rather abbreviated form without going into the details and intricacies covered in Powers's careful analysis—are intended only as examples. They by no means exhibit the full range of interpretive strategies that a mufti might employ in composing a fatwā. But they do give us an idea of how the juristic authority that has been the subject of this chapter actually worked in the type of fatwā composition that was most typical in the postformative period of the development of Islamic law. In particular, we see from these examples how opinion was, so to speak, stacked upon opinion, as later jurists built upon the labors of their predecessors but not without themselves laboring hard to make the law relevant to the real human problems that they had always to deal with.

It was thus through the fatwā that the jurists' law acquired its social relevance. The mufti played a key role in the actual functioning of the law in society.[13] An individual might consult a mufti purely for personal reasons unrelated to an actual dispute with another person. He might, for example, wish to know how to avoid a conflictual situation or a penalty; or he might wish to know more precisely how to discharge a certain ritual duty, which was strictly a matter between him and God. On the other hand, more often than not the individual would be seeking to resolve a dispute. This he might do entirely outside court, as Ahmad and Fatima try to do when they seek a fatwā in the hope of using it to persuade their cousin of the validity of their claim. The fatwā literature abounds with examples of the use of fatwās in the context of private settlement of disputes.

But the mufti also played a key role in instances in which individuals brought their disputes to a judge. The law applied by Muslim judges—that is to say, by qadis—was always in principle, even if not always in fact, the jurists' law, not a law that emerged out of judicial precedent. The only type of precedent that defines the law in the Shariʿa system is, as we have seen, the earlier opinion or fatwā, used as a basis for the later fatwā. This is not to say that a judge was to pay no attention to previous judicial practice. Any judge, upon assuming office, was expected to take over from his predecessor the records of previous court proceedings. The reason for this was simple. A judge was not to hear a case on which judgment had already been made and therefore needed to have access to court records in the event that they were needed as evidence. But previous judgments were not in themselves, at least not in principle, a source of law. The law applied to previous cases was always presumed to be nothing other than the authoritative law of the jurists, their fiqh. The fatwā, not the judicial record, was the conduit of that law.

Ideally, the Muslim judge is himself a scholar in the law and will apply the jurists' law on the basis of his own expertise in it. In reality, however, judges have seldom possessed such expertise, except perhaps in a limited degree, which accounts for the widespread practice among judges of consulting muftis before making a decision. Accordingly, the role of the mufti extends directly into the sphere of judicial decision making, assuring that juristic authority reigns supreme in what is after all the law's surest means of social effectiveness. The juristic literature, in contrasting the role of muftis and judges, frequently assigns to the judge the role of determining the facts and to the mufti the role of applying the law to those facts. For this reason, the judge must be versed in at least that part of the law that lays down rules of evidence, in particular those relating to the attestation of witnesses and to court procedure.

The role of the mufti was seen to be so vital to the interests of Muslim society that in later Islam governments sometimes officially appointed muftis to advise not only the courts but also society at large on major public issues. It was not uncommon for Muslim governments to seek advice from muftis so appointed even on matters of foreign and domestic policy. The mufti thus became the spokesman for the law of the jurists in a wide variety of contexts, keeping alive among Muslims the conviction that God's will for the conduct of human affairs on earth is after all most reliably represented by that law.

# 7 The Moralistic Bent

Anyone who takes up the study of fiqh literature cannot fail to notice a feature of that literature that I shall call the moralistic bent. Although the law contained in the school manuals, commentaries, and fatwa collections accords a large measure of freedom to human beings and takes pains to safeguard their legitimate rights, the primary emphasis of that law lies not so much on the side of rights and freedom as on the side of duties and constraints. The law is in large measure the conscience of every Muslim—a moral code as well as a legal one, as was pointed out in Chapter 1. It is the path of rectitude—the Shariʿa—an individual must follow in order to achieve happiness in this life and in the life to come. Its most fundamental terms emanate from a primordial covenantal encounter between Lord and subject, between divine Addressor and human addressee, in which all rights belong to the Lord and duties alone belong to the subject. Any rights, any measure of freedom, which the subject may enjoy must have been granted to him or her by the Lord.

Within this perspective, personal freedom is, however, by no means without positive value. The Muslim jurists acknowledge that there is a large sphere in which human beings must be able to conduct their own affairs so as to achieve maximal advantage for themselves. Humans are presumed to be endowed with an intelligence that enables them to define and pursue ends beneficial to themselves, and self-initiated efforts to achieve those ends are seen as indispensable to true self-fulfillment. Though humans are in principle slaves of God, their existence is not meant to be slavish. God's slaves are in many ways self-determining free agents; they are clearly not automatons.

But in all human social life, freedom must have its limits, and Islamic law stands in contrast to the liberalism of the West in the drawing of these limits. The spirit of Islamic law is in the balance more communalistic and directive, less individualistic and facilitative, than that of Western law. The Muslim jurists were animated by a social vision that they firmly believed to be of divine provenance and that they saw the law as always serving. This social vision is implicit in the five cardinal values of the law discussed in Chapter 4: religion, life, offspring, property, and rationality. These values were, of course, normally discussed as topics in their own right in the rather limited context of discussion of analogy and were linked to a specific method of analogical reasoning that not all analogists shared, not to mention the opponents of analogy; and these discussions are found in the literature of uṣūl al-fiqh, not the literature of fiqh. That this is so does not, however, detract from their suitability as indicators of the social vision that animated all the jurists. Those analogists who discussed them systematically, after all, believed them to be firmly rooted in the foundational texts and clearly evident to anyone who reflected deeply upon those texts. Although the specific method of analogy that entailed reference to these values may have been controversial, the values themselves could hardly have been a matter of controversy.

It is significant that while the five values are not universally listed in a particular order, the first and second to be mentioned are usually religion and life. The Arabic term here translated as "religion," namely *dīn*, has a wide range of meanings but generally, at least in the writings of the Muslim jurists and theologians, refers to the total body of beliefs and practices, including ritual practices, to which individuals adhere as a matter of duty toward God and of affiliation with a particular religious community. Dīn comprises in particular the five acts of worship that constitute the famous "pillars" of Islam: confession of faith, ritual prayer, alms, fasting during the month of Ramadan, and pilgrimage to sacred places in the vicinity of Mecca. The specific duties entailed in these acts of worship comprise the ritual law, discussion of which fills the opening chapters of every fiqh book.

Worship is not a realm in which one expects to find the accent on human freedom or rights. In worship one is extolling and serving one's Lord, and in so doing one is expressing one's subordination to the Lord. Worship flows from the realization that one is indeed a creature and subject to the dominion of the Creator. One does not choose this status any more than one chooses who shall be one's Lord or decides whether to have a Lord. In worship one is carried back to the primordial covenantal moment in which all rights lie on the side of the addressing Lord and all duties lie on the side of the addressed subject. Through worship one is keeping one's self and one's life in proper perspective. "Thee do we worship" (*iyyāka naʿbud*), declares the worshiper at the beginning of each of the five daily ritual prayers.

Worship encompasses not only the realm of overt ritual—the physical acts the worshiper performs—but also the inner realm of intention and belief. Without intention (*niyya*) no ritual act is valid. Mind and body must both be involved in serving the Lord. Even the confession of faith—the most pervasive ritual in the entire system of worship and the one must crucial to Muslim identity—has both an outer and inner aspect. One confesses with one's mouth "There is no god but God, and Muhammad is the Messenger of God." But this confession is hypocrisy and sham of the highest order if it is not the expression of genuine inner belief. Belief, the assent of the mind to the verities contained within the confession, is as much a part of worship as the actual recitation of the words of the confession. Again, all is duty. One does not choose what to believe. The truth about God and about his Messenger is not for humans to take or leave. It is man's duty to embrace and declare it. Believers are those who have performed this duty, unbelievers are those who have not. Not only must the two cardinal tenets be embraced; so also must all truths that follow from those tenets. To confess that Muhammad is the Prophet of God is to declare belief in all that the revelation of which he was the bearer contains in the way of teachings about God and his prophets, about history, about the Day of Judgment and the life hereafter.

The pervasiveness of the confession of faith within the Islamic religion is due to its being a vital component of three of the four other pillars of Islam. It is part of the call to prayer voiced by the muezzin from atop the minaret and part of the ritual prayer itself, and since the ritual prayer is an indispensable part of the pious activities that occur during the fast and the pilgrimage, the confession of faith becomes a virtually omnipresent mark of the religion.

This religion is crucial not only to the life of the individual Muslim but to the common life of Muslims as a community. The classical jurists all shared a view of human community that made religion the primary foundation of such community, which they variously called *umma, milla,* or *diyāna.* The last of these terms is in fact a cognate of *dīn.* Religion-based communities are, for classical Muslim authors in general, the primary actors on the stage of history. History is in fact the story of the succession of such communities. The Muslim community is the youngest of these communities and the one destined to remain intact until the Day of Judgment. Preservation of the Islamic religion is thus tantamount to preservation of Muslim community.

The law of the jurists assures the preservation of the Islamic religion in various ways. It does not compel humans to embrace the religion in the sense of providing penal sanctions against those who do not. Whether a non-Muslim chooses to be a Muslim or not is an issue that the law leaves entirely in the realm of private deliberation. But the law clearly gives the religion of Muslims a predominant position within the domain of public life. The social order envisioned by the jurists is a mosaic of religion-based communities—Muslim, Jewish, Christian, Zoroastrian, and others—that live peacefully side by side but in the context of a public life designed to give preeminence to the religion of Muslims. In the cities of the medieval Muslim world, the different religious communities lived in their respective residential quarters; but the public area of the city—the area in which the marketplace and official buildings were located and in which people of all faiths assembled to do business—had a definite Islamic character.

An important symbol of this Islamic character was the congregational mosque, where Friday prayer services were conducted. The main congregational mosque of a city was usually located adjacent to the city's marketplace; it towered over Muslim and non-Muslim alike, although it was a place of worship for Muslims alone. The law made the ruler or his delegate responsible for the holding of Friday services and for seeing to it that shops were closed and business suspended during the services. Anything that interfered with or undermined this all-important collective expression of commitment to the religion of Islam could be subjected to punitive action. Although all other daily performances of the ritual prayer were left to the conscience of the individual Muslim, the Friday congregational prayer was a clear public duty for Muslims, and participation in it could, if the need arose, be enforced. Muslim places of business were to be closed during the Friday service, and offenders could be punished.

Churches, synagogues, and other non-Muslim places of worship were restricted to locations outside the central public areas of the city. Usually they were located in the residential quarters where those who frequented them lived. The law placed restrictions on the building of new non-Muslim places of worship, even though these restrictions were not always enforced. In principle, non-Muslim communities remained constant, while only the community of Muslims was free to grow by way of proselytization. New mosques could therefore be built as needed, but non-Muslim places of worship could for the most part be only repaired or replaced.

To the extent that the law allowed non-Muslims to remain faithful to their ancestral faiths we may say that it granted freedom of religion. But it was a freedom that was subject to many qualifications.[1] Non-Muslims enjoyed the protection of the Muslim state only by virtue of a contractual relationship predicated upon payment of a communal tax. They were not allowed to show disrespect for Islam or for things sacred to Muslims, nor were they permitted to drink wine or eat pork in public. They could not marry Muslim women, ride on horseback, bear arms, perform religious services in a loud voice, or attempt to convert Muslims. Muslims, on the other hand, were not free to change their religion. Any Muslim who renounced Islam and persisted in his renunciation despite efforts to convince him of the truth of Islam and wrongness of his renunciation was subject to the death penalty. Determined apostates posed a serious threat to the religion and could not be allowed to live lest they have a pernicious influence on others.

Warfare was justified entirely with reference to religion. The jurists divided the world between two realms, the abode of Islam and the abode of war. The abode of Islam embraced those areas in which the Muslim community held the reins of power and government was Islamic; the abode of war embraced all other areas. That latter was so named because only in these areas could warfare rightfully be undertaken. Warfare within the abode of Islam amounted to civil strife among Muslims and was anathema to the jurists. Security within the abode of Islam, however, required that the Muslim government exercise policing functions and that rebellions launched by unworthy claimants to power be put down. These functions did not technically constitute warfare in the true sense, for which the Arabic designations were *ḥarb* and *jihād*.

Warfare against non-Muslims living outside the abode of Islam was not only permitted but was a communal duty (*farḍ al-kifāya*). The ultimate objective of all warfare was to incorporate the entire world into the abode of Islam, and until this objective was achieved (if it would ever be), Muslims were duty bound to engage in warfare whenever there was a reasonable prospect of success. Warfare was not, however, a duty that rested upon every Muslim. Rather, it was, as a communal duty, normally discharged by Muslim armies on behalf of the community as a whole. When the prospects of success were poor and the interests of the Muslim community were likely to be jeopardized rather than served by war, it was acceptable for the Muslim government to establish treaties of peace with non-Muslim powers. Such treaties were always to be regarded as temporary, however, since peace could in principle never be permanent until the abode of Islam encompassed the entire world.

Warfare did not necessarily entail fighting. The jurists were very clear in their demand that the Muslim commanding authority issue a call to the enemy either to embrace Islam (which would be tantamount to submission) or to submit as non-Muslims to Muslim rule. If the latter alternative was chosen, the enemy agreed to live within the interreligious Islamic social mosaic and to pay a special tax to the Muslim state in return for a protected status. Ideally, therefore, warfare would produce its desired result peacefully and without bloodshed. Combat was always to be a last resort.[2]

The law of war and peace and the constitutional theory erected by the Muslim jurists thus derive their justification in large part from a social vision in which the Islamic religion formed the foundation of the ideal social order and preservation of that religion was a paramount value. The purpose of war was to make the world safe for Islam, to create (as in the earliest days of Islam), maintain, and enlarge a domain within which the religion of Muslims was secure against malicious forces that might oppose it. True peace was possible only where the religion was secure, in other words, within the abode of Islam.

Preservation of the religion was also assured, on the domestic front, by certain aspects of family law. The Muslim family is well defined in the law of the jurists. All male members and those female members born within the family are necessarily Muslim. Only females who become members through marriage may be non-Muslim, providing they had never previously been Muslim. Although a Muslim man could marry a non-Muslim woman, marriage to a Muslim woman was preferable. A Muslim woman, on the other hand, could under no circumstances marry a non-Muslim man. The structure of family life was essentially patriarchal. A wife's religious affiliation was not nearly as crucial as the husband's, for a wife's role vis-à-vis children was limited to physical nurturing in the early years of life, whereas the responsibility for religious education and upbringing of children belonged solely to the husband and other males of the family. Typically boys—and occasionally girls—began learning to recite the Qur'an shortly after reaching the age of seven. Children learned to perform the duties of worship by observing and imitating their Muslim elders. Inheritance law—a subject to which we will return shortly—made provision only for Muslim members of the family.

"Life" is my rendering of the Arabic term *nafs,* which embraces a host of meanings including "self," "psyche," "soul," "animus," "living being." It is not life in an abstract biological sense that is meant by *nafs* but rather the life of the individual person. There can obviously be no worship, no religion, without living worshipers. Unlike sharīʿa, which has God as its subject, dīn (religion) has the human as its subject. In order for dīn to be preserved, nafs must therefore be preserved.

This second cardinal value of the law lies at the core of much of the family law.[3] Life begins in the midst of the family. A newborn child is an utterly dependent being; if its life is to be preserved, responsible adults must provide food, clothing, and shelter. These three necessities are what the Muslim law of maintenance (*nafaqa*) is meant to guarantee. This law of maintenance presupposes a patriarchal family structure. Only adult male members of the family are expected to be fully independent beings capable of maintaining themselves without assistance from others. But their duty under the law includes maintenance not only of themselves but also of dependent members of the family, that is to say, children as well as adult females.

Both children and adult females may be owners of property and recipients of income derived from property. This ability does not, however, diminish their right to maintenance, since they are assumed not to be in a position to earn an ongoing livelihood. For them property is a security against future need. The proper place of children and adult females is in the home. Home is the setting in which children grow up and in which adult females provide for their basic needs. Adult females are thus nurturers and providers of care in an environment of food, clothing, and shelter supplied by adult males. Adult males are themselves also recipients of this care. Normally, adult females are members of the Muslim family by virtue of marriage, although where a daughter does not marry after reaching adulthood she retains her right to maintenance by her father until she does marry. Divorced adult females may also return to the families of their parents with a right to maintenance.

But the life of the individual not only must be sustained by means of food, clothing, and shelter but must also be protected against those who would extinguish it without just cause, in other words, would-be murderers. Here again the setting of the patriarchal family is decisive, for the Muslim law of homicide operates within this setting. Homicide does not belong within the domain of criminal law, strictly speaking; it is not an offense against society as such calling for public prosecution.[4] Rather, it belongs under the rubric of a *lex talionis* in which the family unit—or, more precisely, the *ʿāqila*, which comprises certain male agnates—is the primary actor; it is an offense against the family, and the family must decide how to deal with it. The *talio* is a right, not a duty, and the family—more specifically a near male relative of the victim acting on behalf of the family—may or may not exercise it, although in the normal course of events it predictably will. The slogan of the lex talionis as it relates to homicide is "a life for a life," although the victim's family may elect to receive blood money in lieu of the life of the offender. Forgiveness is also an option for the victim's family.

The talio gives the family the right to demand the death penalty but does not empower the family to execute it without due process. The proper implementation of the death penalty is the responsibility of the state, as is the review of evidence and the determination of guilt. The courts' role in homicide cases is thus more civil than criminal. They uphold and enforce private decisions of families.

Within the setting of patriarchal family life as envisioned by the Muslim jurists, the talio operates as a highly effective deterrent to homicide and as a means of preserving life. Every individual, including the one inclined to take the life of another, is part of a tightly knit extended family unit. The murderer therefore does not act alone but rather represents his family in an act inimical to another family, for the victim too represents a family. All human life is embedded in the web of kinship. Just as the family cradles life during the crucial years of its formation, so it affords protection of life throughout the longer span of time between birth and natural death. When one kills without cause, one therefore is as much accountable to one's own family, which incurs responsibility for appropriate action, as to the family of the victim. Therein lies the deterrent force of the talio within a society founded on ties of kinship.

Muslim family law bristles with the spirit of moral directiveness, and concern for the preservation of the life of the individual in large measure explains why. Only the patriarchal extended family can function with optimal effectiveness as the cradle and safe haven of human life. Any restructuring of the family along other lines can be said most assuredly to be contrary to the spirit of Islamic law. Family life requires a hierarchy in which females and children are under the authority of males, although males must exercise that authority responsibly and with kindness. Males are endowed with the mental and physical qualities that suit them for this role. The same qualities that make for success in earning a livelihood in the world outside the family equip males to provide leadership and direction within the family. Within the nuclear unit, it is the husband/father who provides this leadership; within the larger extended family, adult males form a hierarchy in which leadership is exercised by the more senior males. (A woman, it should be noted, remains part of her original biological family inasmuch as her father or brother still functions as protector of her interests.)

The law's commitment to maintaining the integrity of the extended family is especially apparent in the lex talionis, which we have just discussed, as well as in the law of inheritance, a salient feature of which is the restriction of bequests to one-third of an estate. Muslim inheritance law works on the principle of fixed shares, and while first consideration goes to members of the nuclear family, other relatives as well are assured entitlements in amounts and under conditions stipulated by the law and calculated according to a highly complex system. A person facing death cannot dispose of his earthly goods as he pleases; the interests of the family take precedence over his personal wishes.

The law presupposes that membership in a family is a natural condition among humans and that individuals will rarely become totally bereft of family connections. When this unlikely condition does occur as a result of warfare, plague, or other disasters and the individual is without the means to sustain life, as can occur especially in the case of orphans and widows, he or she then comes under the care of the community as a whole by virtue of an entitlement to a share in goods donated for charitable purposes. The law guarantees that a certain level of provision for such unfortunate persons will always be available by imposing on those with means the duty of *zakāt*, a progressive tax on merchandise or wealth the revenue from which is designated for partly charitable or religious purposes. Otherwise the law leaves the welfare of these persons in the hands of voluntary benefactors on the supposition that benevolence will always be for Muslims a supreme form of piety. The Qur'an itself, in innumerable passages, makes it clear that those who from their wealth provide for the destitute attain greater closeness to God.

Closely allied to the life of the individual as a value that the law seeks to preserve is progeny (*nasal*). Humans not only live their own lives in this world; through sexual reproduction they give rise to lives other than their own. Although some individuals may not marry, the classical jurists considered marriage to be the normal ultimate state of human beings, and they saw marriage as inevitably resulting under normal circumstances in offspring. Through progeny human life—and with it the worship of God and communal life of the faithful—continues from generation to generation. To the extent that the law is concerned with the preservation of life across generations, it is bound to be concerned with the preservation of progeny.

But progeny is more than a mere continuation of life across generations considered in the abstract. Progeny is always the progeny of particular persons. Just as one has one's own life to consider, one's *nafs,* so one must give consideration to one's offspring, or *nasal.* In keeping with the patriarchal structure of the family, progeny is reckoned in patrilineal terms. It is the man who has *nasal,* not the woman. The woman is the necessary partner in procreation, but the offspring is reckoned to be the man's. The justification for this patriarchalism has already been intimated.

Preservation of the patrilineal progeny requires first of all that procreation occur solely within the bounds of legal marriage. A social order in which men and women could have sexual intercourse freely and at will was unthinkable to the classical jurists. In such a situation men would be unable to identify their offspring, and chaos and corruption of human life would ensue. Nowhere in the fiqh literature is the moralistic bent of the jurists more evident than in the sections that deal with marriage and sexual behavior. Marriage is for them largely a means of regulating human procreation in such a way that the identification of offspring and assignment of responsibility for nurture and maintenance will be assured. Since paternity is presumptive, the law must lay down the conditions for a valid presumption. Decisions about paternity cannot be left to the whims of individuals.

Marriage is the all-important ground for a presumption of paternity. According to the commonly accepted rule, a man is presumed to be the father of a child if the child is known to have been born to his wife at least six months after their marriage. This presumption holds even if he did not have access to her during the time when she was likely to have become pregnant. Where the child's birth occurs within the first six months of marriage or there is doubt about the time of its occurrence, the husband's acknowledgment of paternity prevails over any presumption of illegitimacy provided that a valid rebuttal of the acknowledgment, such as proof of the nonoccurrence of the marriage, is not made. Thus the law in effect reduces the incidences of illegitimacy, avoiding the undesirable consequences that the illegitimacy of the child has for child and parents. In the event that the illegitimacy of the child is established, however, harm to the child is mitigated by the fact that the child becomes affiliated with the mother's family, which must assume responsibility for its care.

Extramarital and premarital sexual intercourse—the accursed and much dreaded *zinā*—so threatens the patrilineal system of family relations that the law imposes the harshest imaginable sanctions against it, namely death by stoning for offenders who are or have been married and flogging for offenders who as yet have never been married.[5] Here the talio is entirely inoperative. The punishment in this case is fixed by the law and cannot be altered in any way or withdrawn. The families of the offenders play no role. In the classification of the jurists, it is an offense against God himself, and the punishment is divinely ordained. A proven murderer thus has, at least in principle, a better chance of averting punishment than does the proven sexual offender.

As is well known, the rules of evidence that apply to conviction of unlawful sexual intercourse make it extremely difficult to prove that such an offense has occurred. Among the restrictions is the well-known requirement that four duly qualified upright witnesses be able to testify to having visually observed the actual coitus, the man's penetration of the woman. Considering that false accusation of unlawful intercourse is punishable by flogging and that any accusation that cannot be supported by the above-mentioned type of evidence is considered false, one is given to understand that the punishments stipulated by the law were seldom actually applied. Nonetheless, the harshness of the punishment constitutes a statement in and of itself—a statement of the heinousness of the offense and of the law's extreme abhorrence of it. We must also bear in mind that where there is a suspicion (as opposed to formal proof) of unlawful intercourse, the law of the jurists allows judges to establish discretionary punishments—in contrast to the fixed punishments mentioned above—for sexual misconduct other than actual intercourse, in respect to which the rules of evidence are not so prohibitive.

Since the law views sexual intercourse outside marriage with such abhorrence, it adopts a highly regulatory and moralistic position regarding relations between the sexes. Without denying that men may be sexual objects in the eyes of women, it is more concerned with women as sexual objects in the eyes of men. Men need to be in the world outside the home for purposes of work or doing business. Therefore women should remain in their homes as much as possible, venturing out only when there is a strong necessity for doing so and always with the permission of their husbands and in the company of a male relative. When they do leave their homes, women must be dressed in a modest fashion dictated by the law.

The regulations regarding dress constitute an especially telling part of the law as it bears on relations between the sexes. In many of the fiqh works, the subject of dress is dealt with under the heading of "looking" (*naẓar*):[6] what a man is permitted or forbidden to see of the body of a woman and what a woman is permitted or forbidden to see of the body of a man. Both men and women are, as the preceding words imply, subject to a dress code. This code, however, requires a more extensive covering of the female body than of the male body. The operative concept in the dress code is that of *ʿawra,* which may best be translated as "private area." In a public setting, the area of a man's body designated as private by most jurists extends from just below the navel to just below the knee, whereas the private area of a woman's body includes all parts except the face and palms. The jurists make it clear that they regard looking at the body of a member of the opposite sex as a stimulus to sexual desire. Since sexual desire (*shahwa*) is allowable only in the context of marriage, the dress code serves the purpose of keeping desire where it belongs and preventing it from occurring elsewhere.

In a public setting, dress restrictions are maximal. The jurists in fact define the private area of a woman's body differently for different categories of persons that might be in her company. In the public setting, she is exposed to men unrelated to her, men in whose eyes she might be a prospect for marriage. In relation to such men, she is defined as a "stranger" (*ajnabiyya*). The obligation to avoid stimulation of sexual desire among men and women who are strangers to each other rests equally upon the two sexes; men should not be looking at strange women and women should not allow themselves to be looked at by strange men. The dress code is the law's way of facilitating adherence to this norm. On the other hand, the law is not so restrictive as to prevent a woman, provided she adheres to the dress code, from venturing out of her house to conduct business or to testify or litigate in a court.

Within the home, things are different. A woman here will not be in contact with strange men but only with men who are unmarriageable to her as well as with women and children. In such a setting, the private area of a woman's body diminishes, but certain parts should still not be seen. Here the concern is not so much with arousal of sexual desire as with propriety. Persons whom she may not marry are presumed not to experience sexual desire for her and may therefore freely enter her company. Only in the company of a husband is no part of the woman's body private, just as no part of his body is private.

Preservation of a person's life and progeny is thus largely the function of the patriarchal family, for which reason the law carefully regulates family life and relations between the sexes. But no individual or family can survive without a reasonable assurance that the necessities of life—food, shelter, clothing—will be available. This assurance is provided by the institution of property, the fourth core value of Islamic law. Just as the jurists cannot conceive of the primary responsibility for nurturing and protecting human life from birth to death as falling on any institution but the family, so they cannot conceive of the wherewithal for this responsibility as secured by any means other than private property. Preservation of private property is thus crucial to the social order envisioned by the jurists. Individuals must be able to have full control over resources vital to their existence and must be assured that others cannot deprive them of those resources arbitrarily against their will. In no way can communal or public property or resources take the place of private ones. Islamic law is a law strongly committed to the inviolability of the private sphere as the proper context for the living of human life.

Baber Johansen has emphasized the fact that in Islamic law the individual proprietor is the prototype of the legal person.[7] The society envisioned by the jurists is not only a society of family members; it is also a society of proprietors. The legal person is the one capable of bearing rights and obligations, preeminent among which is the right of property and the obligations that have to do with property. From the point of view of the law, the world contains two complementary categories: proprietors and property. The proprietors are the human beings; property potentially embraces everything in the world that is not human with few exceptions. Slaves, it is true, have some of the attributes of property, but these attributes are not intrinsic to their nature as humans. When they are manumitted, they regain their full human essence as proprietors. As a leading jurist of the Hanafi school declared: "The human being was originally created to be a proprietor."[8] It is thus unnatural for a human being to be other than a proprietor.

The proprietor is always an individual. Islamic law does not know the concept of the corporate person and therefore does not allow property to be owned by legal entities presided over by a changing personnel. It does provide for joint ownership,[9] although it treats this arrangement strictly as a convergence of rights of individuals. Within the family, ownership by a single individual is the rule. A wife typically has property separate from the property of her husband; and children too may acquire their own property, and although the property is placed under the guardianship of the father, this is done in a manner that protects that property from misuse by the father. Inheritance law is designed to divide property among heirs in the form of separate shares.

In order to maximize the benefits they receive from their properties, the human proprietors must be able to enter into exchange relationships. No individual can at any given time be in possession of all the things required to meet basic needs or to enhance the quality of life. An important function of property, therefore, is to serve as the means whereby one can acquire goods and amenities through exchange. Involvement in exchange relations is therefore by definition a part of human proprietorship.

The law makes generous provisions for the facilitation of beneficial exchange transactions. Contracts of exchange in fact are a major preoccupation of the jurists, and discussions of this subject fill many pages in the books of fiqh.[10] It must be remembered that Islamic law was developed at a time when commercial life was rapidly expanding. The Arab conquests in the seventh and eighth centuries had the effect of mobilizing material resources and creating new and unprecedented opportunities for trade within a vast area blessed with relatively peaceful conditions and safe roads. Many of the jurists themselves were merchants or tradesmen or came from families engaged in trade or crafts and brought to their study of law a natural interest in matters related to the marketplace.

Fundamental to Muslim juristic thinking about contracts of exchange is the principle of the just exchange, or the exchange of items having equivalent market values. The market value of any item is understood to be variable and to depend on current market conditions. Typically, the exchanges the jurists have in mind are exchanges of goods for money, in other words sales in the ordinary sense of that term. The just exchange is thus typically the sale/purchase of a commodity at a fair market price. By insisting on a fair price and on equivalent values of items exchanged, the jurists seek to assure that no individual will have an advantage over another individual in the marketplace. Muslim contract law displays a marked abhorrence of exploitation. When God's creatures trade with one another, they must adhere to the principle of balance; no one's gain should be another's loss, and vice versa. Property is a sacred trust, the foundation of human life and well-being, and must not be jeopardized through unfair dealings.

This is not to say that profitable enterprises are disallowed. But such enterprises are defined as resale and presuppose a wholesale-retail relationship. One may purchase an item and then sell it at a profit, provided that the profit is fair. Again, fairness is determined by current market conditions. If the original purchase is a purchase of raw materials for the production of finished goods, one may include expenditures on human labor in the cost to which profit is added. The final transaction remains under the heading of resale for profit. In such a transaction the profit earned by the vendor is seen to be balanced by some sort of advantage to the buyer such as convenience or readier access to the commodity.

It is in their discussions of unlawful gain, the Arabic term for which is *ribā*, that the moralistic bent of the jurists becomes especially pronounced.[11] Although this term is frequently translated as usury, its meaning is somewhat broader. The loan of a sum of money with a charge for interest is seen as a type of exchange in which a given sum of money is exchanged for a larger sum of money with a delay in the completion of the exchange. Essentially the same type of exchange occurs when a given amount of wheat, for example, is exchanged for a larger sum of wheat with a delay in the completion of the exchange. Here too there is for all practical purposes a loan with interest.

Since exchanges were classified as ribā with reference to the items exchanged, the jurists, instead of attempting to produce exhaustive lists of ribā-occasioning categories of items, focused on broader characteristics. The Hanafi jurists, for example, considered items in an exchange to be ribā-occasioning if they were (1) fungible in relation to each other, as when gold is exchanged for gold or wheat for wheat, and (2) either weighable (as is gold) or measurable by volume (as is wheat). The other schools defined the decisive characteristics somewhat differently. Behind these juristic discussions was a desire to enable persons to distinguish the unlawful ribā exchange from the lawful mutually beneficial exchange and the lawful loan. Where items exchanged exhibited the characteristics that defined ribā-occasioning items, the advantage enjoyed by one of the parties to the exchange seemed to the jurists not to be balanced by a significant advantage to the other party. In the case of nonfungible items, this problem of imbalance would tend to be less obvious. One can also detect behind the scruples of the jurists a basic apprehensiveness about profiteering on what amounted to loans of items most vital to human well-being.

Not only was unfair advantage of one of the parties eschewed by the jurists; so also was uncertainty regarding the item received in an exchange, that is to say, the consideration. It is important to understand that the uncertainty here under consideration is an uncertainty deliberately built into a contract of exchange, a man-made uncertainty. It arises from the fact that the consideration is not exactly specified but is made contingent upon factors over which the parties have no control. An important rule of Muslim contract law is that the consideration must be *maʿlūm*, "known," "defined," "fixed in advance." Under this rule, gambling is strictly forbidden, as is speculation when it entails payment of money for an undetermined return.

Lawful profitable enterprises, which, as we have noted, are placed under the rubric of resale for profit, entail of course a degree of risk, and the Hanafi law permits investment partnerships that allow several people to combine their capital for the purpose of investment in such enterprises while at the same time sharing the risk.[12] But in this case the risk is not due to uncertainty within the exchanges themselves. When one or several people purchase goods for the purpose of resale, the items exchanged both in the original purchase and in the resale are defined in the contract. The risk is due to factors over which the parties have no control. If, for example, they invest in the purchase of tapestries and in the transporting of those goods via caravan, a number of unforeseen events may occur between the purchase of the tapestries and hire of the caravan on the one hand and the sale of the tapestries in the distant market on the other. The caravan may be waylaid and robbed or destroyed by an earthquake, or the prices in the distant market may so fluctuate as to result in an overall loss. But such are the vicissitudes of life. They are quite unlike the uncertainty and risk that humans may deliberately impose upon themselves or each other by means of ill-conceived, indeterminate contracts.

If unfair advantage, exploitation, and uncertainty in transactions pertaining to property were abhorrent to the Muslim jurists, the wrongful appropriation of property and damage to property were all the more so. The especially heinous offense known as *sariqa* (usually translated as "theft") was made subject to the grim penalty of amputation of the hand.[13] (In Chapter 5 we considered the hermeneutical issues surrounding this penalty.) As with the penalty of stoning for adultery, however, this penalty was subject to highly restrictive conditions that rendered its application difficult from a procedural point of view and rare in actual occurrence. The penalty could be applied only if the theft had occurred in a private home or guarded place and the thief had been apprehended after having both entered *and left* the place in a stealthy manner. Furthermore, the value of the stolen item had to be above a certain amount, and the thief must not have stolen out of genuine need. Nonetheless, despite these restrictions, the penalty of amputation constituted, like the penalty of stoning, a pronouncement of the law on the extreme heinousness of an offense deemed to be highly injurious to the vital interests of human beings. Just as the law was willing to take an extreme measure to assure that procreation remained within the bounds of legal marriage, so the law was willing to take an extreme measure to assure that the transfer of possession of property occurred within the bounds of legal transactions.

Armed entry of private homes with the intent of robbery was placed in a separate category that also included highway robbery, the category of brigandage (*qaṭʿ al-ṭarīq*). The penalty for brigandage was even more severe: amputation of a hand and foot. Highways served largely as trade routes, and the severity of this penalty indicates the degree to which the jurists regarded safety from armed attack both in travel and while at home as vital to human well-being.

The last of the five cardinal values of the law is *ʿaql*, human rationality. In their dealings with one another—their commercial transactions, their disposal of property, their marrying of one another, their conduct of family life—as well as in their engagement in the acts of worship, human beings must be in full possession of their rational powers. Sanity is in fact a condition of validity of human transactions. Retarded and mentally ill persons are therefore barred from entering into transactions. The sane must accordingly not be allowed to jeopardize their sanity unnecessarily. The law consequently seeks to protect sound minds against all those things that would temporarily and unnecessarily inhibit their functioning.

The clearest expression of the law's abhorrence of irrationality is to be found in the famed penalty for drinking khamr (wine), a flogging of eighty lashes. The majority of jurists, as we have earlier noted, used the method of analogy to apply the prohibition along with the penalty to intoxicating beverages in general. The drinking of such beverages was included among the six offenses considered to be offenses against God and society and as punishable, therefore, by the public authorities without any demand from private parties (talio). The other five offenses have already been considered in this chapter: unlawful sexual intercourse, false accusation of unlawful sexual intercourse, theft, highway robbery, and apostasy.

Most jurists considered the drinking of any amount of an intoxicant to be forbidden and punishable by flogging, even an amount insufficient to cause actual inebriation. This attitude has in fact been the most commonly held position among Muslims in general down to the present time. The drinking of a small amount, on this view, paved the way to drinking of larger amounts, and any act that might lead to a definite offense was an offense in itself. Within the Hanafi school, however, a minority view allowed the drinking of intoxicants other than khamr in moderation, that is, up to the point where inebriation occurred. Only the drinking of khamr was forbidden wholesale, since it alone was specifically forbidden by name in the Qur'an. Among the jurists who held this view, the principal interpretive issues had to do with the definition and criteria of inebriation.[14]

Thus far in this chapter we have discussed the principal manifestations of what I have called the moralistic bent of the Muslim jurists. No discussion of this topic can, however, be considered complete without some mention of two important features of Muslim juristic doctrine that may at first blush seem inconsistent with the moralism we have been exploring but in fact are not, at least in my view. The first of these features is the tendency of the jurists to extend the notion of legal validity to a certain range of morally dubious acts. A good example is provided by Muslim divorce law. A saying attributed to the prophet Muhammad affirms that "of all things legally permissible divorce is the most detestable."[15] Not only was divorce in general morally repugnant in the eyes of the jurists; certain divorce procedures countenanced by the law were more repugnant than others. At the bottom of the scale was the procedure in which a man unilaterally divorces his wife by uttering the divorce formula, "I divorce you," three times on a single occasion rather than monthly over a period of three months, as was preferred. The Hanafi jurists castigated this procedure as deviant and pronounced the man who used this procedure a wrongdoer.

And yet even this most despicable of procedures was granted legal validity. In order to understand how the Muslim jurists could at the same time condemn and grant legal validity to a human action or transaction, it is necessary to recall a point discussed in the first chapter of this book. The jurists had multiple categories to work with. An act might be morally repugnant without being forbidden, just as an act might be morally desirable without being required or obligatory. "Forbidden" and "obligatory," we must remember, were categories belonging to both the moral domain and the legal. Any act that was legally forbidden was also morally forbidden. It could not be otherwise, since God was the one who forbade and what God forbade could not but be forbidden both legally and morally. The categories "desirable" and "repugnant" (or, to employ the terms used in Chapter 1, "recommended" and "disapproved"), on the other hand, must be regarded as belonging to the domain of morality alone.

To speak of a human act as repugnant while at the same time granting it legal validity keeps legal validity within the realm of the legally permissible (*jā'iz* or *halāl* as distinct from *mubāḥ*). In the Islamic system of categories, forbidden and permitted are contraries; repugnant and permitted are not. We must not fail to appreciate the enormous gap that separates the repugnant from the forbidden in the Islamic system. The repugnant, unlike the forbidden, entails no liability to punishment in this world or the next. It is neither a legal offense nor a moral sin. Rather it is a sort of moral shortcoming, a failure to achieve moral excellence.

The fact that the jurists made extensive use of the categories "repugnant" and "desirable" (or "disapproved" and "recommended") shows just how seriously they took their role as moralists-cum-jurists within Muslim society. When an act that was permissible and legally valid entailed a compromise of piety, a falling short of higher levels of moral excellence, the jurists took pains to point this out. The categories in question gave them the opportunity to make moral declarations beyond the sphere of law in the strict sense. It especially gave them the opportunity, when faced with acts whose moral quality they questioned but whose validity seemed to be a matter of social necessity, to grant validity to such acts while keeping their own moral integrity intact. Whether an act was forbidden or merely repugnant could become, for the jurists, a difficult hermeneutical issue, and the debates we find in the fiqh literature over this issue as it pertains to particular acts could be charged with enormous significance for a school's or individual jurist's doctrine.

But in some cases the jurists appear to grant validity even to acts that are forbidden. Here legal validity is obviously *not* kept within the realm of the legally permissible. Schacht speaks of a tendency of the jurists to fuse validity with permissibility and invalidity with forbiddenness but then notes that this fusion did not always obtain.[16] It seems that the jurists were uncomfortable with the thought that an act might at the same time be valid and forbidden inasmuch as they sought to get around this anomaly by showing that "valid" and "forbidden" apply to different aspects of an act or situation. To cite Schacht's example: in the case of a sale concluded at the time of the call to the Friday prayer, the sale as such is distinguished from the act of concluding it at that particular time. The former is valid, the latter forbidden; the vendor's property is transferred to the buyer, but the parties are liable to punishment, in the world to come, if not in this world, for having concluded the sale when they did. But even in the rare cases where such a distinction is not made and a forbidden act appears to be declared valid, the moralistic spirit of the jurists remains, I think, uncompromised. At least it can be said that in such cases the forbiddenness of the act is not allowed to slip out of view. To the contrary, the jurists take pains to call attention to it. Furthermore, there could sometimes be ways of justifying legal validity without diminishing the forbiddenness of an act.

In some cases the jurists leave the forbidden aspect of an otherwise valid or permissible act in the domain of a person's relationship to God without carrying it into the domain of law. As I noted in Chapter 1, "forbidden" is a legal category only to the extent that it is relevant to the judicial process and enforceable by means of sanctions supplied by the state. In cases where these criteria do not obtain, "forbidden" becomes a purely moral category. Thus to the extent that the conclusion of a sale during the call to prayer on Friday is punishable not in this world but only in the world to come, it is a purely moral offense and not a legal one.

Baber Johansen gives several examples from Hanafi literature in which the jurists consciously leave forbidden aspects of otherwise legally valid arrangements within the domain of a morality lying beyond the realm of the law.[17] One of these relates to the contract of sharecropping (*muzāraʿa*), in which a landlord supplies land and seed and the cultivator supplies labor. According to Hanafi doctrine, the landowner has the right to withdraw from the contract any time prior to the sowing of the seed, in which case the cultivator has no contractual entitlement to compensation for the labor expended on plowing and preparing the soil for seeding. As Johansen explains, labor is not a commodity in Hanafi law. The landlord does have, however, according to the jurists, a duty *before God* to compensate the cultivator for his labor, even though he has no duty to do so under the terms of the contract. Since neglect of duty is forbidden, one can say that in the eyes of God the landlord is forbidden to withdraw from the contract without compensating the cultivator. To the extent that the jurists regard a landlord as facing the consequences of noncompensation in the world to come and not in this world, they are leaving the matter in the realm of a morality with which law in the strict sense is not concerned.

In a second example cited by Johansen, an individual who has wrongfully appropriated land belonging to someone else enters into a contract of lease with a third party. Despite the invalidity of his claim to the land, the lessor nonetheless enjoys under Hanafi law an entitlement to the rental income from the land, not the true landlord, the reason being that he, and not the landlord, entered into the contract with the lessee. But if the lessor is a God-fearing person, he will not keep the rental income for himself, since he has a duty before God to donate the income to charity. If he fails to perform this duty, then again, as in the first example, he will face the consequences in the world beyond. The matter, again, is left in the domain of a morality that is beyond the pale of the law.

In both of these examples, what the contract law does not require—compensation of the laborer, donation of rental income to charity—*is* required morally. This is not to say that contract law is not itself a part of the divinely ordained moral system. It is, and the Qur'an itself makes it clear that God expects people to abide by their contractual commitments and that those who do not will face consequences in the world beyond quite apart from the consequences that they may face in this world. But where contracts do not confer duties, or where they confer rights, a morality that is beyond the law may intervene, imposing duties or superseding rights. By going to great lengths to point out the full moral implications of human acts, including those that lie beyond the realm of law, the jurists remain true to the moralistic spirit under discussion in this chapter.

The second feature of Muslim juristic doctrine that may seem to call this moralism into question is the willingness in certain instances—and particularly in the case of the Hanafi jurists—to resort to "legal devices" (*ḥiyal*) in order to circumvent prohibitions of the law. These legal devices can seem to the casual observer to be a way of permitting the forbidden. The jurists who developed them, however, would surely have insisted that they were not in fact permitting the forbidden, since to provide a way to circumvent the forbidden is not to permit it. Their reasoning can best be understood from the most commonly cited example of such a legal device. We have noted that the taking of interest on a loan (ribā) was strictly forbidden by the jurists. Yet some such arrangement was clearly vital to commercial life in medieval Islam, and Muslim merchants in fact charged interest on loans on a wide scale. In order to keep within the letter of the prohibition while at the same time facilitating the practice of the merchants, jurists commonly condoned the so-called double sale (*bayʿatān fī bayʿa*), which accomplished the same result as ribā without actually constituting ribā from a strictly technical point of view. According to this arrangement, one person sold a particular object to another person at a certain price; then immediately he bought the object back from the other person at a greater price payable at some future time. As Joseph Schacht has noted, the ribā transaction was thus replaced with two separate transactions, each in itself perfectly permissible, the combination of which produced the same result as the forbidden transaction.[18]

According to Schacht, the jurists developed hundreds of such legal devices, which covered a wide range of human transactions. Many of them were extremely complex, requiring the expertise of specialists, and whole treatises were devoted to them. Commonly, students of Islamic law regard them as a way of honoring the letter of the law while achieving a result that is out of keeping with its spirit. Schacht described the legal devices as "legal means for [achieving] extra-legal ends."[19] It is therefore tempting to see in these devices an accommodationist spirit that dilutes the moralistic trend that we have been considering.

In reality, however, the concern not to violate the letter of the law and to keep its prohibitions intact reflects a recognition of the sacredness of the law that lies at the very heart of the moralism of the Muslim jurists. Although the title of this book may suggest that our interest in these pages is in the spirit of the law considered as something that overrides the mere letter, the fact of the matter is that for the jurists, letter and spirit can never be in genuine conflict if by "letter" one means the clear, unambiguous pronouncements of the authoritative texts and if by "spirit" one means a divinely ordained principle derivable from those same texts. In any case, the Arabic of the jurists includes no set of twin terms that carries a history of meaning quite like that of "letter" and "spirit," the usage of which in the West has no doubt been heavily influenced by St. Paul. Accordingly, the notion of a "spirit of the law" in this book does not entail an opposition between spirit and letter. It can be argued, I think, that insistence upon conformity to the dictates of the texts upon which the law is based is an integral part of that juristic mentality that we are here calling the "spirit of Islamic law."

But a jurist—and the layperson guided by him—often has choices. The Qur'an, in the same verse in which it forbids the taking of interest, explicitly permits buying and selling, thus setting up a contrast between unlawful *ribā* and lawful *bay*ʿ. If one and the same transaction can be reasonably classified either as a single transaction entailing a taking of interest, or as a combination of two separate transactions each constituting a legitimate sale, and if the latter classification seems in a given situation to be in the best interests of the parties concerned, then no compromise of the moralistic bent is entailed in the choice of the latter classification. The authors of the many legal devices that we find in Muslim jurisprudential literature surely did not see themselves as deliberately setting aside prohibitions of the law or as engaging in interpretive trickery or deception. Rather, they were, as all Muslim jurists routinely do, exploring alternative ways of looking at particular human transactions.

But is it not the case that the jurists saw the prohibition against usury and kindred transactions (*ribā*) as serving the cause of preservation of property and prevention of exploitation? Were not, then, those jurists who created the legal device of the double sale undermining one of the cardinal purposes of the law? Here it is important for us to recall how the notion of cardinal purposes worked for the jurists. We have in this chapter used the widely accepted five purposes of the law as a framework for exploring the moralistic outlook of the Muslim jurists, and I have no doubt that this has been a valid procedure. We must remember, however, a point made in an earlier chapter: the five purposes were not themselves, for most jurists, principles upon which one could directly base a judgment about a particular case. At most, they were considerations that a jurist could use in seeking to determine which feature of a case was the "cause" (*ʿilla*) of the rule governing that case, and some jurists were not willing to give the five purposes even this role.

The five purposes of the law have in this chapter helped us understand the social vision that animated the Muslim jurists and undergirded their moralism. This moralism, however, remains in the final analysis a moralism of obedience to the will of the one God and Lord of the universe. Inductive examination of the foundational texts could lead to the conviction that God's design was to effect the realization of a social order predicated upon preservation of religion, life, progeny, property, and rationality. But God knew best how to implement these purposes through concrete rules; it was not for man to create such rules. Faithfulness not only to God's purposes but also to God's rules was the best course for the jurist to follow. If a given transaction could be classified either as a loan with interest or as a double sale and the latter classification was chosen as the one most propitious in a given situation, no disobedience had occurred. A jurist might, in keeping with an animus shared by all jurists, abhor exploitation but remain convinced that a given transaction capable of classification either as usurious lending or double sale entailed no exploitation and in fact best served the interests of proprietors in the marketplace. Both the rule forbidding ribā and the rule permitting sales (including double sales) were, after all, rules of divine law in the thinking of the jurists who accepted the device of the double sale. God knew best which rule applied in a given case, and it was the toilsome task of the jurist to read the mind of God to the best of his ability.

# 8 Private and Public Dimensions of the Law

A cursory look at the chapter headings of a typical fiqh work and at the number of pages encompassed by the various chapters reveals a striking feature of Muslim juristic doctrine, namely the far greater attention and care given to matters of private law than to matters of public law. This is not to say that the jurists were uninterested in the latter. To the contrary, they were well aware of the importance of public interests and of the role of government in safeguarding and promoting those interests. But their discussions of matters of public law are interspersed among much more extensive discussions of private law issues, and furthermore these discussions are marked by an interest in public law only insofar as it impinges upon the lives of private individuals. In the realm of private law the jurists strove to be as comprehensive as possible. The drive toward comprehensiveness is not evident in the discussions of public law matters.

This contrast may be due to the circumstances under which the jurists originally began to develop the law. When the earlier juristic circles first emerged, the Islamic imperial edifice—the caliphate—was already in place and was governed by administrative, military, and criminal regulations that were either elaborated in the wake of the conquests or inherited from the preceding imperial regimes. As was noted in Chapter 1, the Umayyad caliphs took their role as builders of a new Islamic governmental order very seriously. Accordingly, they exercised energetic control over public law and policy. The early jurists, on the other hand, found themselves primarily caught up in issues relating to private disputes. The role socially cut out for them was, generally speaking, that of advisers to private individuals, not to persons of power and authority.

As a result, a kind of bifurcation took place in the development of public and private law. On the one hand, the Islamic imperial regime forged the institutions and administrative rules it needed, some of which came squarely within the purview of the jurists and some of which did so only tangentially or not at all. On the other hand, the jurists fashioned a predominantly civil law, incorporating only those elements of public law that they saw as vital to the Shariʿa-based legal order of which they were the expositors. In the fiqh literature as such, we find discussions of penal law, fiscal law, the law of war (*siyar*), judicial administration (but only as it relates to the qadi), and the status of non-Muslims living under Muslim rule. But the discussions are far from exhaustive or systemic, and the focus is generally on aspects of these topics affecting the interests of private individuals. Individuals are presumed, for example, to want to know what actions constitute punishable offenses and what the punishments are so as to avoid them. Taxes are discussed largely in terms of how they are to be distributed and whom they are to benefit. Rules governing warfare are discussed on the grounds that participation in military campaigns is a potential duty of every Muslim and that a knowledge of the rules is therefore in his interests. The strictly administrative side of these components of public law is only scantily dealt with, if at all.

Constitutional organization as such was a matter of great interest to the Muslim jurists, although we do not find discussions of it in the classical fiqh manuals. The primary places for such discussion were two: chapters of theological *summae*[1] and treatises devoted especially to the subject, the classic and most renowned of these treatises being "The Principles of Government" (*al-Aḥkām al-Sulṭāniyya*) of al-Mawardi. The inclusion of constitutional organization within the purview of theology tells us something of great importance about the attitude of jurists—especially those who looked with favor on theological discourse and participated in it to some extent—toward this subject. The discipline of theology dealt with matters considered most fundamental to the Muslim religion, and theology was in fact often called *ʿilm uṣūl al-dīn*, "the science of the fundamentals of religion." Among these fundamentals were the existence, oneness, and attributes of God; the prophethood of Muhammad; and doctrines relating to the eschaton (resurrection, final judgment, etc.) and to the afterlife. Only when such fundamentals had been established through argumentation and grounded in sound epistemological principles could the ongoing work of the practical disciplines, such as law and jurisprudence, be said to have a proper theoretical foundation.

Constitutional organization—that is to say, the caliphate and the constitutional arrangements for its establishment and theoretical grounds of its authority—was thus considered to be among the fundamentals belonging to the sphere of theological discourse rather than among the more subsidiary matters belonging to the disciplines of fiqh and uṣūl al-fiqh. Although the confession of faith used by Muslims in worship is a very simple one, embracing only affirmation of God's unity and the prophethood of Muhammad, the Muslim creed elaborated in theological writings contains a much broader spectrum of articles. Affirmation of the authority of the ruler and his delegates and of the duty of Muslims to obey those in authority is in reality a part of the Muslim creed, a part of the system of beliefs that defines one as a Muslim.

Thus, even though these matters were not discussed in the fiqh books, they were presupposed to underlie all that the authors of those books wrote about, and allusions to them (if not discussions of them) appear here and there throughout the literature of fiqh. The ruler—whether called caliph or designated by some other title, such as imam or sultan—is indeed quite ubiquitous in that literature and appears in connection with a variety of topics and especially at those points where public law impinges on the discussions of the jurists.

All authority, including the authority to govern, is for the Muslim jurists of divine provenance and must therefore be shown to be grounded either directly or indirectly in revelation. Since government is a prerogative belonging to God, the ruler governs on God's behalf and is indeed the instrument of God's dominion on earth, as the title of caliph (*khalīfa*, "vicegerent") implies. The process of appointment to this high office must therefore likewise accord with the divine will. It is with regard to the nature of this process, however, that a fundamental disagreement between Sunni and Shiʿi thinking occurs.

The Sunni view is that God has established an essentially electoral procedure for the appointment of the ruler and that the relationship between the ruler and his subjects is contractual. The election of the ruler is a duty that in principle rests upon the community as a whole, although only those who meet certain qualifications laid down by the jurists and theologians may execute the task of election. They act on behalf of the larger community. Their primary qualifications are two: moral integrity and expertise in the religious sciences, including law. Since any jurist in good standing among Muslims meets these qualifications, the electors can be said to be for all practical purposes the jurists themselves. It is not surprising that a juristic constitutional theory would assign to scholars the important task of singling out a person for the high office of ruler.

The reason why scholarly expertise is considered requisite for this task is that the selection of an individual to be God's vicegerent on the earth calls for sound judgment of the sort not possessed by ordinary people. Some Sunni jurists likened the contract between the ruler and his subjects to the marriage contract. Just as in a marriage a woman's guardian exercises the judgment of a mature elder in seeking a man suited to be the woman's husband, so the scholars of the Muslim community, acting as guardians, seek a man suited to be ruler of the community. Just as a candidate for marriage to a woman must possess certain qualifications, so also must a candidate for the highest office among Muslims possess certain qualifications. These qualifications are carefully delineated in the writings on constitutional organization.

Mawardi enumerates seven such qualifications: moral integrity, scholarly expertise, soundness of hearing, vision and speech, bodily integrity, administrative and governing ability, prowess in military matters, and descent from the Arab tribe of Quraysh, the tribe of the prophet Muhammad.[2] The first two are, as noted above, requisites of the electors. The rationale for requiring that the electors be scholars is that it takes a scholar to know a scholar, not to mention the scholarly expertise required in the testing of genealogies and evaluation of other relevant attributes. The ruler of the Muslims is thus in principle a scholar-prince, one learned in law and theology as well as in statecraft and warfare.

Once the scholar-electors have completed their task of selecting a ruler for the Muslims, it is the duty of the rest of the community to swear their allegiance to him, thus completing the contractual process upon which legitimate rulership is based. As with every contract, this contract engenders rights and duties pertaining to both parties. The ruler has the right to demand absolute obedience from the community in all matters falling under his authority. His duties embrace the following, in Mawardi's reckoning: (1) maintenance of the religion of Islam, (2) settlement of disputes between litigants, (3) maintenance of security of life and property, (4) implementation of the legal penalties, (5) fortifying the frontiers, (6) conduct of warfare into enemy territory, (7) collection of revenues, (8) proper use of treasury funds, (9) appointment of trustworthy officials, (10) personal supervision of the affairs of government. The community has a right to all the benefits implied in these duties, for example the right to security of life, of property, and of religion. In return, the community must render obedience to the ruler's orders.

Juristic theory does not specify any particular number of electors as requisite for a valid contract of rulership. In fact, most jurists considered that the electoral role could be fulfilled by as few as one elector. The primary requirement of the theory was that scholarly expertise be applied to the task of selecting a ruler. One elector's expertise in this matter could be as effective as that of several or of many. The theory envisioned a scenario in which a ruler dies and an elector or electors step forward and select a successor. This action, once completed, was deemed final, and no other electors were permitted to repeat the action. Whoever among the qualified electors acted first acted with finality and on behalf of the rest of the community, including both scholars who participated and nonscholars.

If the electors could be as few as one and if the preceding ruler possessed the requisite scholarship and moral integrity (which in principle he would), then what objection could be raised if prior to his death a ruler chose someone to be his successor? The answer of the majority of Sunni jurists was that no objection could possibly be raised, since the judgment of a duly appointed ruler was as competent as that of any scholar, and the fact that the decision occurred before the ruler's death did not militate against its competence. Thus was shaped a rationale for the appointment by Muslim caliphs of their successors. Naturally, the caliphs chose sons or other close relatives. Among the jurists, however, the dynastic principle was carefully avoided by means of the language of election. Any son who succeeded his father as caliph enjoyed authority not by virtue of his being the son of the deceased caliph or member of the royal family but solely by virtue of the deceased caliph's election of him. And the election was always, in principle, ratified by the community through a swearing of allegiance.

Although this theoretical construct was always somewhat removed from actual political reality, it became more and more so as the centuries passed, prompting the jurists to introduce modifications and adaptations. The first great challenge to the original theory came in the form of usurpation of the caliph's power by Muslim warlords, chiefly the Buwayhids and, after them, the Seljuks. In order to make sense of such a situation, Mawardi himself devised the notion of "governorship by seizure," according to which any Muslim prince who was able to seize the reins of power in any region of the caliphal empire acquired entitlement thereby to investiture in the office of governor in that region by the caliph. In this manner the caliph became a mere legitimizer of a political arrangement not of his own making whereby a warlord, posing as the caliph's delegate, functioned as the effective head of government.

A much greater challenge to classical constitutional thinking came with the conquest of Baghdad in 1258 by the heathen Mongols and the Mongol repudiation and destruction of the caliphate. Although a remnant caliphate was retained in Egypt, the caliphate as a universal institution of Sunni Muslims ceased to exist, and Muslim jurists and theologians found themselves having to alter constitutional theory in more profound ways. Two figures are most prominent in this process.[3] First, Badr al-Din Ibn Jamaʿa, writing in Egypt in the late thirteenth and early fourteenth centuries and apparently ignoring the puppet caliphate maintained there, allowed the caliphate itself to be acquired through seizure of power. On this view the "elective" (*ikhtiyāriyya*) caliphate was one of two types, the other being the "coercively acquired" (*qahriyya*) caliphate. The former was the ideal type, but it belonged to past days; in the present it was the latter type, and it alone, that Muslims could reasonably hope for. The one who acquired the caliphate by force might not be in possession of the qualifications that distinguished the elected caliph, but Muslims should accept his rule as legitimate as long as the essential functions of Muslim government were being carried out under his auspices.

A younger Egyptian contemporary of Ibn Jamaʿa—nineteen years younger, to be exact—went a step further. This was Ibn Taymiyya, whose career as a rather radical Hanbali malcontent forms an intriguing episode in Muslim intellectual history. Ibn Taymiyya saw no need to postulate a caliphate at all. The caliphate for him was a historic institution that had lasted thirty years. With its demise in 661, the year of the death of the last of the "rightly guided" (*rāshidūn*) ʿAli ibn Abi Talib, had occurred the demise of ideal government but not of valid government. Valid government as such did not require the title of caliphate as an underpinning of its legitimacy. Legitimacy had to do with function, not with any process of appointment or even with any particular qualifications demanded in advance. The proof was to be in the pudding. As long as the one holding the reigns of power ruled at least ostensibly in the name of Islam and as long as the essential functions of Islamic government were being carried out, the Muslim community should render obedience to him. Ibn Taymiyya's thinking is much like that of Ibn Jamaʿa but takes the additional step of excising the notion of the caliphate—of a rulership harking back to earliest times—altogether from its argument for the legitimacy of present government.

As this discussion intimates, the Sunni jurists shared a general abhorrence of political revolution. They were all, almost without exception, political conservatives and upholders of the status quo, even to the extent of regarding tyranny as better than revolution. In general, they insisted that the ruler must be a Muslim, although a few later jurists dropped even this requirement.[4] The ultimate and final sine qua non of Sunni theory was that the ruler enable the time-honored institutions of Muslim society, and especially the law and institutions associated with it, to function with reasonable efficiency. If this was the case, then government was legitimate and deserving to be called "Shariʿa government" (*al-siyāsa al-sharʿiyya*), to use the term made especially popular through the writings of Ibn Taymiyya.

Shiʿi thinking about government is in certain respects similar to Sunni thinking, despite important differences in the realm of constitutional theory. The hallmark of Shiʿi theory is, of course, the belief in the Prophet's designation (*naṣṣ*) of ʿAli ibn Abi Talib as the first caliph and its assessment of the three caliphs who preceded him—as well as of all subsequent caliphs recognized by the Sunnis—as usurpers. By virtue of the Prophet's action, the true caliphate belonged henceforth, according to the Shiʿis, to ʿAli and his house, the *ahl al-bayt.* The transmission of rule occurred through the designation by each caliph—or imam, the title preferred by Shiʿis—of a member of the house of ʿAli to succeed him. Shiʿis accordingly reject altogether the notion of elective caliphate (not to mention Ibn Jamaʿa's notion of the caliphate acquired by seizure).

But there is more to the difference between Sunni and Shiʿi thinking. For Shiʿis, the imams are blessed with the quality of infallibility such that their actions and pronouncements constitute, along with those of the Prophet himself, the Sunna, which is the second source of Shariʿa norms after the Qur'an itself. The imams are therefore, for Shiʿis, successors to the Prophet not only with respect to their role as rightful political heads of the community but also with respect to their role as spiritual guides and sources of divinely inspired teachings.

Nonetheless, there remains a fundamental similarity between the general course of Shiʿi thinking over the centuries about political authority and that of the Sunnis, for the great majority of Shiʿis—those who came to be called Twelvers—were, like the Sunnis, ultimately destined to live in a world devoid of ideal rulership. If one places the terminus ad quem of Sunni thinking in the outlook of Ibn Taymiyya, then we may say that Sunni and Shiʿi thinking, despite the differences in theoretical approaches, ended up at much the same place. Both for Sunnis and for Twelver Shiʿis, the caliphate/imamate became in time a thing of the past, and Muslims had to make do with governments that imposed themselves on them. Twelver doctrine declared that the Twelfth Imam had entered into a state of "occultation" (*ghayba*) some years after the middle of the ninth century and, after having communicated with his followers for a limited time through special agents, was now represented in the world by the religious scholars of his community. The Twelver posture toward existing government became remarkably similar to the Sunni posture. Like the Sunnis, the Twelvers eventually for the most part (there are some exceptions) exhibited a tendency to accommodate and legitimize existing government as long as it enabled them to live in accordance with the Shariʿa. They too, like the Sunnis, came to judge governments according to the degree to which they accorded respect to and supported the scholars of the law, who were seen as carrying on many of the functions originally invested in the caliphate. And they too, like the Sunnis, tended in the end to be politically conservative and disenchanted with radical or revolutionary ideas.

For Muslim jurists in general it is simply impossible to think and to write about Islamic law without envisioning some sort of Islamic political authority and government in the background. Although the jurists were moralists in large degree, they were also scholars of the law who had a keen interest in all those things that make law law, especially judicial process and mechanisms of enforcement. They could not imagine themselves constructing a law that was purely theoretical and belonged entirely to the realm of the ideal. The law that they developed was expressly designed for persons living in Muslim territory under Muslim rule—in a domain that they generally called the *dār al-islām*, "abode of Islam." (Non-Muslims living in the dār al-islām were subject only to those parts of Islamic law that governed their obligations toward the Muslim polity.) Many Muslims of course lived outside that domain, and the jurists knew it; but a world entirely devoid of such a domain was unthinkable to them and inconsistent with their most fundamental beliefs, their theology. And if any lands constituted that domain, it was surely the lands in which the majority of jurists lived, the lands in which those who ruled called themselves Muslim and built impressive architectural monuments to prove it, including mosques and centers of religious learning.

The authority of the ruler can only be, in the thinking of the jurists, absolute. Governing authority is indivisible; all officials of government derive their authority from the ruler, whose delegates they are. They hold office only in accordance with his wishes and may be dismissed at any time. They are extensions of his will. A wise ruler will of course choose capable administrators and benefit from their counsel, but original earthly authority is his alone to wield.

The absolute character of the ruler's authority stems from the absolute character of the rights he represents and defends. These are not his rights as an individual, nor are they the rights of government or the state. Muslim juristic thinking does not know the concept of the corporate person and therefore does not regard the state or the people as a legal entity. Only individuals may be bearers of rights and obligations. Among these individuals is God Himself, who is a bearer of rights only and who, to some extent, replaces the state or body politic as a bearer of rights. The state qua state can never be party to a dispute or make a claim against a party. Thus, when one pays taxes or serves in the military, one is discharging an obligation toward God, not toward society. Accordingly, the ruler represents and defends nothing less than the rights of God.

The nonrecognition of the state as a legal entity and possible party to disputes helps to account for the absence of a developed criminal law in the writings of the Muslim jurists. Strictly speaking, the concept of crime as understood in Western societies does not exist in their thinking. There is no such thing as an offense against the state or against society, since these have no status in the law. Certain of the offenses that in Western law are counted as crimes are treated as offenses against God, whereas others are treated as injuries of man to man and as subject to what amounts to civil action. The offenses against God are violations of his rights. These include, quite naturally, the right, as God, to order and regulate man's worship of him. God's rights are thus intimately bound up with the interests of organized religion as expressed in ritual. But they are also intimately bound up with the interests of the family and of the social order.

These interests transcend the interests of individuals qua individuals, and as such they can, given the nonrecognition of corporate persons, be maintained only with reference to divine rights. Thus fornication (*zinā*, which includes both premarital and extramarital sexual intercourse) and false accusation of fornication are both offenses against God because they undermine God's ordaining of marriage as the means for legitimate procreation and perpetuation of the family across generations. Theft is an offense against God because it militates against the security of property upon which the well-being of the family and of society depends. The drinking of intoxicating beverages is an offense against God because it interferes with rationality, which is an essential ingredient of the social order and of proper worship of God and disposition of the assets that he has conferred upon his human creatures.[5]

Homicide and bodily harm, on the other hand, are lumped together under the heading of offenses against human parties and thus seem to acquire a tortlike character. Even in cases where retribution in the form of the death penalty is demanded, the offense (viz. homicide) retains this tortlike character inasmuch as satisfaction is still a purely private concern and a matter of choice and can be ordered by a court only after proceedings initiated by a kinsman of the victim.

Public interests are thus coterminous with the rights of God, and the ruler has the duty of seeing to it that the rights of God are not violated. As the above comments on homicide and bodily harm show, however, the rights of God do not pervade every area of human life. They are absolute, but not all-encompassing, which is to say that they are absolute only in the areas of human life where they hold sway. Accordingly, the authority of the ruler is absolute only within its proper domain.

Alongside the domain of God's rights (*ḥuqūq allāh*) stands the domain of the rights of human beings (*ḥuqūq al-ʿibād*), the rights that they have vis-à-vis each other. Baber Johansen has in recent times written especially insightfully on the relationship between these two categories of rights in Muslim juristic thought.[6] He has called attention to a striking feature of that thought, namely its concern to protect the rights of private persons against unjustified encroachments of the governing authority and to delimit the rights of God carefully so as to rob government of any pretext for such encroachments. Here we encounter once again the preoccupation of the Muslim jurists with private law and interests. In accordance with this preoccupation, the jurists sought to keep the rights of God in their proper place.

There is nothing irreverent or disrespectful of God in this attitude. Private law is as much God's law as public law, and the rights of men are as much of divine provenance as God's own rights. As was noted in Chapter 1, all rights belong originally to God. In the primordial covenantal encounter between God and humans, God as Lord has all the rights and humans as his subjects have none. Whatever rights humans have in the present world, they therefore acquire from God; they have these rights solely by his will. Zeal for the safeguarding of the rights of humans against unjustified intrusions into human life in the name of God's rights is therefore perfectly in keeping with the divine will. In social terms, this endeavor translates into safeguarding the sphere of rights of humans against the authority of the temporal ruler. Along with the preoccupation of the jurists with the private affairs of humans, then, goes a preoccupation with keeping the public authority within its divinely ordained limits. Public law is treated very largely from this perspective.

As Johansen has pointed out, the rights of humans represent the sphere of free human interactions. The prototypical legal person is the proprietor, and the juristic ideal posits a large sphere of exchange relations subject to the principle of the just exchange. It is not the prerogative of the political authority to intrude upon this sphere except when called upon to do so by private individuals. When a private party feels that his rights have been violated, he may bring his case to a judge, and if necessary the judge's decision will be enforced by means of sanctions. But this function of enabling individuals to realize their rights in the face of violations by other individuals is carried on only at the behest of the individual whose rights have been violated. Individuals are encouraged to settle their differences out of court.

Justice in the realm of exchange relations must therefore be realized through private initiative. When an individual feels that he has been the victim of an unjust exchange—say, an unfair price—it is up to him to decide what course to follow. Since a right has been violated, he should first seek a private settlement but, failing this, may choose to turn to the public authority for assistance. The presupposition of the jurists in regard to exchange relations is that human beings are for the most part rational persons who will pursue their interests in a fair and enlightened manner, and the posture toward the realm of exchange relations enjoined by the jurists upon the government may be described, not incorrectly, as laissez-faire. The thinking of the Muslim jurists is at this point fairly consonant with the outlook of classical liberalism.

The rights of humans and the rights of God cannot, as Johansen notes, operate simultaneously. The penalty of amputation for theft is, for example, considered to be a right of God. When an owner of stolen property reports the theft to the authorities, he creates an opportunity for the authorities to satisfy a right of God. He thus in effect relinquishes his own right in the matter and cannot demand compensation. Generally, however, when both categories of rights impinge on a particular case, the rights of humans should, according to the jurists, take precedence. A private individual may choose if he wishes to play the role of defender of God's rights, bringing accusations to the court against persons known to have violated God's laws against fornication, theft, the drinking of intoxicants, apostasy, and so on. But the individual is under no obligation to assume this role, especially if his interests are best served through refraining. Juristic thought leaves much to the Day of Judgment (*yawm al-dīn*), when justice will be perfectly meted out by God himself.

The procedural rules governing the application of the fixed penalties (*ḥudūd*) are in any case patently obstructive, as was observed in the previous chapter, and may be more correctly interpreted as safeguards for the individual than as facilitations of penal justice. Again, the backdrop of the Day of Judgment allows the jurists to be lenient in their protection of individuals in this world. We are thus presented here with the anomaly of a process that makes God's rights much more difficult to satisfy than the rights of humans. The justification for this was that since God cannot suffer loss or damage, the nonrealization of his rights is not a hardship for him. He retains in all cases his dignity as Lord.

The concern to protect the private individual against the harshness of the penal code may be illustrated with the case of fornication (*zinā*, a category covering all premarital and extramarital sexual intercourse). The jurists require that the accusation be brought before the judge within one month of the offense, that the accusation be supported by four trustworthy witnesses who can testify to having seen coitus take place, that the witnesses be made liable to the statutory qur'anic punishment, flogging, in the event the court does not uphold the accusation, and that the witnesses cast the first stones. The jurists also recommend that witnesses refrain from witnessing and that the offender not confess but rather turn to God for forgiveness. They even allow a confession, having been made, to be retracted subsequently.

The areas where the public authority may intrude upon the lives of individuals without waiting upon a private initiative are four: the collection of taxes, the regulation of the behavior of people in public places, the recruitment of persons to bear arms, and the maintenance of public worship. But the taxes mandated by the jurists were quite limited, and military conscription became for all practical purposes a matter of no concern to the average person, because there was a special military class in most areas of the Muslim world throughout most of the Middle Ages. The public authority had the responsibility of seeing to it that the Friday congregational services were properly conducted—the ruler or his governor in fact were to lead services in the main mosque of the major cities—and that shops were closed. As for the regulation of behavior in public places, known in Arabic as *ḥisba,* this impinged on a limited range of public offenses such as the use of fraudulent measuring devices by merchants, indecent exposure of the body or mingling of the sexes, and public imbibing of intoxicants, to mention a few major examples.

Thus we find in the writings of the Muslim jurists an insistence upon the existence of a Muslim political authority and upon the absolute character of that authority coupled with a careful delimitation of the sphere in which that authority and the awesome power that supported it could rightfully be exercised. The social order described in the previous chapter could not be realized without an Islamic government; but on the other hand it could best be realized by an Islamic government that knew where the limits of its authority lay. Public law was to be in the service of private law and of free human interaction regulated by private rights.

# Epilogue

In writing this book I have continuously pondered the question of tense. Generally speaking, I have employed the past tense but not without considerable misgiving. Does not Islamic law belong as much to the present as to the past? Is not the spirit of Islamic law about which I have written as much alive today as it ever was? Why should I write as though it were a thing of the past?

Part of the reason why I have employed the past tense, I suppose, is that the great classical works of Islamic jurisprudence—works that are regarded as definitive even now—belong most definitely to the past, and the most authoritative ones, to the fairly remote past. One who works entirely in these classical writings, as I do, is altogether likely to treat Islamic law, together with the spirit that informs it, as a medieval phenomenon.

But there is more to the matter. In days past, Islamic law—the law articulated in volumes of fiqh and in collections of fatwās—enjoyed a pride of place in Muslim societies that in the modern world it no longer has. By "days past" I mean the days before the Muslim world came under the political and cultural ascendancy of the West, days preceding the onset of a modernity fashioned by the West. The law of the jurists was, it is true, not always implemented with perfect fidelity or consistency in those premodern or medieval days. As Schacht and others have pointed out, the impact of this law on Muslim society was always uneven. Its hold was greatest in the realms of personal status, inheritance, and endowments. The jurists' law of property and of contracts and obligations was universally respected and influential but was usually observed selectively, especially among merchants, who not infrequently required greater flexibility than most jurists could allow. Penal law, tax law, and the law of warfare, as fashioned by the jurists, had the least impact on Muslim societies, owing to the infringement upon these parts of the law by governments that freely developed policies and administrative arrangements consonant with their perception of their interests and of societal exigencies.

In the sphere of judicial decision making, the impact of formal rules laid down by the jurists depended on the strength of the mufti-qadi connection. Where the role of mufti was more institutionalized under the auspices of the state, the impact of rules was presumably greater. But as appointees of the political authorities qadis were formally independent of the circles of those who studied the law. According to juristic theory, the qadis were to apply fiqh law; in actual practice, they often freely took into account the norms of local custom (*ʿurf*). Furthermore, the political authorities characteristically retained for themselves the right to maintain alternative jurisdictions represented by the so-called "courts of wrongs" (*maẓālim*); these courts, over which the ruler himself or local governor might directly preside, made no pretense of being bound to the fiqh law.

But notwithstanding these infringements and limitations on the actual working of the jurists' law among Muslims, that law was for Muslims in general the only true law of Muslim society, since it alone could claim to represent as faithfully as was humanly possible the holy law of God. Throughout the centuries that stretch from the time of the prophet Muhammad to the dawn of the modern age, there was no way for Muslims to think about law except monotheistically, and from that central monotheistic vision all those features of Muslim legal thought that have been subsumed in this book under the heading of "the spirit of Islamic law" followed as conclusions from a premise. The world of medieval Islam lavished vast amounts of money and architectural talent on the building of institutions of legal education (madrasas), and at those institutions the jurists' law—their fiqh and the fatwās that flowed from that fiqh—was studied. Whatever role custom or state policy may have had in the lives of Muslims or in the decision making of qadis, it could be conveniently ignored or placed on the periphery as far as legal education and the juristic exposition of the law was concerned. If as a result the law was in some measure more an ideal than a social reality, then it was a solidly institutionalized ideal firmly woven into the fabric of Muslim thought. But it was not just an ideal; it *was* in very large measure a social reality. The spirit of medieval Islamic law is the spirit of a monotheism concerned as much with the social effectiveness of the law as with truth in the law.

Since the engulfment of the Muslim world in the West's modernity, the situation has changed drastically. Certain things, it is true, seem at first blush to be much as they always were. The traditional law of the jurists continues to have a strong hold over family relations, for example; and in those areas where the jurists' law never enjoyed full sway in times past, we should hardly expect to see a turn toward greater implementation in modern times. The unevenness of the law's impact on Muslim society is thus still very much in evidence, although the factors that make for this unevenness and the actual patterns of unevenness are now very different; and, furthermore, even those parts of the law that are still in force have been profoundly affected by legislative reform. What most truly makes the modern situation different from times past, however, is the fact that the pride of place enjoyed by the jurists' law in those times must now be called into question and with it the strength of the monotheistic spirit that inspired the thinking of jurists and of Muslims in general about the law. If in the medieval past the jurists' law was subject to infringements that could be ignored or played down—perhaps even to some extent justified with reference to the true sources of the law—that law has in the modern period been subject to infringements of a more serious kind, the infringements of Western law and political ideas. As a result of years of colonial administration, most Muslim countries now have legal systems that are essentially European in provenance. The Islamic law of personal status remains in force in most areas only by virtue of legislative enactment and incorporation into civil codes inspired by European models and containing many modifications of the traditional law. Criminal, commercial, and other codes have been almost entirely imported from Europe.

But the most far-reaching change has to do with the way lawmaking and the authority underlying it are understood. Joseph Schacht described this change in the following words:

> Whereas a traditional Muslim ruler must, by definition, remain the servant of the sacred Law of Islam, a modern government, and particularly a parliament, with the modern idea of sovereignty behind it, can constitute itself its master. The legislative power is not any more content with what the *sharīʿa* is prepared to leave to it officially or in fact; it wants itself to determine and to restrict the sphere left to traditional Islamic law, and to modify according to its own requirements what has been left. This has led to an unprecedented relationship between Islamic and secular law.[1]

And yet, although the monotheistic spirit that informed the law of the classical Muslim jurists is in decline in the modern world, it is by no means dead. The concept of a divinely ordained Shariʿa is so central to Islam that it is likely to remain in some way alive as long as there are Muslims in the world. But how are Muslims to understand the Shariʿa, and how are they to implement it in their lives? One approach that is rapidly gaining ground involves treating the Shariʿa entirely as a moral code, as a source of moral guidance, and not as the foundation of an actual legal system. For Muslims living in Western countries in particular, this may seem the only viable approach; but it can make sense also to Muslims in traditionally Muslim countries who see their own legal systems as essentially secular and who are quite willing to accept the secular democratic understanding of sovereignty and the lawmaking process that seems to undergird those systems. This way of thinking presupposes that henceforth Islam will provide moral guidance within settings in which that moral guidance, however influential within Muslim family and communal life, can no longer count on the backing of the law. With no legislation to arrest the tendency among segments of contemporary society to abandon traditional norms, adherence to Islam's moral guidance will necessarily depend more and more upon the strength of the individual will and of communal institutions outside the state.

Among many Muslims, especially among those commonly dubbed

fundamentalists, the monotheistic spirit continues to find expression, as in former days, in a demand for a monotheistic polity in which God's law has the force of real positive law. For these Muslims Islam can truly be all that it is meant to be only within the context of an Islamic state, a state in which Islamic law is enforced and serves to guarantee a certain measure of realization of Islamic moral norms in public as well as private life. Some who think along these lines may be content with the degree to which Islamic law is implemented in their countries, especially if they live in countries that have embarked on programs of Islamization. Many others, however, are pursuing more aggressive reformist—in some cases, revolutionary—agendas in their efforts to remain true to their Islamic ideals.

Anyone who browses in bookstores in virtually any Arab or other Muslim country—or has opportunity to see the exhibits at the international book fair held annually in Cairo—cannot fail to be impressed with the great number of books on Islamic law that are continually being published. Many of these are modern editions of major classical works, without which the work of scholars such as myself would be extremely difficult. Others are contemporary studies of Islamic law based on research in the classical works. The sheer volume of such publications indicates that interest in the traditional jurists' law is widespread throughout the Muslim world.

This interest is not entirely academic. Frequently, the classical writings are called *turāth,* a heritage. A heritage is something from which one expects to derive benefit. Millions of Muslims in our world are unwilling to dismiss as irrelevant to modern life the great legal tradition that generations of jurists of the past fashioned through arduous interpretive effort and from a sincere desire to live according to the will of God. To the extent that the jurists' law is truly regarded as a heritage, something of value from the past, the spirit that informed this law is bound to remain in some measure alive.

# NOTES

## 1. The Formation of Islamic Law

1 In my own efforts to understand Paul's thinking about the law I have been especially guided by E. P. Sanders, *Paul, the Law, and the Jewish People.*

2 On the use of this title by the Umayyads and their religiopolitical aspirations, see Crone and Hinds, *God's Caliph.*

3 This amalgam of legal traditions forms the principal subject of Patricia Crone's study in her *Roman, Provincial, and Islamic Law.*

4 Schacht, *Introduction to Islamic Law,* 23–26.

5 Ibid., 28–33.

6 Ibid., 57–59.

7 See Calder, *Studies in Early Muslim Jurisprudence.*

## 2. Divine Sovereignty and Human Subordination

1 The grounding (*tawaqquf, istimdād*) of jurisprudence in theology was customarily established in the opening sections of the works on uṣūl al-fiqh. See, for example, Ghazālī, *Mustaṣfā,* 1:5; Āmidī, *Al-Iḥkām,* 1:9; Ibn al-Ḥājib, *Mukhtaṣar,* 1:33; Maḥbūbī, *Tanqīḥ,* 1:20; Shawkānī, *Irshād,* 20.

2 See G. Makdisi, *Ibn Qudama's Censure.*

3 The classical expression of these arguments is found in a treatise of the renowned Muslim theologian Abu'l-Hasan al-Ashʿari. See McCarthy, *The Theology of al-Ashʿari,* 6–8.

4 The locus classicus for the doctrine of the fiṭra is the prophetic saying "Every child is born in [a state of] fiṭra; it is his parents who make him a Jew or a Christian or a Zoroastrian." Wensinck, *The Muslim Creed,* 42.

5 The definition of *īmān* as *taṣdīq* has a long history in Islam and is of fairly early origin. See Watt, *The Formative Period of Islamic Thought,* 129–34; McCarthy, *The Theology of al-Ashʿari,* 75 (Arabic text); Elder, *A Commentary,* 116–17.

6 For a fuller account of the various arguments that were used in kalam circles to prove the creation of the world, see Wolfson, *The Philosophy of the Kalam,* 373–455.

7 See Macdonald, *The Development of Muslim Theology,* 315–51.

8 The discussion of this topic that follows is based on an earlier study en-

titled "Covenant and Law in Islam." See Firmage, Weiss, and Welsh, *Religion and Law*, 49–83.

9 Rāzī, *Tafsīr*, 3:106.

10 Ghazālī, *Mustaṣfā*, 1:55ff.; Rāzī, *Maḥṣūl*, 1:123–46; Āmidī, *Iḥkām*, 1:113ff.; Ibn al-Ḥājib, *Mukhtaṣar*, 1:199ff.; Bayḍāwī, *Minhāj*, 1:111–16; Ibn al-Subkī, *Jam'*, 1:54ff.

11 Reinhart, *Before Revelation*, 43–56.

12 Bihārī, *Musallam*, 1:25. Ansari is the commentator on Bihari's *Musallam al-Thubūt*.

13 Modarressi, "Rationalism and Traditionalism," 142.

## 3. The Textualist/Intentionalist Bent

1 Modarressi, "Rationalism and Traditionalism," 142.

2 Muẓaffar, *Uṣūl al-Fiqh*, 1:236–40. For a general account of Shi'i thinking about the role of reason in jurisprudence, see 1:205–356 and 3:121–34.

3 Ibid., 3:126.

4 The foregoing overview of Muslim thinking about the miracle of the Qur'an is based largely on Āmidī, *Ghāyat al-Marām*, 341–60. See also Baghdādī, *Uṣūl al-Dīn*, 182–84; Juwaynī, *Irshād*, 345–53; Guillaume, *Summa philosophiae*, 446–60 (Arabic text).

5 See, e.g., Grunebaum, *A Tenth Century Document*. Grunebaum's study focuses on elaborations on the miraculous character of the Qur'an in a treatise by Abu Bakr al-Baqillani. See also Larkin, *The Theology of Meaning*.

6 Ghazālī, *Mustaṣfā*, 1:129; Āmidī, *Iḥkām*, 1:226; Ibn al-Ḥājib, *Mukhtaṣar*, 2:17–18; Maḥbūbī, *Tanqīḥ*, 2:15; Bihārī, *Musallam*, 2:2–3.

7 Muẓaffar, *Uṣūl al-Fiqh*, 3:61.

8 The idea that the Qur'an contains the most fundamental principles of the law—an idea expounded most systematically by the Maliki jurist Abu Ishaq al-Shatibi—is discussed by Wael Hallaq in "The Primacy of the Qur'an in Shatibi's Legal Theory," in Hallaq and Little, *Islamic Studies*, 69–90. The article is reprinted in Hallaq, *Law and Legal Theory*.

9 On the traditional Muslim view concerning the history of the qur'anic text, see Said, *The Recited Koran*.

10 For a fuller account of this argumentation, see Weiss, "Knowledge of the Past."

11 Wael Hallaq discusses the subject of tawātur ma'nawī in this context of

Muslim theory of knowledge in his "On Inductive Corroboration, Probability, and Certainty in Sunni Legal Thought," in Heer, *Islamic Law and Jurisprudence*, 3–31. The article is reprinted in Hallaq, *Law and Legal Theory.*

12 Sarakhsī, *Uṣūl*, 284ff.; Bukhārī, *Kashf*, 2:680–88; Ghazālī, *Mustaṣfā*, 1:132–39; Ibn Qudāma, *Rawḍa*, 49–52; Rāzī, *Maḥṣūl*, 4:227–70; Āmidī, *Iḥkām*, 3:20–46; Bayḍāwī, *Minhāj*, 2:21–29; Maḥbūbī, *Tanqīḥ*, 2:2–3; Bihārī, *Musallam*, 2:113–20; Shawkānī, *Irshād*, 46–48.

13 Because the law cannot represent the divine willing of human behavior, Āmidī takes to task those Muʿtazilis who defined "command" (*amr*) as the willing of an act (*irādat al-fiʿl*). Āmidī, *Iḥkām*, 2:201–2.

14 Ghazālī, *Mustaṣfā*, 2:189; Āmidī, *Iḥkām*, 3:92.

15 The breakdown of language into its meaning-bearing components and the classification of the *lafẓ-maʿnā* correlations is the subject of my article "*ʿIlm al-Waḍʿ*."

16 Stanley Fish, "Play of Surfaces: Theory and Law," in Leyh, *Legal Hermeneutics*, 299–301.

17 Both the origin (*mabdaʾ*) and the transmission (*naql*) of the lugha are discussed at length in many of the classical works of jurisprudence (uṣūl al-fiqh). See Ghazālī, *Mustaṣfā*, 1:318–22; Rāzī, *Maḥṣūl*, 1:181–92, 203–17; Āmidī, *Iḥkām*, 1:104–12; Ibn al-Hājib, *Mukhtaṣar*, 1:192–98; Bayḍāwī, *Minhāj*, 1:151–65; Ibn al-Subkī, *Jamʿ*, 1:269–71; Shawkānī, *Irshād*, 12–17.

18 These are discussed in Weiss, "Origins of Language."

## 4. The Venture Beyond the Texts

1 Ghazālī, *Mustaṣfā*, 1:325ff.; Āmidī, *Iḥkām*, 3:273–74; Ibn al-Ḥājib, *Mukhtaṣar*, 2:308–9; Bayḍāwī, *Minhāj*, 2:141–42; Ibn Qudāma, *Rawḍa*, 166–69; Shawkānī, *Irshād*, 204.

2 I explain my justification for this translation in Weiss, *The Search for God's Law*, 555–56.

3 Calder, *Studies in Early Muslim Jurisprudence*, 1–9.

4 Schacht, *The Origins of Muhammadan Jurisprudence*, 180–89. In these pages Schacht gives numerous examples of these maxims.

5 The classic study of the Zahiri school is found in Goldziher, *The Zahiris*. On the ideas of the most illustrious representative of this school after its founder, see Arnaldez, *Grammaire et théologie*.

6 Zysow, "The Economy of Certainty."
7 Weiss, *The Search for God's Law*, 551–654.
8 Ghazālī, *Mustaṣfā*, 2:234ff.; Ibn Qudāma, *Rawḍa*, 147–54; Rāzī, *Maḥṣūl*, 5:21–58; Āmidī, *Iḥkām*, 4:38–57; Bayḍāwī, *Minhāj*, 2:119–26; Bihārī, *Musallam*, 2:311–16; Shawkānī, *Irshād*, 199–204.
9 Zysow, "Economy of Certainty," 373–94. Cf. Āmidī, *Iḥkām*, 3:289; Ibn al-Ḥājib, *Mukhtaṣar*, 2:228; Maḥbūbī, *Tanqīḥ*, 2:62–63; Shawkānī, *Irshād*, 207.
10 Zysow, "Economy of Certainty," 335–64.
11 Ibid., 351. This method of identifying a cause was called *ta'thīr*, while the method entailing linkage to a higher purpose was called *munāsaba*. Those jurists who embraced the munāsaba method often saw it as including ta'thīr, and hence we find discussions of *ta'thīr* in the section of their writings that dealt with *munāsaba*, not in a separate section. There seemed to be no reason why one could not establish linkages with higher purposes and at the same time set up types. See, for example, Ghazālī, *Mustaṣfā*, 2:296–306; Rāzī, *Maḥṣūl*, 5:157–98; Āmidī, *Iḥkām*, 3:387–423; Bayḍāwī, *Minhāj*, 2:156–64; Maḥbūbī, *Tanqīḥ*, 2:69–79; Ibn al-Subkī, *Jamʿ*, 2:273–85; Shawkānī, *Irshād*, 214–19. Others (according to Zysow's research, largely Hanafi jurists of Central Asia) preferred to adhere to the ta'thīr method without becoming involved in higher purposes. In their case, ta'thīr was kept distinct from munāsaba.
12 Ghazālī, *Mustaṣfā*, 2:288–90; Rāzī, *Maḥṣūl*, 5:139–54; Āmidī, *Iḥkām*, 3:364–80; Ibn al-Ḥājib, *Mukhtaṣar*, 2:234ff.; Baydāwī, *Minhāj*, 2:144–56; Bihārī, *Musallam*, 2:295–300; Shawkānī, *Irshād*, 210–13.
13 The references for the discussion of these methods in the juristic literature appear in note 11.
14 Wael Hallaq, "On Inductive Corroboration, Probability, and Certainty in Sunni Legal Thought," in Heer, *Islamic Law and Jurisprudence*, 3–31 (see especially 24–31, which deal with induction in relation to the five purposes of the law), and "The Primacy of the Qur'an in Shatibi's Legal Theory" in Hallaq and Little, *Islamic Studies*, 85–90. Both articles are reprinted in Hallaq, *Law and Legal Theory*.
15 That God takes human interests into account is argued with particular thoroughness by Āmidī in *Iḥkām*, 3:411–23.
16 The subject of *ʿāda* looms especially large in Ghazālī's discussion of *munāsaba* in *Mustaṣfā*, 2:302ff.
17 On the relationship between ʿilla (cause, occasioning factor) and ḥikma (purpose, rationale), see Āmidī, *Iḥkām*, 3:290ff.; Rāzī, *Maḥṣūl*, 5:287ff.;

Bihārī, *Musallam*, 2:274. I have discussed this subject in greater depth in *Search*, 572–82.

18 Makdisi, "Logic and Equity," 74.

19 Ibid., 73.

20 Shāṭibī, *Muwāfaqāt*, 4:134–36. Cf. Makdisi, "Logic and Equity," 79–80.

## 5. Probabilism and the Limits of Certainty

1 For discussions of abrogation in the literature of *uṣūl al-fiqh*, see Ghazālī, *Mustaṣfā*, 1:107–28; Ibn al-Qudāma, *Rawḍa*, 36–46; Rāzī, *Maḥṣūl*, 3: 277–381; Āmidī, *Iḥkām*, 3:146–260; Ibn al-Ḥājib, *Mukhtaṣar*, 2:185–204; Maḥbūbī, *Tanqīḥ*, 2:31–39; Bayḍāwī, *Minhāj*, 2:422–49; Ibn al-Subkī, *Jamʿ*, 2:74–94; Bihārī, *Musallam*, 2:53–96; Shawkānī, *Irshād*, 183–97.

2 On the role of the context in the Muslim interpretation of texts, see Wael B. Hallaq, "Notes on the Term *Qarīna* in Islamic Legal Discourse," *Journal of the American Oriental Society* 108 (1988): 475–80. The article is reprinted in Hallaq, *Law and Legal Theory*.

3 The following account of Muslim text/transmitter criticism is based primarily on Āmidī, *Iḥkām*, 2:47–100. See also Ghazālī, *Mustaṣfā*, 1:140–73; Ibn Qudāma, *Rawda*, 52–66; Rāzī, *Maḥṣūl*, 4:351–475; Ibn al-Ḥājib, *Mukhtaṣar*, 2:58ff.; Bayḍāwī, *Minhāj*, 2:37–70; Maḥbūbī, *Tanqīḥ*, 2:3–12; Bihārī, *Musallam*, 2:131–80; Shawkānī, *Irshād*, 48–71. An excellent modern overview of the traditional "science of hadith" is found in Siddiqi, *Hadith Literature*.

4 The translation of this hadith is Arthur Jeffery's. See his *A Reader on Islam*, 108.

5 A comprehensive discussion of Muslim thinking about the trustworthy person may be found in Farhat J. Ziadeh, "Integrity (*ʿAdālah*) in Classical Islamic Law," in Heer, *Islamic Law and Jurisprudence*, 73–93.

6 Juynboll, *Muslim Tradition*, 161–90.

7 Āmidī attributes this position to "Abu Hanifa and his followers." Āmidī, *Iḥkām*, 2:110.

8 On the chronology of this activity, see Juynboll, *Muslim Tradition*, 66–76. Cf. Goldziher, *Muslim Studies*, 164–80.

9 Discussions of the ambiguous (mujmal) and the univocal (ẓāhir) expressions as well as of the metaphor (*majāz*) are to be found throughout the literature of uṣūl al-fiqh. See Ghazālī, *Mustaṣfā*, 1:341–400; Rāzī, *Maḥṣūl*, 1:230–32, 285–94, and 3:155–72; Āmidī, *Iḥkām*, 1:36–47 and 3:9–

90; Ibn al-Ḥājib, *Mukhtaṣar,* 1:138–62 and 2:158–63, 168–71; Bayḍāwī, *Minhāj,* 1:174–75, 217–19, 405–10; Bihārī, *Musallam,* 1:203–7 and 2: 19–42; Shawkānī, *Irshād,* 21–26, 167–77.

10 Literally, "held in a state of suspension." A good example of the use of this term appears in Āmidī, *Iḥkām,* 3:26.

11 My discussion of the interpretive issues pertaining to this verse is based primarily on Āmidī, *Iḥkām,* 3:23–26. Cf. Rāzī, *Maḥṣūl,* 3:171–72; Bayḍāwī, *Minhāj,* 1:409–10; Ibn al-Ḥājib, *Mukhtaṣar,* 2:160–61; Bihārī, *Musallam,* 2:39–40; Shawkānī, *Irshād,* 170; Sarakhsī, *Uṣūl,* 1:129. See also Rāzī, *Tafsīr,* 11:222–29. In the present discussion I use this qur'anic verse to illustrate not only interpretive issues mentioned in these passages but others as well.

12 On the interpretation of the imperative, see Jeanette Wakin, "Interpretation of the Divine Command in the Jurisprudence of Mawaffaq al-Din Ibn Qudamah," in Heer, *Islamic Law and Jurisprudence,* 33–52. For discussions in the works of *uṣūl al-fiqh,* see Ghazālī, *Mustaṣfā,* 1:411–35 and 2:2–32; Ibn Qudāma, *Rawḍa,* 98–115; Rāzī, *Maḥṣūl,* 2:7–306; Āmidī, *Iḥkām,* 2:188–273; Ibn al-Ḥājib, *Mukhtaṣar,* 2:77–95; Bayḍāwī, *Minhāj,* 1:293–339; Bihārī, *Musallam,* 1:367–95; Shawkānī, *Irshād,* 90–109.

13 On the subject of generality versus specificity of expressions, see Ghazālī, *Mustaṣfā,* 2:32–185; Ibn Qudāma, *Rawḍa,* 115–36; Rāzī, *Maḥṣūl,* 2: 307–401; Āmidī, *Iḥkām,* 2:286–495; Ibn al-Ḥājib, *Mukhtaṣar,* 2:101–54; Bayḍāwī, *Minhāj,* 1:345–99; Bihārī, *Musallam,* 1:255–360; Shawkānī, *Irshād,* 112–64.

## 6. Juristic Authority and the Diversity of Schools

1 Schacht, *Introduction to Islamic Law,* 209.

2 Schiller, "Jurists' Law," 1230.

3 Schacht, *Introduction to Islamic Law,* 1.

4 The fullest and most authoritative account of the history of Islamic legal education and its institutions appears in Makdisi, *The Rise of Colleges.*

5 Zysow, "The Economy of Certainty," 463ff.

6 Discussions of the different views of the jurists on correctness, error, and validity in the formulation of the law appear in Ghazālī, *Mustaṣfā,* 2: 363ff.; Ibn Qudāma, *Rawḍa,* 193–200; Rāzī, *Maḥṣūl,* 6:29–58; Āmidī, *Iḥkām,* 4:246–65; Ibn al-Ḥājib, *Mukhtaṣar,* 2:294–98; Bihārī, *Musallam,* 2:380–92; Shawkānī, *Irshād,* 259–63.

7 Ghazālī, *Mustaṣfā*, 1:173–245; Ibn Qudāma, *Rawḍa*, 67–79; Rāzī, *Maḥṣūl*, 4:17–212; Āmidī, *Iḥkām*, 280–407; Ibn al-Ḥājib, *Mukhtaṣar*, 2:29–44; Bayḍāwī, *Minhāj*, 2:73–111; Maḥbūbī, *Tanqīḥ*, 2:41–52; Bihārī, *Musallam*, 2:211–46; Shawkānī, *Irshād*, 71–90.

8 On the various issues pertaining to the mustafti-mujtahid relationship, see Ghazālī, *Mustaṣfā*, 2:387–92; Ibn Qudāma, *Rawḍa*, 205–7; Rāzī, *Maḥṣūl*, 6:69–94; Āmidī, *Iḥkām*, 4:297–319; Ibn al-Ḥājib, *Mukhtaṣar*, 2:305–9; Bayḍāwī, *Minhāj*, 2:297–303; Bihārī, *Musallam*, 2:400–8; Shawkānī, *Irshād*, 265–72.

9 Ṭahānawī, *Kashshāf*, 1156–57.

10 Rāzī, *Maḥṣūl*, 6:70–72; Āmidī, *Iḥkām*, 4:315–16; Bihārī, *Musallam*, 2:404; Shawkānī, *Irshād*, 269–71.

11 Jackson, *Islamic Law and the State*. The pages that are most relevant to the present discussion are 69–96.

12 Powers, "Fatwas as Sources" (see the Bibliography) and "The Art of the Legal Opinion," in Masud, Messick, and Powers, *Islamic Legal Interpretation*, 98–115.

13 For a broader treatment of this subject, see Masud, Messick, and Powers, *Islamic Legal Interpretation*, 3–32.

## 7. The Moralistic Bent

1 On the status of non-Muslims (*dhimmīs*) within the Islamic state, see Khadduri, *War and Peace*, 175–201.

2 The major introductory work on the Islamic law of war and peace is Khadduri, *War and Peace*.

3 A useful recent survey of Islamic family law may be found in Nasir, *The Islamic Law of Personal Status*. For a shorter survey, see Abu Zahra, "Family Law," in Khadduri and Liebesny, *Law in the Middle East*, 132–78, and Schacht, *Introduction to Islamic Law*, 161–68.

4 That this is so is clear from Farrukh, *Public and Private Law*, 163-70. On the subject of homicide, see also Awa, *Punishment*, 69–90; Joseph Schacht, *Introduction to Islamic Law*, 181–87.

5 Awa, *Punishment*, 13–20; Farrukh, *Public and Private Law*, 117-20; Schacht, *Introduction to Islamic Law*, 178–79.

6 The subject of "looking" as it pertains to dress is dealt with in Hsu, "Dress in Islam."

7 Johansen, "Secular and Religious Elements," 283–89.

8 Ibid., 284.

9 Joint ownership was the basis of a type of partnership called *sharikat al-milk* (proprietary partnership). See Udovitch, *Partnership and Profit*, 17–39.

10 A broad overview of Islamic law of contracts may be found in Rayner, *The Theory of Contracts.* See also Subhi Mahmasani, "Transactions in the Shari'a," in Khadduri and Liebesny, *Law in the Middle East*, 144–60.

11 On the subject of ribā and ventures entailing uncertainty and risk, see Saleh, *Unlawful Gain.*

12 The classic treatment of this subject continues to be Udovitch, *Partnership and Profit.*

13 Awa, *Punishment*, 2–12.

14 See Hattox, *Coffee and Coffeehouses*, 46–57, 148–56.

15 Fyzee, *Outlines of Muhammadan Law*, 139.

16 Schacht, *Introduction to Islamic Law*, 122.

17 Johansen, "Die sündige, gesunde Amme," 264ff. On one point my view differs from Johansen's: he seems to juxtapose "legal" (*gesetzlich, gerichtsverbindlich*) and "moral/religiomoral" (*moralisch, religiös-moralisch*) as mutually exclusive, self-contained spheres or "semantic fields." As I indicate in the previous paragraphs, I prefer to speak of a distinction between a legal-moral domain and a domain of morality that lies beyond temporal law (considered, of course, as Islamic categories) and am uncomfortable with the notion that the Muslim jurists posited a purely legal domain distinct altogether from the moral domain. This difference of viewpoint is, I think, largely terminological and not substantive.

18 Schacht, *Introduction to Islamic Law*, 79.

19 Ibid., 78.

## 8. Private and Public Dimensions of the Law

1 For example, Baghdādī, *Uṣūl al-Dīn*, 271–93; Juwaynī, *Irshād*, 424–34; Āmidī, *Ghāyat al-Marām*, 361–92; Guillaume, *Summa philosophiae*, 478–97.

2 Māwardī, *Aḥkām*, 1–7. See also Ann Lambton, *State and Government*, 83–102; Rosenthal, *Political Thought*, 27–37; Kerr, *Islamic Reform*, 19–54.

3 On both of these figures (Badr al-Din ibn Jamaʿa and Ibn Taymiyya), see Lambton, *State and Government*, 138–51, and Rosenthal, *Political Thought*, 43–61.

4 Lewis, *Political Language*, 91–116; see especially 106–7.

5 References to literature dealing with the Islamic penal system and with the law of homicide and bodily harm (see next paragraph) have been supplied in the notes to Chapter 7.

6 See Johansen, "Secular and Religious Elements," 289–301, and "Eigentum, Familie, und Obrigkeit," 61–73.

## Epilogue

1 Schacht, *Introduction to Islamic Law,* 101.

# GLOSSARY OF MAJOR ARABIC TERMS

*Ahl al-ḥadīth:* People who specialize in the collection, memorization, and study of *ḥadīth.*

*Ahl al-ra'y:* People who rely on their own sense of equity in their formulation of the law.

*'Aql:* Human reason; human rationality.

*Dīn:* Religion, worship.

*Falsafa:* The philosophical tradition in Islam.

*Faqīh* (pl. *fuqahā'*): A scholar versed in fiqh.

*Fatwā* (pl. *fatāwā*): A legal opinion offered as a response to a question.

*Fiqh:* The law considered as a product of juristic interpretation of or extrapolation from foundational texts.

*Ḥadīth:* Narrative material containing sayings of the prophet Muhammad (or some other authority figure of early Islam) or accounts of his deeds.

*Ḥarb:* A state of warfare between an Islamic state and a non-Muslim enemy.

*Ḥukm* (pl. *aḥkām*): A categorization of a human act; a rule of law.

*Ijmā':* The consensus of mujtahids on a point of law.

*Ijtihād:* The interpretive toil of a jurist attempting to formulate the law on the basis of the foundational texts.

*'Illa:* The aspect of a case that causes or occasions the application of a rule of law to that case.

*'Iṣma:* Infallibility, the state of being protected against error.

*Isnād:* The supplying of a sanad.

*Istiftā':* Solicitation of a fatwā; adherence to the legal doctrine of a mujtahid (see also *taqlīd*).

*Istiḥsān:* The preference for one analogy-based rule over another.

*Istiṣlāḥ:* The consideration of human welfare (*maṣlaḥa*) in the preferring of one rule over another.

*Jihād:* The pursuit of legitimate warfare.

*Kalām:* Theology; theological discourse.

*Khamr*: Grape wine.

*Khiṭāb:* Addressed speech; in particular, God's speech considered in respect to its being addressed to humans in a divine-human encounter.

*Lafẓ:* Any meaning-bearing unit of language; vocable.

*Lugha:* Lexical code.

*Madhhab* (pl. *madhāhib*): A school of legal doctrine.

*Madrasa:* A law college.

*Majāz:* Figure of speech.

*Maʿnā:* The meaning of a word or other vocable considered as a lexical datum.

*Maqṣūd* (pl. *maqāṣid*): The authorial intent behind an expression or passage; more broadly, a purpose or objective of the law.

*Maṣlaḥa* (pl. *maṣāliḥ*): A human interest; human welfare.

*Muftī:* A jurist who gives fatwās.

*Mujtahid:* a jurist who possesses the qualifications entitling him to engage in ijtihād.

*Murād:* The authorial intent behind an expression or passage.

*Nabīdh:* Date wine.

*Nafs:* Soul, self; the life of the individual.

*Naṣṣ:* A foundational text; in Shiʿi usage, the Prophet's appointment of ʿAli ibn Abi Talib to be his successor.

*Qāḍī:* The judge responsible for the application of Shariʿa law.

*Qiyās:* An analogy between cases considered as a justification for the formulation of a novel rule.

*Ra'y:* An individual jurist's own sense of equity.

*Ribā:* An exchange of a given amount of a fungible commodity (grain, precious metal, etc.) for a larger amount of the same commodity with a delay in the completion of the exchange; broadly, an exchange of money or fungibles of unequal amounts that gives unfair advantage to one of the parties.

*Sanad:* The chain of transmitters of a ḥadīth text.

*Shariʿa:* The totality of moral and legal norms ordained by God.

*Sunna:* The authoritative custom of the prophet Muhammad (and, for Shiʿis, of the Imams) as reflected in his (their) sayings and deeds.

*Taqlīd:* Adherence to the legal doctrine of a mujtahid.

*Tawātur:* A process of transmission that guarantees the authenticity of the text transmitted.

*ʿUrf:* Customary practice of a given region or group.

*Uṣūl al-fiqh:* The theoretical and methodological principles underlying the jurists' formulation of the law.

*Waḍʿ:* The primordial assignment of a vocable to its meaning.

*Waḥy:* The prophetic experience of receiving divine revelation.

*Ẓāhir:* A univocal expression.

# BIBLIOGRAPHY


Āmidī, Sayf al-Dīn al-. *Al-Iḥkām fī Uṣūl al-Aḥkām.* 4 vols. Cairo: Dār al-Kutub al-Khidīwiyya, 1914.

———. *Ghāyat al-Marām fī 'Ilm al-Kalām.* Edited by H. M. 'Abd al-Laṭīf. Cairo: al-Majlis al-A'lā li'l-Shu'ūn al-Islāmiyya, 1971.

Arjomand, Said A., ed. *Authority and Political Culture in Shī'ism.* Albany: State University of New York Press, 1988.

Arnaldez, Roger. *Grammaire et théologie chez Ibn Hazm de Cordoue.* Paris: J. Vrin, 1956.

Awa, Mohamed S. El-. *Punishment in Islamic Law.* Indianapolis: American Trust Publications, 1982.

Azmeh, Aziz al-, ed. *Islamic Law: Social and Historical Contexts.* London: Routledge, 1988.

Baghdādī, Abū Manṣūr 'Abd al-Qāhir al-. *Uṣūl al-Dīn.* Istanbul: Maṭba'at al-Dawla, 1928.

Bayḍāwī, Nāṣir al-Dīn al-. *Mi'rāj al-Minhāj.* 2 vols. A Commentary on *Minhāj al-Wuṣūl ilā 'Ilm al-Uṣūl* by the same author. Edited by S. M. Ismā'īl. Cairo: Maṭba'at al-Ḥusayn al-Islāmiyya, 1993.

Bihārī, Muḥibb Allāh al-. *Musallam al-Thubūt.* 2 vols. With the commentary of Muḥammad al-Anṣārī. [This text and commentary occupies the bottom portion of the pages; the top portion is occupied by Ghazālī's *Mustaṣfā.*] Būlāq: al-Maṭba'a al-Amīriyya, 1913–14. Reprint, Baghdad: al-Muthannā, n.d.

Bukhārī, 'Abd al-'Azīz al-. *Kashf al-Asrār: Sharḥ Uṣūl al-Fiqh li'l-Bazdawī.* 2 vols. Cairo: Maktab al-Ṣanāyi', 1889.

Burton, John. *An Introduction to the Hadith.* Edinburgh: Edinburgh University Press, 1994.

———. *The Sources of Islamic Law: Islamic Theories of Abrogation.* Edinburgh: Edinburgh University Press, 1990.

Calder, Norman. *Studies in Early Muslim Jurisprudence.* Oxford: Clarendon Press, 1993.

Coulson, Noel J. *Conflicts and Tensions in Islamic Jurisprudence.* Chicago: University of Chicago Press, 1969.

———. *A History of Islamic Law.* Edinburgh: Edinburgh University Press, 1964.

Crone, Patricia. *Roman, Provincial, and Islamic Law: The Origin of the Islamic Patronate.* New York: Cambridge University Press, 1987.

Crone, Patricia, and Martin Hinds. *God's Caliph.* New York: Cambridge University Press, 1986.

Elder, Earl E., trans. *A Commentary on the Creed of Islam.* New York: Columbia University Press, 1950.

Farrukh, Omar A. *Ibn Taimiyya on Public and Private Law in Islam.* Beirut: Khayats, 1966.

Faruki, Kemal. *Islamic Jurisprudence.* 2d ed. Karachi: National Book Foundation, 1975.

Firmage, Edwin B., Bernard G. Weiss, and John W. Welsh, eds. *Religion and Law: Biblical-Judaic and Islamic Perspectives.* Winona Lake: Eisenbrauns, 1990.

Fyzee, Asaf A. A. *Outlines of Muhammadan Law.* 3d ed. London: Oxford University Press, 1964.

Ghazālī, Abū Ḥāmid Muḥammad al-. *Al-Mustaṣfā.* 2 vols. [This text occupies the top portion of the pages; the bottom portion is occupied by Bihārī's *Musallam al-Thubūt.*] Būlāq: al-Maṭba'a al-Amīriyya, 1913–14. Reprint, Baghdad: al-Muthannā, n.d.

Goldziher, Ignaz. *Introduction to Islamic Theology and Law.* Translated by A. and R. Hamori. Princeton: Princeton University Press, 1981.

———. *Muslim Studies.* 2 vols. Edited by S. M. Stern. Translated by C. R. Barber and S. M. Stern. London: George Allen and Unwin, 1971.

———. *The Zahiris: Their Doctrine and Their History.* Translated by Wolfgang Behn. Leiden: E. J. Brill, 1971.

Grunebaum, Gustav von. *A Tenth Century Document of Arabic Literary Theory and Criticism.* Chicago: University of Chicago Press, 1950.

Guillaume, Alfred. *The Summa philosophiae of al-Shahrastani.* London: Oxford University Press, 1934.

Hallaq, Wael B. "From *Fatwas* to *Furū'*: Growth and Change in Islamic Substantive Law." *Islamic Law and Society* 1 (1994): 29–65.

———. *Law and Legal Theory in Classical and Medieval Islam.* Brookfield: Variorum, 1995.

———. "Murder in Cordoba: *Ijtihād, Iftā'*, and the Evolution of Substantive Law in Medieval Islam." *Acta Orientalia* 55 (1994): 55–83.

Hallaq, Wael B., and D. P. Little, eds. *Islamic Studies Presented to Charles J. Adams.* Leiden: E. J. Brill, 1991.

Hattox, Ralph S. *Coffee and Coffeehouses: The Origins of a Social Beverage in the Medieval Near East.* Seattle: University of Washington Press, 1985.

Heer, Nicholas L., ed. *Islamic Law and Jurisprudence: Studies in Honor of Farhat J. Ziadeh.* Seattle: University of Washington Press, 1990.

Hourani, George F. *Islamic Rationalism: The Ethics of ʿAbd al-Jabbar.* Oxford: Clarendon Press, 1971.

Hsu, Shui-Sian Angel. "Dress in Islam: Looking and Touching in Hanafi Fiqh." Ph.D. diss., University of Utah, 1994.

Ibn al-Ḥājib, ʿUthmān ibn ʿUmar. *Mukhtaṣar al-Muntahā al-Uṣūlī.* 2 vols. With the commentary of ʿAḍud al-Dīn al-Ījī and the glosses of Saʿd al-Dīn al-Taftazānī and ʿAlī al-Jurjānī. Edited by S. M. Ismāʿīl. Cairo: Maktabat al-Kulliyyāt al-Azhariyya, 1973.

Ibn al-Subkī, Tāj al-Dīn ʿAbd al-Wahhāb. *Jamʿ al-Jawāmiʿ.* 2 vols. With a commentary by Shams al-Dīn al-Maḥallī and a gloss by al-Bannānī. Cairo: Dār Iḥyāʾ al-Kutub al-ʿArabiyya, n.d.

Ibn Qudāma, Muwaffaq al-Dīn. *Rawḍat al-Nāẓir wa-Jannat al-Munāẓir.* Cairo: al-Maṭbaʿa al-Salafiyya, 1965–66.

Jackson, Sherman A. *Islamic Law and the State: The Constitutional Jurisprudence of Shihab al-Din al-Qarafi.* Leiden: E. J. Brill, 1996.

Jeffery, Arthur. *A Reader on Islam.* The Hague: Mouton, 1962.

Johansen, Baber. "Die sündige, gesunde Amme." *Die Welt des Islams* 28 (1988): 264ff.

———. "Eigentum, Familie, und Obrigkeit im hanafitischen Strafrecht." *Die Welt des Islams* 19 (1979): 61–73.

———. *The Islamic Law on Land Tax and Rent.* London: Croom Helm, 1988.

———. "Secular and Religious Elements in Hanafite Law: Function and Limits of the Absolute Character of Government Authority." In *Islam et Politique au Maghreb,* edited by E. Gellner and J. Vatin. Paris: Centre National de la Recherche Scientifique, 1981.

Juwaynī, Imām al-Ḥaramayn al-. *Kiṭāb al-Irshād.* Cairo: Maktabat al-Khānjī, 1950.

Juynboll, G. H. A. *Muslim Tradition: Studies in Chronology, Provenance, and Authorship of Early Hadith.* Cambridge: Cambridge University Press, 1983.

Kamali, Mohammad H. *Principles of Islamic Jurisprudence.* Cambridge: Islamic Texts Society, 1991.

Kerr, Malcolm. *Islamic Reform: The Political and Legal Theories of Muhammad ʿAbduh and Rashid Rida.* Berkeley: University of California Press, 1966.

Khadduri, Majid. *War and Peace in the Law of Islam.* Baltimore: Johns Hopkins University Press, 1955.

Khadduri, Majid, and Herbert Liebesny, eds. *Law in the Middle East.* Vol. 1. *Origin and Development of Islamic Law.* Washington, D.C.: Middle East Institute, 1955.

Lambton, Ann K. S. *State and Government in Medieval Islam*. Oxford: Oxford University Press, 1991.

Larkin, Margaret. *The Theology of Meaning: ʿAbd al-Qahir al-Jurjani's Theory of Discourse*. American Oriental Series, vol. 79. New Haven: American Oriental Society, 1995.

Lewis, Bernard. *The Political Language of Islam*. Chicago: University of Chicago Press, 1988.

Leyh, Gregory. *Legal Hermeneutics: History, Theory, and Practice*. Berkeley: University of California Press, 1992.

Macdonald, Duncan B. *The Development of Muslim Theology, Jurisprudence, and Constitutional Theory*. Reprint. London: Darf Publishing, 1985.

Maḥbūbī, Ṣadr al-Sharīʿa al-. *Tanqīḥ al-Uṣūl*. 2 vols. With a commentary by the author entitled *al-Tawḍīḥ* and a gloss by Saʿd al-Dīn al-Taftazānī. Cairo: Dār al-Kutub al-ʿArabiyya al-Kubrā, 1910.

Mahmassani, Subhi. *The Philosophy of Jurisprudence in Islam*. Translated by Farhat J. Ziadeh. Leiden: E. J. Brill, 1961.

Makdisi, George. *Ibn Qudama's Censure of Speculative Theology*. London: Luzac, 1962.

———. "Legal Logic and Equity in Islamic Law." *American Journal of Comparative Law* 33 (1985): 63–92.

———. *Religion, Law, and Learning in Classical Islam*. Brookfield: Variorum, 1991.

———. *The Rise of Colleges: Institutions of Learning in Islam and the West*. Edinburgh: Edinburgh University Press, 1981.

Makdisi, John, and Marianne Makdisi. "Islamic Law Bibliography: Revised and Updated List of Secondary Sources." *Law Library Journal* 87:1 (1995): 69–191.

Masud, Khalid M., Brinkley Messick, and David S. Powers, eds. *Islamic Legal Interpretation: Muftis and Their Fatwas*. Cambridge, Mass.: Harvard University Press, 1996.

Māwardī, Abu'l-Ḥasan ʿAlī al-. *Al-Aḥkām al-Sulṭāniyya*. Cairo: Matbaʿat al-Waṭan, 1937.

Mayer, Ann Elizabeth. "Law and Religion in the Muslim Middle East." *American Journal of Comparative Law* 35 (1987): 127–84.

McCarthy, Richard J. *The Theology of al-Ashʿari*. Beirut: Imprimerie Catholique, 1953.

Modarressi, Hussein. "Rationalism and Traditionalism in Shiʿi Jurisprudence." *Studia Islamica* 59 (1984): 141–58.

Momen, Moojan. *An Introduction to Shiʿi Islam: The History and Doctrines of Twelver Shiʿism*. New Haven: Yale University Press, 1985.

Muẓaffar, Muḥammad Riḍā al-. *Uṣūl al-Fiqh.* 3 vols. Najaf: Dār al-Nuʿmān, 1971.

Nasir, Jamal J. *The Islamic Law of Personal Status.* London: Graham and Trotman, 1986.

Nasr, Seyyed Hossein, Hamid Dabashi, and Seyyed Vali Reza Nasr, eds. *Shiʿism: Doctrines, Thought, and Spirituality.* Albany: State University of New York Press, 1988.

Powers, David S. "Fatwas as Sources for Legal and Social History: A Dispute over Endowment Revenues from Fourteenth-Century Fez." *Al-Qantara: Revista de Estudios Arabes* 11 (1990): 295–341.

———. *Studies in Qur'an and Hadith: The Formation of the Islamic Law of Inheritance.* Berkeley: University of California Press, 1986.

Rayner, Susan E. *The Theory of Contracts in Islamic Law.* London: Graham and Trotman, 1991.

Rāzī, Fakhr al-Dīn al-. *Al-Maḥṣūl fī ʿIlm Uṣūl al-Fiqh.* 6 vols. Edited by J. F. al-ʿAlwānī. Beirut: Mu'assasat al-Risāla, 1992.

———. *Al-Tafsīr al-Kabīr.* Cairo: Al-Matbaʿa al-Bahiyya, n.d.

Reinhart, A. Kevin. *Before Revelation: The Boundaries of Muslim Moral Thought.* Albany: State University of New York Press, 1995.

Rosenthal, Erwin I. J. *Political Thought in Medieval Islam.* Cambridge: Cambridge University Press, 1958.

Sachedina, Abdulaziz A. *The Just Ruler in Shiʿite Islam.* Oxford: Oxford University Press, 1988.

Said, Labib es-. *The Recited Koran.* Translated and adapted by Bernard Weiss, M. A. Rauf, and Morroe Berger. Princeton: Darwin Press, 1975.

Saleh, Nabil. *Unlawful Gain and Legitimate Profit in Islamic Law.* 2d ed. London: Graham and Trotman, 1992.

Sanders, E. P. *Paul, the Law, and the Jewish People.* Minneapolis: Fortress Press, 1983.

Sarakhsī, Abū Bakr Muḥammad al-. *Uṣūl al-Sarakhsī.* 2 vols. Beirut: Dār al-Maʿrifa, 1973.

Schacht, Joseph. *Introduction to Islamic Law.* Oxford: Clarendon Press, 1966.

———. *The Origins of Muhammadan Jurisprudence.* Oxford: Clarendon Press, 1950.

Schiller, A. Arthur. "Jurists' Law." *Columbia Law Review* 58 (1958): 1225–38.

Shāṭibī, Abū Isḥāq Ibrāhīm al-. *Al-Muwāfaqāt fī Uṣūl al-Aḥkām.* 2 vols. Edited by M. ʿAbd al-Ḥamīd. Cairo: Maṭbaʿat Muḥammad ʿAlī Ṣabīḥ, 1969–70.

Shawkānī, Muḥammad ibn ʿAlī al-. *Irshād al-Fuḥūl ilā ʿIlm al-Uṣūl.* Cairo: Muṣṭafā al-Bābī al-Ḥalabī, 1937.

Siddiqi, Muhammad Zubayr. *Hadith Literature.* Cambridge: Islamic Texts Society, 1993.

Ṭahānawī, Muḥammad ibn ʿAlī al-. Kashshāf Iṣṭilāḥāt al-Funūn. 6 vols. Reprint, Beirut: Khayat, n.d.

Tyan, Emile. *Histoire de l'organisation judiciaire en pays d'Islam.* Leiden: E. J. Brill, 1960.

Udovitch, Abraham L. *Partnership and Profit in Medieval Islam.* Princeton: Princeton University Press, 1970.

Vogel, Frank. "The Closing of the Door of Ijtihad and the Application of the Law." *American Journal of Islamic Social Sciences* 10 (1993): 396–401.

Wakin, Jeanette A. *The Function of Documents in Islamic Law.* Albany: State University of New York Press, 1972.

Watt, W. Montgomery. *The Formative Period of Islamic Thought.* Edinburgh: Edinburgh University Press, 1973.

Weiss, Bernard G. "*ʿIlm al-Waḍʿ*: An Introductory Account of a Later Muslim Philological Science." *Arabica* 34 (1987): 339–56.

———. "Knowledge of the Past: the Theory of Tawātur According to Ghazali." *Studia Islamica* 61 (1985): 81–105.

———. "The Medieval Muslim Discussions of the Origin of Language." *Zeitschrift der Deutschen Morgenländischen Gesellschaft* 124:1 (1974): 33–41.

———. *The Search for God's Law: Islamic Jurisprudence in the Writings of Sayf al-Din al-Amidi.* Salt Lake City: University of Utah Press, 1992.

Wensinck, A. J. *The Muslim Creed.* Cambridge: Cambridge University Press, 1932.

Wolfson, Harry. *The Philosophy of the Kalam.* Cambridge, Mass.: Harvard University Press, 1976.

Ziadeh, Farhat. "ʿUrf and Law in Islam." In *The World of Islam: Studies in Honor of Philip K. Hitti,* edited by J. Kritzeck and R. B. Winder. London: Macmillan, 1960.

Zwaini, Laila al-, and Rudolph Peters. *A Bibliography of Islamic Law, 1980–1993.* Leiden: E. J. Brill, 1994.

Zysow, Aron. "The Economy of Certainty: An Introduction to the Typology of Islamic Legal Theory." Ph.D. diss., Harvard University, 1984.

# INDEX

## *The Spirit of the Laws*

Alan Watson, General Editor

Bernard G. Weiss, *The Spirit of Islamic Law*
Calum Carmichael, *The Spirit of Biblical Law*
John Owen Haley, *The Spirit of Japanese Law*
R. H. Helmholz, *The Spirit of Classical Canon Law*
Geoffrey MacCormack, *The Spirit of Traditional Chinese Law*
Alan Watson, *The Spirit of Roman Law*